ERNST JÜNGER:
A DIFFERENT
EUROPEAN DESTINY

ERNST JÜNGER
A DIFFERENT EUROPEAN DESTINY
DOMINIQUE VENNER

ARKTOS
LONDON 2024

Arktos.com   fb.com/Arktos   arktosmedia   arktosjournal

Copyright © 2024 by Arktos Media Ltd.

All rights reserved. No part of this book may be reproduced or utilised in any form or by any means (whether electronic or mechanical), including photocopying, recording or by any information storage and retrieval system, without permission in writing from the publisher.

ISBN
978-1-915755-91-9 (Paperback)
978-1-915755-92-6 (Hardback)
978-1-915755-93-3 (Ebook)

Editing
Constantin von Hoffmeister

Layout & Cover
Tor Westman

Translation
Roger Adwan

CONTENTS

Prologue: Jünger's Century vii

I. The Founding Experience 1
II. Books in the Shadow of Mars 21
III. Weimar and the Conservative Revolution 37
IV. The German-Russian Alliance 55
V. Franco-German Dialogues 75
VI. The Prussian Socialism of *The Worker* 89
VII. The Myth of Prussia and That of Race 101
VIII. Internal Exile 115
IX. A Farewell to Arms 137
X. From Rebel to Anarch 167

Epilogue: A Different European Destiny 195

To Clotilde, who was the first to read this book; to Pierre-Guillaume Le Roux, who encouraged me to pen it; and to my children, who were in my thoughts while I was writing it.

PROLOGUE

JÜNGER'S CENTURY

MORE THAN any other man's, it was Ernst Jünger's existence that coincided with the European destiny of his own century. He himself suggested that, just like a seismograph, he had been the herald of the successive eras with which he would interact in a state of mutual resonance. From 1914 to 1918, and occasionally beyond, most Europeans would turn out to be bellicose; and so would Jünger, yet without ever giving in to hatred. Following their defeat in 1918, the Germans would proceed to revile the Weimar Republic, seeking refuge in a bruised sort of nationalism; and Jünger himself would, likewise, unrestrainedly renounce Weimar. In a state of distress, the Germans then placed great hope in Hitler, before ultimately falling victim to him. Jünger espoused these fluctuations personally, entering a mindset of premature dissidence. During the Second World War, the hope of an agreement between European nations surfaced among many French people, including resistance fighters, as well as among patriotic Germans. Very early on, and at great risk, Jünger himself would express this very hope. After 1945, a now aching Europe longed to establish a kind of novel humanism while simultaneously protecting itself against the threats that stemmed from the East. Jünger thus imparted these expectations in several of his essays and novels. At a later point, when the disillusionment of a gorged sort of society had spread, his entire work would display itself as an antidote.

A French-Praised German

No other European writer could claim to have witnessed, to such an extent, over so long a period and with such prescience, the fluctuations and tragedies of his century. The difference being that, unlike many of his contemporaries, Jünger never espoused the spirit of an era by sheer opportunism, anticipating it instead without any desire for personal profit.

Born on 29 March 1895, at the dawn of the new century, Jünger would follow the latter from end to end, before parting ways with it as a more-than-centenarian and without having been disfigured by age. Indeed, he died on 17 February 1998, at the hour of the wolf.[1] He was almost 103 years old. His exceptional longevity was such that one would have readily thought him immortal. And immortal shall he undoubtedly be in the memory of future generations. He travelled across the entire century, from beginning to end, suffering the wounds of a tragic destiny yet evading all its blemishes.

Attracted during his youth by the 'inebriating rapture of the scents of evil',[2] he would become a fierce yet hate-free combatant of the Great War, a post-1918 nationalist that never succumbed to aggressiveness, an opponent of Nazism that never disavowed his fatherland, a drug- and alcohol-curious individual who was never robbed of his freedom by such substances, a critic fascinated by technological modernity without being devoured by the latter, and a prestigious writer never taken in by his own glory, having been both committed to and detached from his century and keeping his distance from the latter's degeneracy and infamies.

---

1   TN: The hour of the wolf is the time between night and dawn, when most people pass away.

2   AN: Ernst Jünger, *Sturm* (1923), translated by Philippe Giraudon. Published by Vivaine Hamy Editions, 1991.

When his passing was announced, his memory was celebrated in the French press with surprising unanimity.[3] In Germany, the *Frankfurter Allgemeine Zeitung* pointed out the glowing tribute published by French President François Mitterrand in March 1995, on the occasion of the writer's centenary. In Paris, more and more people lavished him with praise.[4]

During his lifetime, and often early on, his highly personal talent gathered a lot of praise from the likes of André Gide, Marcel Jouhandeau, Paul Léautaud, Jean Cocteau, Julien Gracq, Maurice Nadeau, and many other authors. Unlike the English, for instance, who rather ignored him, the French translated and read his books extensively, often considering him to be the greatest German writer of his time.[5] What a disconcerting mystery it is to be faced with the craze that befell many of our French intellectuals, who usually bristle at what the author of *Storm of Steel* actually symbolises. Exoticism is partly responsible for this. What we can accept from a stranger, we would never tolerate from one of our own. Talent has something to do with it as well, without, however, sufficiently accounting for things. Indeed, many other talented writers have been shrouded in a veil of silence. Nor can we ignore the fact that, despite his Prussian profile, Jünger had the tact to lean on the right side during the so-called 'brown years',

---

3   AN: Limiting ourselves to Parisian dailies, let us mention *Le Figaro* on 18 February 1998, with articles by Frédéric de Towarnicki, Marcel Schneider and Jean-Marie Rouart; *Libération* (on the same day) with articles by Michka Assayas, Claire Devarrieux and Lorraine Millot; *L'Humanité* with a one-page article by Jean-Pierre Léonardini; and *Le Monde* on 19 February 1998, with articles by Jean-Louis de Rambure, Christian Delacampagne and Philippe Dagen.

4   AN: Save for a few rare exceptions, the publication of two *Pléiades* volumes in 2008 dedicated to his *War Journals* also met with a favourable response within the French press.

5   AN: As someone who spoke and read French perfectly, Ernst Jünger was an avid reader of various French authors, whose words he quotes more readily in his own writings than those of his compatriots.

to the point of suddenly coming across as a sort of resistance fighter, which is no small matter. Yet these explanations are all insufficient.

A Prussian Archetype

A translator and a friend of Jünger's, Julien Hervier once suggested that in the immediate post-war period, 'many Frenchmen, guilt-ridden as a result of their defeat, yet developing a kind of superiority complex in connection with the atrocities perpetrated by the Nazis, found in Jünger a positive image of the German man, one that corresponded to their own horizon of expectations: someone horrified by the camps while remaining courageous in war and showing understanding of, and unfailing respect for, the French culture.'[6]

Indeed, many a lettered Frenchman of that period kept a memory of what Jünger had written about the French capital in *A German Officer in Occupied Paris*: 'This city has become a second spiritual homeland for me, for it ever more strongly symbolises everything that I cherish about the old culture.'

The first contact between Ernst Jünger and France reaches far back in time, to the eve of 1914, when the still teenage author of *African Games* crossed the border to join the Foreign Legion. Next came those autumnal mornings in Champagne and the June nights that preceded the attack, when the young helmeted people that fought on both sides of the Artois trench line vowed to meet again once free of their warring obligations, in a newly reconciled Europe.

The recognition that this reputable and highly cultured German benefited from, that of a self-professed friend of both France and its literature, also expresses an implicit return to the state of mutual sympathy which embodied the prevalent rule that governed the interactions between the descendants of the Gauls and the Germans prior to

---

6   AN: An excerpt taken from an article that was originally published in *Revue de Littérature contemporaine* [TN: Contemporary Literature Magazine] in January-March 1989. It later resurfaced in the notes of the second *Pléiades* volume entitled *War Journals II: 1939–1949*, Gallimard 2008, p. 1138, number 3.

the catastrophe of 1870.[7] Thanks to his multifaceted imagination, the harsh beauty of his war books, the mysterious dreaminess of his mature novels, the meditative originality of his diarist writings, the sultry appeal of this drug and alcohol enthusiast, not to mention the poetic resources of a botanist and entomologist, Jünger managed to address a vast array of different readers. If one digs even deeper into the mystery of his lasting success among the educated public, one can wonder if the content of his books does not also reflect a genuinely French sort of unhappiness. One must not forget the fact that France is, alongside Germany, the Western European country that has been most traumatised by the passing of centuries, the one whose own tradition was the most lastingly scarred even before the Revolution. In the turmoil of an era of dereliction, Jünger's works were received as omens or promises of a different destiny.

His unique character is, in fact, the embodiment of an ultimate sort of figure, that of a European archetype that had temporarily disappeared and for whom a secret nostalgia had perhaps endured. In a world saturated with dialectical subtlety and dominated by appearances, Jünger seems credible, having been authenticated by his own life. And it already says a lot when one of the greatest writers of a century and one of the most cultivated ones was simultaneously a young officer of the stormtroopers who sang 'Our Mother War'.[8] It is indeed a rarity that bears within itself the lost unity of arbitrarily conflicting

---

7   AN: As regards the long-term Franco-Germanic agreement and understanding, one can refer to *Die Geburt zweier Völker. Deutsche und Franzosen* [TN: The Birth of Two Peoples: the Germans and the French] by the great mediaevalist Carlrichard Brühl (1925–1997). Published in France by Fayard in 1994.

8   AN: *Our Mother War*, or *La Guerre notre mère*, is the French title given to one of Jünger's early works, entitled *Der Kampf als inneres Erlebnis* (1922), as translated by Jean Dahel for Albin Michel in 1934. This work of his has since been re-translated by François Poncet under the title *La Guerre comme expérience intérieure* [TN: War as an Inner Experience, which is the accurate rendering of the original title], Christian Bourgois, 1997.

natures: the poet and the warrior, i.e. the man of meditation and the man of action.

Although writing has indeed become rather unoriginal, Jünger started off by intensely experiencing what he wrote. He proved himself to be what he truly was through his very actions before recounting them in his books. Next, he substantiated his very soul's hardening through both trials and adversity. When, in the wake of yet another defeat, his homeland was virtually pulled from under his own two feet, he remained upright, even rising to unassailable heights at a time when his country was subject to denial, always ready to reach beyond the limits of proud and discreet piety.

Youth and Mature Books

Readers and critics alike are used to distinguishing between the two authors that Jünger undoubtedly was: a writer of youth books and a very different writer, one that penned mature books. The first Jünger, i.e. the one who authored *Storm of Steel* (*In Stahlgewittern*, 1920) and *The Worker* (*Der Arbeiter*, 1932), wrote his works under the influence of Mars. He preferred unwavering courage to gentleness and inconvenience to comfort. He remained in harmony with the overexcited Europe of the 1920s and 1930s. The second Jünger, inaugurated by *On the Marble Cliffs* (*Auf den Marmorklippen*, 1939) and subsequently upheld by *The Peace* (1945), *Eumeswil* (1977) and many other works, distanced himself from the passions of his now distant youth. Jünger, however, never denied his own essence. Nor had he ever been a man that craved confrontations the way Nietzsche did, despite admiring, pondering and reading many of the latter's books. When he chose to dissent from the positions of the Third Reich, it was from a metaphysical and moral point of view. Akin to water, he espoused the most extreme borders of the century. The consideration that he has garnered has undoubtedly stemmed from the harmony he maintained with the dizzying fluctuations of his era, one that was balanced and righted by an irreproachable sort of conduct.

The intention behind the book introduced by this prologue is to give an analysis of Jünger's works in a manner closely associated with the author's very uncommon life path. This essay also aims to highlight what makes Ernst Jünger the perfect example for revealing the notion of a different European destiny.

Two seemingly contrasting characters meet our eyes in a most enigmatic way, representing the two complementary faces of Europe: that of the soldier who prided himself on having been the youngest person to be awarded the Order of Merit of the Prussian Crown in 1918, and that of the mature man who took pride in having bequeathed his own name to a butterfly.[9]

Ever so different, these two Jüngers seem to belong to two contradictory personalities. They are, in fact, in close symbiosis with the two inverted faces of European destiny: the one that existed before the Second World War and the one that emerged after it. Just like the life of Europe itself, the author's life was cut in half as if by the blow of an axe, resulting in an incredible divide, an unthinkable mutation. In the second period, one can no longer recognise any aspect of what the first had actually been.

A Figure for the Stormiest of Weathers

The trauma was so intense and spiritually unsettling that despite having the most prophetic and most lucid of minds, Jünger himself seemed to have lost his ability to manifest his second sight after the immense disaster that led to his country's defeat and the very erasure of Europe. It thus took him some time to create new timeless 'figures' capable of symbolising what he himself had become and what Europeans could become in a disquieting interregnum. The awakening of the prophetic writer did, however, ultimately come about through the twofold lightning bolt embodied by his *The Forest Passage* (1950) and *The Gordian Knot* (1953), two works that served to prove the intactness of their

---

[9] AN: The *Trachydora juengeri* (Amsel, 1968).

author's vigour. Next came, in 1977, the publication of *Eumeswil*, which, although described as a novel, acts, in fact, as a metaphysical allegory. Indeed, Jünger had just turned eighty-two, showcasing the fact that, just like Goethe and Michelangelo, age had no hold over him, save that of ensuring the fulfilment of his art and capabilities.

A philosophical novel similar in its metaphorical construction to *On the Marble Cliffs*, *Eumeswil* served as a pretext for the creation of a new 'figure', that of the *anarch*, who Jünger distinguishes from and strongly contrasts with the *anarchist*, despite the close connection between the two words. While the anarchist fights power and is dependent on it, the anarch keeps his distance from it without ever being in a state of exile. He observes attentively without becoming involved, occasionally conducting talks with the prince. He is reminiscent of what Jünger himself had become and would remain until his final day. Driven out of history just as Europeans were following the disasters of the first part of the century, the anarch is no longer a historical actor, but an attentive spectator that never displays a wait-and-see attitude. He is thus the very figure that embodies the fate temporarily imposed upon Europeans by Destiny itself.

Perceiving the Present in a Different Way

Despite my not having belonged to his most immediate circle of friends, I did correspond with Jünger for many years, ever since his heartfelt reaction to my sending him *Baltikum*, the very first of my historical works, published in 1974. The subject is indeed very personal to him, as it relates to the adventure that the German Free Corps (*Freikorps*) embarked on after November 1918, and after many other interactions, he ultimately thanked me for having sent him *The Rebel Heart*, a work of remembrance and reflection on my pugnacious and 'Mauretanian'[10] youth. Twenty years passed, and with his firm writing

---

10   AN: Dominique Venner, *The Rebel Heart*, published in French by Les Belles Lettres, 1995. Regarding the interpretation of the term 'Mauretanians' (political

style, he penned a most valuable message of complicity: 'We comrades can readily display our wounds!' The date was 9 January 1995, shortly before his hundredth birthday.

At a later point, namely six years after Jünger's death, I received what could be described as a message from beyond when I discovered the fifth and final volume[11] of his journal, which was published in France during the summer of 2004. This work is a collection of his final writings and one of my books is mentioned on the last page under the date of 15 March 1996. It was one of the final thoughts he ever published. He was about to turn one-hundred and one. This is what he wrote:

> I have finished reading Dominique Venner's *Terror and Political Crimes in the 20th Century*.[12] The book was sent to me by the author several years ago. He actually quotes a sentence of mine, one that I had forgotten about: "The terrorist does not merely strike his victim, but also inflicts a permanent injury upon himself."[13] I had probably thought of Ernst von Salomon, who Venner also quotes because of his involvement in Rathenau's murder.

Next came several comments that would become clearer once one referred to an observation made on page 22 of the same volume and dated 4 February 1991:

> It is regrettable that we have been deprived of a Clausewitz of the civil war, and especially the global civil war in which we have been involved since 1917. [...] I would very much like to add a third volume to my two books entitled *The Forest Passage* and *The Gordian Knot*, but this will remain a simple wish.

---

activists), one should refer to chapter 9.

11 TN: The French title is *Soixante-dix s'efface*, which could be translated as '*Seventy Draws to an End*'.

12 AN: Published in French by Plon, 1988. Jünger had initially read it upon its release. He then wrote to me in order to express his interest and voice his desire to have a translation of it published in Germany.

13 AN: This sentence was actually written in French.

A reflection on this 'global civil war' had been outlined in his book titled *The Gordian Knot*:

> Revolutions imprint themselves more deeply and establish more visible benchmarks than national wars. In this sense, we can say that three giant steps have brought us to the point where we stand today: the Reformation, the French Revolution and the Russian Revolution. For wars are but the protrusions of hidden events whose mass remains underground.[14]

Jünger does not believe that great historical movements could ever be explained through causal rationality alone. His mythical vision of history, which he had long cultivated, encouraged him to believe that the life of different peoples is subject to forces that are far more profound than that:

> High tides result from the fact that the sun and the moon combine their respective effects: the waters then reach beyond all landmarks. What makes our time exceptional is that the disasters of global civil war coincide with one of the flows separated by long ebbs, alongside the paroxysms of the centuries-old struggle between East and West.

Awareness of Destiny

If the journal's final thoughts deserve to be highlighted, it is because they encourage us to take to new heights in order to perceive the present moment differently. They are proof of the fact that, in his perception of the long-lasting ebbs and flows of history and his perfect awareness of the European slumber of his own era, the contemplative warrior that Jünger undoubtedly was did not think for a single moment that such a slumber would be eternal.

In all fairness to the reader, I must in turn reveal why I have undertaken this study of the life and thoughts of Ernst Jünger. Before becoming a historian driven by a profound sort of vocation, keeping away

---

[14] AN: Excerpt from *The Gordian Knot* (1953), translated by Henri Plard and published by Christian Bourgois in 1981, pp. 70–71.

from academic paths, yet displaying a constant concern for historical analysis and bestowing upon history what must be seen as the art of the writer (yes, before this long part of my life), I was initially a young man that became very involved in the adventures of his time, when adventure itself was political. Then I freed myself from it, discovering that my vocation lay elsewhere. Still, I had at least learnt much of what a historian is expected to know. In terms of enabling me to break free of the ancient spells I was under, some of Ernst Jünger's writings proved invaluable to me. It is therefore a moral debt that I am settling here. I will add, however, that the political journey undertaken by the author of *Storm of Steel* begs questions to which it is not easy to find an immediate answer, even when you yourself have had a rather rich 'Mauretanian' experience. And yet the following text does not attempt to evade these questions. Beyond such inquiring, however, this book is especially carried by the idea that what Jünger sets down, both before us and before the future itself, is the example of a 'different European destiny'. Throughout his life, the former soldier presents us with a model of noble behaviour which every young European will be able to adopt as a reference point in future times. In his literary work, he also outlines the pathways of what the future would be like were we to break with what was imposed upon us by the century of 1914. This had to be said, for such was my conclusion as a contemplative historian, one that is haunted by his awareness of destiny.

CHAPTER I

THE FOUNDING EXPERIENCE

SERIOUSLY WOUNDED during the last major German offensive of 21 March 1918, Ernst Jünger spends several weeks on convalescence leave in a hospital. In order to kill time, he undertakes to count his wounds:

> I amused myself once during the monotonous hours on my back by counting the number of times I had been hit. I found that I had been hit fourteen times: six times by rifle bullets, once by a shrapnel bullet, once by a shell splinter, three times by bomb splinters, and twice by splinters of rifle bullets. Counting the ins and outs, this made precisely twenty punctures, so that I might confidently, with that Roman centurion, Holkschen Reiter, take my place in every warlike circle. Certainly I could at any time assert my claim to belong to one order at least, namely, that of the gold wound stripes. This honour did in fact come to me at this very time […] Yet I must confess I had it sewn on my tunic with a certain pleasure.

The Foundation of a Mythical Figure

This, however, was not to be the last of his battles and injuries. No sooner was he back on his own two feet than he took his place at the head of his assault company. He is thus, once again, seriously wounded on 25 August 1918, in the vicinity of Cambrai. This time, the war is definitely over for him. The armistice signed on 11 November came as a surprise to him, at a time when he had been sent to convalesce in his family home of Rehburg, located near Hanover.

Since the start of the war, he had, on a daily basis, transcribed various salient facts and thrilling experiences, all of which were recorded in his notebooks. With the war now over, this raw material would be processed using a personal literary talent that would garner the admiration of Gide, despite the latter's general lack of appreciation of martial narratives. Numerous and characterised by their magnetic intensity, those penned by Jünger would forever constitute the unshakable foundation for the fascination that both the man and the writer would exert upon so many German and French minds, often in sharp contrast to his belligerent intoxications. His stories and meditations on the war would also serve as the unyielding bedrock that would effortlessly pave the way for the oneiric and literary wanderings that defined his second life, the one that would commence at the turn of the 1930s, following the enthusiasm and disillusionment of his radical political commitments. This point cannot be overemphasised. Indeed, without his war exploits and their literary form, never would Jünger have attained the mythical dimension that would ultimately be his own. Neither his privileged position in Paris during the Occupation, at the General Staff of the German forces, nor the relations he forged in the brilliant French literary circles of the time would have been possible without the prestige of the writer-warrior.

Without his *Storm of Steel*, Ernst Jünger would never have been able to achieve his later fame and influence. First and foremost, the man and the writer came to be through war and the books on war that strengthened his very founding experience. What Jünger drew from this experience, until the day of his death, was a very legitimate sort of pride, one which he never denied. Any thoughts on Jünger can therefore only be channelled through one's precise understanding of what this experience actually was, an experience that was preceded by his childhood and education years.

An Attentive and Wise Father

As already mentioned, the future writer was born in Heidelberg on 29 March 1895. Descending from a Lower Saxon peasant lineage, his father, Ernst Georg Jünger (1868–1943), was, at the time, working at the city's university as an assistant to the German chemist Victor Mayer. He would later go on to establish an analytical testing laboratory and a pharmacy, thus ensuring that his family enjoyed a comfortable life of affluence. Born Karoline Lampl, his wife (1873–1950) was born into a Catholic peasant family from Franconia. She would bear him seven children, of which Ernst was the eldest. Since two of his little brothers, Hermann and Felix, would pass away at a young age, the family would ultimately be left with five children. An essayist, a poet, and the author of numerous works, Friedrich Georg (1898–1977) would, to the end of his days, maintain a close relationship with his elder brother, thanks to their intimate intellectual complicity.[1] The other three children were Johanna Hermine (1899–1984), whose beautiful regular features can be seen in their family photo; Hans Otto (1905–1976), a future physicist; and Wolfgang (1908–1975), who would grow up to be a geographer.[2]

---

1   AN: Friedrich Georg Jünger's memories (until 1926) can be found in his book entitled *Grüne Zweige. Ein Erinnerungsbuch* [TN: Green Branches — A Memory Book] They were originally published in 1951 by Carl Hanser, Munich and later included in the twelve-volume edition of the works of the same author (Klett-Cotta, Stuttgart). To date (December 2008), none of Friedrich Georg Jünger's books have been translated into French.

2   AN: Regarding Ernst Jünger, his biography and his work, one can refer to the very rich documentary display (comprising introductions, chronologies and notes) produced by Julien Hervier for the two volumes of the *War Journals* in the Pléiade edition (Gallimard, 2008). One can also consult Julien Hervier's work entitled *Two Individuals against History — Pierre Drieu La Rochelle and Ernst Jünger* (Klincksieck, 1978). Other reference materials include Banine's *Ernst Jünger and His Many Faces* (L'Âge d'Homme, Lausanne, 1989) and Alain de Benoist's *Ernst Jünger — A Biobibliography* (Guy Trédaniel, 1997). In 2009, these were the most complete works in the French language alongside 'File H' — *Ernst Jünger*, produced under the direction of Philippe Barthelet (L'Âge d'Homme, 2000). One must also add to the list the small and precious photo

Though, at their mother's request, the children were indeed baptised, they would not receive any religious education, thus fulfilling the wishes of their father, who was unwaveringly rationalistic.

With regard to his father, whom he admired and who often guided him well beyond his years of adolescence, Ernst would always speak with affection. Having learnt of the serious illness that was to claim his father's life, Ernst noted the following in his *Journal* on 9 January 1943: 'One day I would like to describe him like a mother possessing male intelligence — with a deeper sense of justice.' This attentive father would give him his first botanical paraphernalia, thus giving rise to a devouring passion that would extend to all insects. Much later, his friend Banine would be left wondering whether entomology had not been the only true passion that Ernst Jünger had ever had. In the meantime, fatherly talks helped to broaden the child's horizons. In his *Journal*, Ernst would state:

> Not a day went by without my father speaking to me of Alexander the Great or Napoleon, to whom he had dedicated a whole section of his vast library.

Just like Goethe, his father felt sympathy for the French and made certain that Ernst learned their language. He even organised for him a language stay with a French family, at a time when Ernst was still very young.

A Cultured Duffer and Dreamer

The young boy's first school report was marked with the words 'does not pay sufficient attention'. This observation would often be found in future reports. Indeed, Ernst seemed to be the very embodiment of those imaginative and talented duffers who, ever impervious to mathematics yet passionate about literature, prove to be full-blooded

---

album created by François Lagarde (Gris Banal Editions, 11, rue Louis-Braille, 34000 Montpellier). Other works will be mentioned as references when the time comes.

authors. It was to his mother that he owed his passion for reading, a mother who had bequeathed to him her flights of the imagination. Although he rejected any and all subject matters that bored him, he did learn proper Latin and Greek and composed poems that he then sent to the local press. At a very young age, he read the works of Alexandre Dumas, Karl May's adventure tales, and even Jules Verne. Already eclectic, he also read the Bible, which piqued his interest with its stories of Bedouins, murders and raids. He also read *The Arabian Nights*, the *Icelandic Edda*, Hesiod and Homer, all of which would leave a deep and contradictory mark on him. Later, during his adolescence, he would read Nietzsche and Maurice Barrès, whose writings would impact him in a most lasting way, but also Oscar Wilde, Edgar Allan Poe, Stendhal, Balzac, and Baudelaire.

Prior to the great initiatory ordeal of the war, he would experience, in a perfectly disorderly fashion, an extensive sort of mental training resulting from a direct access to a variety of texts and authors. They affected him, awakening a plethora of ideas and emotions while also promoting his mastery of both German and French, and thus an uncommon ability to express thoughts or feelings alike. In the classic sense of the word, he actually completed his studies of the humanities, albeit in a non-academic way. His mind underwent a profound process of enrichment and enlightenment, to an extent that would become rare a century later. Accompanied by his favourite brother, furthermore, he would enjoy first-hand experiences of the sometimes dangerous world of wild nature. His development was therefore particularly rich and balanced while remaining foreign to school conventions.

Forbidden Games and Wildness

Every summer, the long holidays would offer Ernst and his younger brother Friedrich Georg the opportunity to experience what they themselves felt was real life. Indeed, their father had bought a large house in Rehburg, located to the northwest of Hanover. Free of their boarding school prison, and thanks to this new place of residence and the country which surrounded it, both boys would discover a wilderness paradise. Within an hour's walking distance from their house lay an immense and shallow lake, *Steinhuder Meer*, from which flowed a stream between the woods and marshes, with not a single house or village in sight. 'All of this bestowed upon us a feeling of unexpected happiness', wrote Friedrich Georg, 'for there was no one to impose any limits on us.'

Far from their parents, the boys would turn this isolated and manforsaken land into their own forbidden playgrounds. Their domain was immense, comprising forests, lakes, marshes, and abandoned quarries. They were thus able to greatly vary their endless explorations, sometimes even having a brush with death. They made their way through an inaccessible jungle, their legs lacerated by brambles. The favourite location, however, were the marshes. They went through it naked, coating their bodies with mud to protect themselves from horseflies and mosquitoes. They bathed among the reeds and ran across a grassy surface that wobbled underfoot. At times, they would suddenly sink into a black mud that sucked them in and from which they had every difficulty to pull themselves out. It was their favourite game, the most dangerous one, a game their parents knew nothing of. Whenever the grassy carpet gave way and the boys sank, screaming in fear and excitement, they would wonder whether they could, once again, escape with their lives. Exhausted, they would then lie down on the grass, in the sun, talking over and over again. Wearing their backpacks, the two brothers also joined a *Wandervogel* group (meaning 'migratory birds'), an important youth movement at the time, one that was libertarian and *völkisch*[3] and advocated both ecology (before the term was even coined) and a return to nature, far from all cities and the bourgeois world.

---

3   AN: *Völkisch* is a word that has no equivalent in French except for 'popular' in its ethnic and deep-rooted sense. It cannot be expressed using the term 'racist', owing to the latter's narrow and negative meaning.

In his autobiographical novel entitled *Die Zwille*,[4] Ernst Jünger humorously recounted the achievements of the bunch of rascals of which he acted as leader. He and his brother dreamt of discoveries and tropical countries. Back then, the colonial adventure was at its peak and popular literature sang its praise. Africa thus seemed to be the continent where the wildest dreams could come true, an Africa that was partly unspoilt and still sparsely populated: the one mentioned in the memories of adventurers such as Stanley. The two brothers devoured these stories, ever indignant that 'civilisation', this desecration of all that is wild, had been introduced into the African Eden. To missionaries, doctors and European colonisers, they very much preferred 'Arab slave traders […], the descendants of Sinbad the sailor; rich and dignified figures in a world of magic. To burn villages, hunt down slaves and roll people's heads in the sand — wasn't that their very right?'[5]

The Legion and the African Dream

'To me,' said Ernst Jünger, 'Africa was the pinnacle of all that is wild and primitive, the only possible arena where one could lead a life whose very scope mirrored that of the life I intended to have. And it seemed obvious to me that I should go there as soon as I had secured my freedom.'

In November 1913, aged eighteen, he had every intention to provide himself with such freedom. Absconding from his father's house on a night of pouring rain, he secretly departed for France, crossing the border and heading towards Verdun to join the Foreign Legion. What attracted him to it was not the prospect of martial adventures. Thanks to its exotic aspect, the Legion would instead serve as the passageway

---

4   AN: *Die Zwille* [TN: The Catapult] (Ernst Klett Verlag, Stuttgart, 1973), translated by Henri Plard under the title *Le Lance-Pierres*, La Table Ronde, 1974, Folio reissue.

5   AN: Comments published by Armin Mohler in his book on Ernst Jünger entitled *Die Schleife* [TN: The Bow], as quoted by Banine, op. cit., pp. 18–20.

that would allow him to realise his African dream. Having arrived in Verdun, the boy felt his resolve and enthusiasm wane. To put an end to this state and prevent any possible retreat, he proceeded to burn his own bridges by throwing his [German] marks[6] into a sewer. Then, upon meeting the very first police officer, he asked the latter how to get to the Legion's recruiting office.[7] On 3 November 1913, he filled out an enlistment form while lying about his age. A few days later, he took a train to Marseille and, from there, to Sidi-bel-Abbès, where he was incorporated into the 26th training company. The plain and trivial reality he discovered was truly far removed from his dreams. Instead of the desert he had long imagined, a dreary barracks. His first exercise consisted in moving stones from one corner of the courtyard to another. After three weeks, he felt smothered by despair. With an older comrade, he proceeded to desert the Legion so as to reach the Africa that the walls of the barracks had kept hidden from him. The two fugitives would be promptly brought back by the natives, who received a bounty for this type of work. Ernst thus found himself locked up in the regimental prison of Bel-Abbès.

It was his father that would end up getting him out of this predicament. Having been warned by a kind soul and making use of all his connections, his providential father went to Berlin, specifically to the Foreign Affairs Office, which dealt with such matters. Using as a pretext the fact that Ernst, a minor, had lied about his age, he managed to cancel his son's enlistment, obtaining his repatriation. He then sent him a telegram that ended with the following recommendation: 'Have your photo taken.' Thanks to this, the photo, depicting Ernst in the Foreign Legion uniform, would find its way into the future writer's visual saga. Ever wise, his father avoided any and all reproach. He even went as far as to promise his son a place in a German expedition to

---

6   TN: The currency in Germany at the time.
7   AN: Ernst Jünger would leave behind a highly romanticised account of this adventure, *African Games*, translated by Henri Thomas, Gallimard, 1944, 'Folio' reissue.

Kilimanjaro, under the condition of his passing his *Abitur* (A levels). What a privilege it was to have had such a father as one's guide!

The Delusions of a Joyful War

There would ultimately be no expedition to Kilimanjaro. At the beginning of the summer of 1914, the assassination in Sarajevo of an Austrian archduke, heir to the Habsburgs, precipitated all of Europe into the bloodiest of wars. Patriotic passions set Germany and all other European countries ablaze. Ernst Jünger and his brother Friedrich Georg rushed to be enlisted. On the third day of the war, they were incorporated into the 73rd Hanoverian Rifle Regiment, the 'Prince Albert of Prussia' regiment, whose members wore a blue armband stamped with the word 'Gibraltar', in commemoration of the military feats accomplished at the end of the 18th century. What followed were several weeks of intensive training, the kind that the German imperial army was good at dispensing. And on 27 December 1914, the 'Gibraltar regiment' set off by train towards the military front of Champagne. Ernst Jünger writes:

> I had slipped into my pocket a small notebook meant to become my journal. I knew that the things awaiting us were unique, and I was heading towards them with great curiosity.

This notebook, along with those that followed it, would constitute the material of a future book — the first, the most famous, the most translated and the most read by entire generations of readers: *In Stahlgewittern* (Storm of Steel). He would go on to prove that the 'duffer' Jünger had had excellent literature teachers and that he had made the most of their teaching by adding a very personal style and perspective.

The very first page of the book already expresses the initial impetus to join the commencing war:

We had left the classrooms, the school benches, the workbenches, and the brief weeks of training had fused us into one great body burning with enthusiasm. [...] We had set out in a rain of flowers to seek the death of heroes. The war was our dream of greatness, power, and glory. It was a man's work, a duel on fields whose flowers would be stained with blood. There is no more beautiful death in the world (as a song once said). Ah, above all, don't stay at home — be part of this sacred communion.[8]

Considering that these notes were taken in great haste, the literary effect is quite remarkable indeed! We will soon be returning to the manner in which these Jungerian 'journals' were penned.

Disillusionment quickly set in, hastened by the shocking impact of reality. To serve as its quarters, the regiment is assigned a pitiful town in Champagne, comprised of around fifty houses and located in a flat, rainy and cold part of the countryside. Some French shells rain upon the village, causing approximately ten deaths in the company. 'The war had shown its claws and torn off its pleasant mask.' The incident would swiftly dampen the belligerent enthusiasm of those young soldiers.

The Chronicler of the Great War

On that same evening, the regiment sets out, heavily loaded, towards the trenches which are beginning to spread in coils across the chalky soil of Champagne. 'Then in silence and in single file we went across country through the night, in a landscape studded with clumps of woodland.' Gunshots startle the young soldiers. A rocket gains speed and whistles by. A stray bullet flies overhead, emitting a light humming sound that is followed by a cry. 'How often since then have I gone up the line in a mood half of excitement and half of melancholy through scenes of utter desolation!'

What follows are hours of sentry duty in shivering conditions and exhausting chores to lay out trenches and construct shelters. Dawn

---

8   AN: Unless explicitly stated, all the quotes included in the current chapter are taken from Jünger's *Storm of Steel*.

breaks, casting its light upon exhausted human forms, mud-smeared men that throw themselves on the rotten straw inside leaking shelters, which were all but simple holes dug into the chalky soil.

> After a short while with the regiment we had pretty well lost the illusion with which we had set out. Instead of the dangers we had hoped for, only mud and work and sleepless nights had fallen to our lot, and the conquest of these called for a heroism that was little to our taste. Worst of all, however, was the boredom, which was more annoying to the soldier than the proximity of death.

For Jünger and his regiment, real war and combat would come at a later point, when, at the beginning of 1915, they were directed towards Les Éparges. Wounded for the first time on 24 April, the young soldier is sent on convalescence leave to a hospital in Heidelberg. At the insistence of his ever-wise father, he would undergo military training in Döberitz to become a commissioned officer. He would emerge from it in September, having attained the rank of officer cadet, which would then be upgraded to that of lieutenant at the end of November. In his notebook, Jünger would take brief notes of everyday events, some routine-like and others far deadlier.

The accuracy characterising these daily notes would go a long way in terms of endowing the stories to come with a great deal of vigour. They comprised descriptions of both the terrain and missions, the names of the officers and men closest to Jünger, including their physiognomy and character traits, and the circumstances surrounding their injury or death under the sustained shelling of the enemy's artillery. A born diarist, Lieutenant Jünger would, whenever given a moment of respite, organise his notes, at a time when the memories were still fresh. To these he would later add various reflections to highlight the meaning behind each amusing or terrible incident.

We are thus granted the opportunity to read these lines, penned after numerous days in the nightmarish Battle of the Somme during the summer of 1916, and undoubtedly improved afterwards:

> The sunken road now appeared as nothing but a series of enormous shell holes filled with pieces of uniform, weapons, and dead bodies. The ground all round, as far as the eye could see, was ploughed by shells. You could search in vain for one wretched blade of grass. This churned-up battlefield was ghastly. Among the living lay the dead. As we dug ourselves in we found them in layers stacked one upon the top of another. One company after another had been shoved into the drum fire and steadily annihilated. The corpses were covered with the masses of soil turned up by the shells, and the next company advanced in the place of the fallen.

This Battle of the Somme would result in young Lieutenant Jünger being injured two further times and receiving the Iron Cross First Class during the month of December.

The Rescue of His Beloved Brother

The meticulous chronology established by Julien Hervier for the publication of the first volume of the *War Journals, 1914–1918*, by Pléiade, allows us to keep precise track of the very highlights of Jünger's life as a troop officer. As early as the end of December 1916, he is appointed company commander. In a letter to his parents in February 1917, he expresses indignation at the suggestion made by his father who, anxious to limit his exposure to enemy fire, advises him to seek out the position of aide-de-camp.[9] He rejects what he considers to be a slacker's act of cowardice, one that would turn him into a lackey. At the head of his own company, he was at least his own master, depending only on his direct superior.

Following his participation in several battles during the spring of 1917, his independence, not to say his insolence as an officer of the front line, would earn him a three-week sentence for his ruthless treatment of home front officers.

In July of the same year, when facing the British during the battles at Langemark on the Flanders front, he set off to find his brother

---

9   TN: This French expression has long been used in the English language to refer to a military officer who spends his time helping his superiors.

Friedrich Georg when the latter had been seriously injured. A bullet had punctured his lung and another shattered the joint of his forearm. He remained on the ground, sometimes unconscious, sometimes coming to amidst the dull and powerful shock of explosions. Three men would locate him and carry him to a shelter, as the English continued their advance, preceded by moving artillery fire. Friedrich Georg described the scene:

> In the middle of all this misery came some unexpected help: a young officer, covered in soil from his helmet to his boots, stuck his head through the door, casting a careful look inside. I only recognised him once he bent down over me, for even his face was concealed by the mud: it was Ernst…

And here is how Ernst himself tells the story:

> My brother lay among a crowd of groaning stretcher-cases in a place that stank of death. He was in a sad plight.

His main concern was to evacuate his brother at all costs prior to the arrival of the English.

> We tied him in a ground-sheet, and stuck a long pole through it, which rested on two of the men's shoulders. I squeezed his hand again, and the sad procession started on its way.

Evacuated, hospitalised and ultimately saved, Friedrich Georg would be discharged, thus escaping the storms of steel, while his brother, already wounded so many times, underwent repeated rebirths to participate in increasingly incredible battles. Between two slaughters, taking advantage of some rare moments of rest, he read the works of Ariosto.[10]

---

10   TN: Ludovico Ariosto was an Italian poet who, among other things, coined the term 'humanism'.

Mowed Down during the Great Battle

Soon came the great German offensive of 21 March 1918 on both sides of the Somme, which General Ludendorff, the unofficial commander-in-chief, expected to be pivotal in terms of deciding the very outcome of the war and forcing the Allies to accept the compromise of a peace treaty. Colossal artillery forces were assembled along an eighty-kilometre front, at a rate of 225 cannons and mortars per kilometre. The goal was to crush the English trenches, after which the assault troops would rush forward, preceding the bulk of the infantry that would occupy the conquered land and achieve the intended advance. As for Lieutenant Jünger, he commanded his own assault company.

At the specified moment, a hurricane of artillery broke out, an event described in the following manner in *Storm of Steel*:

> A curtain of flames was let down, followed by a sudden impetuous tumult such as was never heard, a raging thunder that swallowed up the reports even of the heaviest guns in its tremendous reverberations and made the earth tremble. This gigantic roar of annihilation from countless guns behind us was so terrific that, compared with it, all preceding battles were child's-play.

The officers of the assault troops stood in the shelters, watch in hand. At the selected time, they climbed over the railing, followed by their men.

> We drew our revolvers and crossed our wire, through which the first casualties were already trailing back.

The dividing line between the two armies offered a spectacle that none would ever see again. With a frightful rumble that resounded along a front extending over dozens of kilometres and comprised of lightly equipped companies, the shock troop battalions marched towards enemy lines across an almost lunar ground surface. Jünger writes:

The fury now rose like a storm. Thousands of men had undoubtedly already fallen. The red mists were traversed by spectral breaths.

It was a *no man's land* that now teemed with attackers wearing steel helmets. They marched towards the burning curtain, as the enemy's artillery now returned fire.

> In my right hand I gripped my revolver, in my left a bamboo riding-cane. [...] The tremendous force of destruction that bent over the field of battle was concentrated in our brains. [...] It reached us with such vigour that I was overcome by a feeling of happiness; one of serenity.

Jünger would remember the next hours as acts of madness committed in a drunken-like state. For the first time, one could see hand-to-hand fighting involving enormous human masses.

> In the very transport of victory I felt a sharp blow on the left side of my breast. Night descended on me. I was finished!

Not quite. Although a bullet had pierced his chest and lung, the young officer would be evacuated in the nick of time and would once again survive. The sheer incredible luck that never left his side even decreed that a friend of his would end up finding his map wallet, which contained all of his precious notebooks.

Final Battle, Final Injury

Having recovered from his injury after several weeks in hospital, Jünger returned to the front on 4 June 1918. A few weeks later, during the month of August, a new battle would break out in the vicinity of Cambrai.

> How often in years gone by we had stepped out into the western sun in a mood the same as now! Les Éparges, Guillemont, St.-Pierre-Vaast, Langemarck, Passchendaele, Mœuvres, Vraucourt, Mory! Again the carnival of carnage beckoned.

At a much later point, a witness would write to him to discuss the premonitions of one of his men: 'You know, I think that the lieutenant will kick the bucket today!' Having poorly recovered from his injuries, Jünger would in fact feel terribly weakened. He even considered the attack to have failed. In a state of trance, he felt as though he were a stranger to himself.

Despite everything, he leads his men forward at a brisk pace, leaping over holed-up gunmen, as an English machine gun takes him to task. Just as he is jumping over a trench, a shock breaks his momentum, as if he were a bird in flight:

> Letting out a great cry, a clamour through which it seemed as if I were exhaling all the air in my lungs, I spun around and fell, amidst a tinkling sound of metal. At the very moment when I felt I had been hit, I understood that the bullet had severed life at its very root […]. As I collapsed heavily on the ground surrounding the trench, I was overcome by the certainty of being inevitably doomed. Yet, strangely enough, this moment was one of the very few where I can say that I was truly happy; for at that very moment, as if by the light of a flash of lightning, I understood my life in its most complete structure…

If we are now summarising what can be read directly and obviously more completely on the pages of Jünger's *Storm of Steel*, it is for the purpose of highlighting the author's accumulating ordeals and sensations whose memory would remain indelible.

The young officer would regain consciousness shortly thereafter and in the same place, as cries ring out around him: 'Stretcher-bearers! The company commander is wounded!' A soldier then leans over him, unbuckling his belt and opening his tunic. Two round stains glisten in the middle of his right pectoral and on his back. Suffocating, his only hope is to fall, once and for all, into darkness.

Suddenly, a hurricane of fire is unleashed by the enemy's lines. A fellow officer comes and stands by his side. While firing away, he comments on their situation and its development. Jünger listens to him as if through a layer of fog and understands that things are going wrong.

CHAPTER I. THE FOUNDING EXPERIENCE

Terrified, he hears people scream: 'They're through on the left! We're surrounded!'' The injured officer then feels his energy flare up again. Clinging to the rough edges of the trench, he slowly pulls himself back up on his feet, as the blood accumulating in his lung trickles from his wounds. As the blood pours out, he feels relieved. Bare-headed, his shirt open and his pistol in hand, he observes the battle.

The English are now everywhere. A group of attackers can be seen moving behind him, pushing prisoners whose arms are in the air. In complete control of the situation, the enemy had cut off the final trench, opening the noose.

> We were surrounded by a circle of Germans and English and called upon to throw down our weapons. I urged those nearest me in a weak voice to fight it out to the death. Friend and foe were fired on alike. Some who surrounded our little band were shouting, some were dumb. [...] I looked at the two officers who were with me in the trench. They smiled back and with a shrug let their belts fall to the ground.

Jünger goes on to comment in a most soberly fashion: 'There was left only the choice of being taken or being shot.' Crawling through the trench and taking advantage of the surrounding confusion, he walks, with faltering steps, towards the German lines.

> Two Englishmen who were taking a haul of prisoners of the 99th Regiment to their own lines barred my way. I shot the nearest one in the middle of the body with my revolver. He collapsed like a dummy figure. The other blazed his rifle at me and missed.

These intense efforts would expel the blood from his lungs in a series of obvious spasms. 'I could breathe more freely, and set off at a run over the open beside the trench.'

With a light machine gun, the English now have him in their line of fire. Although many men are killed around him, he himself is miraculously spared, as he continues to stagger forward. His good fortune would lead him to the only way out of the noose that the English were now tightening. Weakened to the point of falling, he collapses into an entrenchment held by his own countrymen. Cries resound as he is rescued. He is wrapped up in a tent canvas that would serve as a stretcher. Some of his company's men escort him, ducking to evade the bullets. The man carrying the back of the stretcher is shot straight in the head and killed. A tall blonde member from his company hoists him on his back: 'I'll take you on my back, sir. Either we'll get through or, at worst, we'll lie where we fall.'

They would not succeed in this endeavour. Indeed, the rescuer himself is killed, collapsing under Jünger's weight. A second volunteer hoists him onto his shoulders. Bullets fly by, but they are ultimately very lucky: saved by the falling dusk, they reach a German aid-station.

Worthy of Merit

'Next day began the usual journey by stages to the rear', Jünger comments philosophically, accustomed by now to such evacuation procedures. 'The terrible journey by car to the war hospital brought me to the edge of the grave. Then I was in nurses' hands and resumed my reading of *Tristram Shandy* at the very passage where the order of attack had interrupted me.'

Nearly a century later, a century that seems to have flown by in the blink of an eye, the stories told by those who witnessed the Great War are now many. None, however, could ever compare to the accounts given by Lieutenant Jünger. Beyond the obvious stylistic qualities, what is most striking about this young man is that although war did not spare him in any way, his descriptions are characterised by a staggering absence of complaints, compassion or moral judgement. In his accounts, life and death, laughter and suffering are intermingled. One thus draws from them a deep feeling of serenity and peace, despite all the fury of action.

Back at the hospital, the suffering of the wounded is alleviated by the constant expression of concern, in combination with the effects of morphine and Burgundy wine. Jünger would receive a heartfelt telegram from the general commanding his division, an unexpected honour by any means. The telegram mentions an exceptional proposal addressed to the emperor himself, requesting that Jünger be presented with an award:

> Lieutenant Jünger is regarded by his entire division as the bravest leader, one who can ask anything of his men and who is followed blindly by his own company […]. The shining example he has already set on countless occasions is, in these difficult times, so superior that I feel compelled to nominate this young officer, who has proven himself to be the equal of our most brilliant aviation pilots, for our highest award — that of the Order of Merit.

Quite a glowing tribute, I must say! The requested decoration would be granted on 22 September 1918, when Jünger was twenty-three years old.

Six weeks later, the armistice is signed. Having neither been utterly crushed nor occupied, Germany is forced to accept defeat, turmoil and humiliation.[11]

---

11 AN: For a more profound understanding of the war and everything relating to it, readers should refer to the *Dictionnaire de la Grande Guerre, 1914–1918* [TN: Dictionary of the Great War, 1914–1918], published under the supervision of François Cochet and Rémy Porte, Robert Laffont, "Bouquin" collection, 2008.

CHAPTER II

BOOKS IN THE SHADOW OF MARS

CONVALESCING IN the family home in Hanover, Lieutenant Jünger begins to carry out the formatting of the sixteen notebooks in which he had, on a daily basis, noted his memories of the great ordeal. Casting his eye over those notes, his father displays great enthusiasm. Convinced of the exceptional quality of his son's testimony, he offers to publish it all himself. As regards the publisher's name, it would be that of the gardener, Robert Meier.[1] With Stendhal's *The Red and the Black* in mind, Ernst, for his part, initially considers titling his book *The Red and the Grey*, the latter being the colour of the German field uniform. Soon, however, his recollections of ancient Icelandic sagas would inspire him to opt for the highly evocative title of *In Stahlgewittern* (Storm of Steel).

Initiation into Terror

In the meantime, the initial material contained in the notebooks begins to take on the shape of a journal, a literary genre that would forge Jünger's reputation as a writer more than any other and to which he

---

1 TN: A part of the edition had a sticker on it: 'Verlag Robert Meier/Leisnig i.Sa.', meaning Robert Meier Publishing House. It was all a joke, because Robert Meier was their gardener, who took charge of the book's distribution.

himself would remain faithful beyond his one-hundredth birthday. Many other combatants of the Great War had also undertaken to keep a diary to preserve the memory of the exceptional experience they were about to go through. Most would give up after a few days or weeks, but not Jünger. Not that his quickly scribbled notes had been written in the form that would ultimately be found in the book. Julien Hervier reveals that just like the other ones, but to a greater extent, Jünger's first journal, *Storm of Steel*, involved a considerable amount of re-writing with an obvious literary intention. The war, a paroxysmal existential experience, was thus not only the 'mother' of the soldier, but also that of the writer. There is no doubt that Jünger was a born writer or almost, but it was the war that offered him the opportunity to open his mind to things and reveal the gifts he bore within. Remembering the great offensive of 21 March 1918, during which he was seriously injured for the first time after being hit in the lungs, Jünger thus offers us a philosophical and poetic transposition of this ordeal:

> The Great Battle also marked a turning point in my inner life, and not only because I considered our defeat to be henceforth possible. At the fateful hour when the struggle for a distant future had begun […], a formidable concentration of forces had led me, for the first time, to the very chasms of alien forces superior to the individual. It was something that differed from my previous experiences; it was an initiation that would do more than just open up the burning dens of terror. At that moment, as if from the top of a chariot ploughing the ground with its wheels, we also saw spiritual energies rising from the earth.

Storm of Steel

Originally bearing the caption *Excerpts from the Diary of a Shock Troop Commander* and, from the fourth edition onwards, simply *War Journal*, the work does not meet the definition of what one usually considers a journal to be. Written, for the most part, in chronological order, it does not mention any dates, and the reader is often at a loss to put a date, even an approximate one, to the events and circumstances reported by the author. Jünger himself would not withhold the fact that, to him, the literary concern of the artist prevails over the memoirist's concern for accuracy. As much out of modesty as for the sake of keeping a certain distance, the author deliberately redacted from his journals all exceedingly personal notes that were present in his original notebooks.[2] For instance, he erased any mention of his relationships with women almost completely. In *Storm of Steel*, he merely alludes to his romance with a young French woman nicknamed 'Joan of Arc'. He also avoids passing any unfavourable judgments upon his superiors or war in general, although the notebooks strongly criticise the staff officers that indulge in the practice of armchair heroics. Jünger is indignant at their lack of awareness of the realities of the front and the absurdity of certain orders that sacrifice the lives of soldiers. Let us take the date of 23 July 1918:

> To be able to write a few sleep-inducing sentences for the home front, we sacrificed the very bones of seven riflemen; and this happened despite the fact that our position's complete lack of tactical value was widely known, thanks to my reports and those of others.

Such comments would be deleted in *Storm of Steel*, where the author takes on the appearance of a model officer, an officer who, in the truthfulness of the original notebooks, wondered at times when 'this shitty war' would end.

The preface to the 1924 edition acknowledges with a certain level of humour what differentiates the notebooks penned on location from the later text written with literary intent:

> It was a strange activity indeed to be in my comfortable seat, deciphering the scribbles contained in these notebooks, whose cover was still plastered

---

2   AN: Jünger's original notebooks were deposited in the archives of Marbach. A scientific comparison with the author's published works was conducted by John King in *'Wann hat dieser Scheißkrieg ein Ende?' Writing and Rewriting the First World War*, Edition Antaios. Schnellroda, 2003, pp. 263 et seq.

with the dried mud of the trenches and covered with dark stains that I could no longer determine to have been blood or wine.[3]

Rewriting the Journals

In the eyes of certain commentators, this rewriting of Jünger's journals would raise the question of their authenticity. I consider this to be a fake issue, since the author is not a high-ranking actor in the war whose decisions or thoughts have a historical impact, but merely an insignificant witness to an immense tragedy. Upon reading the journals, one may certainly wonder if the thought attributed to a particular date was truly conceived at that precise moment or rather imagined and subsequently written. Even if the latter case were true, such complements would only result from a legitimate mental effort or equally legitimate literary concerns. From one edition to another, Jünger sometimes made substantial changes. In his comments published in the Pléiade edition, Julien Hervier has demonstrated that, to Jünger, 'no text is completely immutable.' Such constant rewriting efforts were very real indeed in the stories of the Great War and less usual in the case of World War II diaries. Those interested in such details can, just as Julien Hervier did in exemplary fashion for the Pléiade edition, always refer to Jünger's notebooks and his book's successive editions to compare the content and draw any conclusions that satisfy their curiosity.

Regarding *Storm of Steel*, it is informative to note that unlike the third edition (1924), the first two (those of 1920 and 1922) do not contain any partisan commentary. The third one was, particularly in its preface, visibly influenced by its time and by a painful awareness of defeat awakened by the French occupation of the Ruhr in 1923, as well as by the great crisis that followed and lasted until the Munich putsch in November. This edition is therefore more politicised from a

---

3   AN: Segment translated and shared by Julien Hervier in his introduction in *War Journals I: 1914-1918*, p. XVI.

nationalist perspective than the previous ones.[4] Following Hitler's rise to power in 1933, Jünger would delete all political comments so as to prevent any exploitation at the hands of the new regime's propaganda. As pointed out by Hervier, the editions that came out after 1934 are thus paradoxically closer to the 1920 and 1922 editions than to the one published in 1924.[5]

In 1920, in accordance with his previously mentioned intention, Jünger's father had two thousand copies printed of what would constitute the first edition of *Storm of Steel*. A few were sent to reviewers. A laudatory article soon attracted people's attention to the book and word of mouth did the rest among the combatants of the war. A second edition, expanded and reworked, was published in 1922, this time by a Berlin publisher. The work extended its reader base to reach a wider public. It would subsequently be reissued numerous times and be given reprints that would bring in a part of the rather meagre income that its author would enjoy over the following years.[6]

Our Mother War

Unlike so many other Germans of his generation, Ernst Jünger was not demobilised after the defeat of November 1918. Nor did he participate in the turbulent adventures of the Free Corps. What was left of the old army did not want to let go of such a promising young officer. In the defeated and chaotic Germany of the 1920s, infantry Lieutenant Jünger would punctually take up his service every morning at the Reichswehr barracks in Hanover. And every evening, having withdrawn into his

---

4   AN: It was initially translated into French in 1930 by Lieutenant-Colonel Fernand Grenier (1881–1939) and published by Payot.

5   AN: Current French editions, including Henri Plard's translation for Librairie Plon in 1960, reflect the very sobriety pervading the first two versions of 1920 and 1922.

6   AN: According to Eva Dempewolf, the author of a doctoral thesis on Jünger (*Blut und Tinte*), the print run given to *Storm of Steel* in Germany reached a total of 410,000 copies at the time of her doctoral thesis (1992).

room, the young officer would proceed to tirelessly write in order 'to give meaning to what human lowliness regards as nonsense'.

As in the work of other European writers of his generation, war would, even in allusive form, remain present in many of his later writings, writings that would fail to reach the intense heights of the works of his youth, which embody the indestructible foundation of both his existence and his fame. Jünger, in the meantime, had resumed his initial *Storm of Steel* efforts, penning three other books in a completely different way.

He first publishes *Our Mother War* in 1922, adopting the title of the first French edition. A new French translation, published in 1997, would revert to the German, albeit less poetic, title, *War as an Inner Experience*. In this book, Jünger intends to demonstrate that despite the overwhelming nature of war, one must not accept to be its victim. He gives the example of those he calls 'lansquenets', those reckless and brazen warriors that neither fear the harshness of the warfront nor ever managed to weaken. 'Filled with strength to the very brim', they did not hesitate to don their werewolf attire as they 'rushed howling across the deserted fields', expanding the boundaries of their mortal human condition. The energy of the fight drove them forward as much as intoxication provided by combat, wine or erotic impulses. They thus experienced the most extreme states of consciousness, the perception of which would be broadened at a much later point in *Annäherungen. Drogen und Rausch* (1970).[7]

What Ernst Jünger would retain from Hölderlin's poetry is the impression that the human adventure takes place in a world whose meaning remains hidden. Thanks to art, however, it is indeed possible to decipher it. Art, in fact, allows us to sense the mysterious universal order that embraces men instead of rejecting them; which is why Jünger writes the following in *Our Mother War*: 'That we should kill

---

7   TN: Approaches: Drugs and Intoxication.

men is inconsequential, for they will have to die one day — but we have no right to deny them.'

Fire and Blood

In October of 1924, a new story entitled *Das Wäldchen 125*[8] would see the light of day, ultimately being published in 1925. At the time, the author was no longer part of the *Reichswehr*, having been discharged on 31 August 1923. He thus enrolled at the University of Leipzig, joining the Department of Natural Sciences. He would spend some time attending the lessons of Hans Driesch (1867–1941), a biologist and neo-vitalist philosopher, and participate in the courses of philosopher Felix Krüger (1874–1848). He would then go on to study zoology in Leipzig until 1925 and work at the Anton-Dohm Zoological Institute in Naples until April. No longer receiving his officer's pay and suffering, just like his compatriots, from the extreme inflation caused by the occupation of the Ruhr, Jünger's only source of livelihood was a meagre military pension and his royalties as an author. These practical concerns, later aggravated by his marriage to Gretha von Jeinsen (Perpetua in his *War Journals, 1941–1945*) on 3 August 1925, probably stimulated his intention to publish new books.

One year after *Copse 125*, a book that we shall soon be returning to, a rather brief story entitled *Feuer und Blut* (Fire and Blood), would be published at the end of 1925. In it, Jünger tackles an episode from *Storm of Steel* by developing it further and granting it a new form. The intention here seems twofold. It is certainly literary, but one also notices that the author wants to justify his commitments as well. He selected a particularly heroic episode of the Great Battle, which began on 21 March 1918. Whereas *Storm of Steel* mainly used the past tense (a tense that relates to one's memories), the new book is written in the present tense as if to render its reflections more current, as highlighted

---

8   TN: Copse 125.

in the short prefaces of 1925 and 1926. In the latter, Jünger explicitly urges his comrades to become the founders of a new State:

> Love for one's homeland, comradeship, courage and discipline are all expressed through the State; in other words, [the State] must be organised in harmony with national, social, military and authoritarian axioms — for it is on these four principles that the nationalist programme is based.[9]

All the political content of the text would be expunged by Jünger after 1961, for the publication of his works. In accordance with his wishes, it is this amputated version, one that is free of political passages, which would be translated into French (at Christian Bourgois in 1998 and at Pléiade in 2008).

On 9 January 1926, Jünger sent his book to Hitler with the following dedication: 'To our national Führer, Adolf Hitler.' The recipient would respond with a warm thank you shortly afterwards. As for us, we will later be returning to this episode to focus on the relationship between these two men, whose destinies are very different indeed.

Although an undeniable literary success, *Fire and Blood* does not, in our eyes, have the philosophical and historical significance of *Copse 125*, published a year earlier.

Deciphering *Copse 125*

Of the three works which, in the aftermath of *Storm of Steel*, developed the author's new reflections on the experience of war, it is *Copse 125* which, despite its innocuous title, commands special attention, insofar as it allows us to perceive, in a most complete fashion, the worldview that its author espoused at that time.[10]

---

9 AN: A passage quoted by Julien Hervier in the French edition of *War Journals I, 1914–1918*, p. 782.

10 AN: *Copse 125* (*Das Wäldchen 125*), translated by Th. Lacaze, Payot, 1932. Reprinted by Éditions du Porte-Glaive (Paris, 1987) and once again by Payot in 1995, with a preface by Philippe Barthelet.

In this book, Ernst Jünger skilfully combines an utterly precise account of a week spent in the trenches of the summer of 1918 with various reflections whose metaphysical dimension does not, this time around, prevent him from criticising the army's high command and staff officers. Jünger explains in the introduction:

> My sole aim was to talk about a small sector (that of *Copse 125*, a mere point on the map of our General Staff) in order to describe, without any concern for the text's literary form, all the forces and reactions through which the men of our time face one another in combat and which do not stop in any way where the trajectory of the projectiles ends.

One must believe Jünger, since he insists on the absence of literary concern. Nonetheless, *Copse 125* is written in a language that alternates between crystal-clear clarity and cryptic mysteriousness, a feature that is both characteristic of and responsible for the book's very appeal.

Like most of Jünger's works, *Copse 125* offers us several reading layers. At first glance, it comes across as a graphic testimony describing the extreme experience of trench warfare for the generation who experienced it and emerged from it radically transformed. It is, however, necessary to situate the book in its own time and remember that Jünger penned this text in a defeated but by no means crushed Germany, a Germany permeated by intense currents of conflicting forces, at a time when the *Baltikum Freikorps* and the Spartacist militias were fighting for control of the streets.[11]

Like his compatriots, the writer is faced with the ever more cruel consequences of Germany's November 1918 defeat: inflation, an economic and political crisis, the occupation of the Ruhr by the French army (since January 1923), the attempted putsch by Hitler and Ludendorff on 9 November, the conflict between the Reich's central

---

11 AN: Dominique Venner, *Histoire d'un fascisme allemand. Les Corps francs du Baltikum et la révolution conservatrice* [TN: History of a German Sort of Fascism. The Baltikum Freikorps and the Conservative Revolution], Pygmalion, 1996, reprinted in 2002.

authority and the states' desire for autonomy (which led to the implementation of a state of emergency from 27 September 1923 to 1 March 1924), the Germans' almost ubiquitous awareness of being crushed by the unjust conditions of the Treaty (*Diktat*) of Versailles (28 June 1919), and the perceived powerlessness of the Weimar Republic. In Jünger's case, these torments overlapped with the despairing idea that the immense sacrifices of the war had all come to nothing.

Tribute to Hermann Löns

It is in response to this fate that *Copse 125* was penned, a fact that would ultimately be understood by readers. The first edition, published at the end of 1924, would enjoy a relatively large print circulation of 16,000 copies; a second version, with amputated nationalistic passages as implemented in *Storm of Steel*, would be published in 1935, once again in a total of 16,000 copies. A third version (4,000 copies) would be released in 1961 by Ernst Klett, as part of the author's *Works*, pending the 1978 edition (2,000 copies) by the same publisher, this time for the *Complete Works*. The final version reinforced literary coherence while removing the initial nationalistic tone. In France, a first translation by Th. Lacaze was published by Payot in 1932. It adopted the original version from 1925. Its only missing passages are, unfortunately, those that appertain to Hermann Löns (1866–1914), a writer that remains rather unknown to the French public.[12] A volunteer in 1914 despite his advanced age of forty-eight, Hermann Löns was killed in front of Reims on 26 September of the same year. The first translation was reprinted without permission by Editions du Porte-Glaive in 1987[13] and

---

12   AN: One of the best historical novels by Hermann Löns is of *völkisch* inspiration and titled *The Werewolf* (*Der Wehrwolf*, 1908). It was translated and prefaced in French by Jean-Paul Allard and published by Art et histoire d'Europe in 1986. It revolves around an incident that occurred during the Thirty Years' War in a peasant community in Lower Saxony, where Hermann Löns came from.

13   AN: At the time, Jünger wrote to me, stating that he was very annoyed by this 'pirate' edition. Still, it had at least the merit of making the original text and all

re-published by Payot & Rivages in 1995, with a foreword by Philippe Barthelet. Last but not least, a new translation by Julien Hervier consistent with the latest version of the author's *Complete Works* would be published by Christian Bourgois in 2000.

Upon reading *Copse 125*, it is difficult not to be immediately struck by a surprising paradox. If one compares two of the most striking war testimonies of the period, written by two often closely connected authors, one discovers that despite the French victory of 1918, *La Comédie de Charleroi*[14] by Pierre Drieu La Rochelle[15] gives the impression of having been written by the defeated, whereas *Copse 125*, written in the aftermath of the German defeat of 1918, seems rather like a book penned by the victorious. The latter clearly reflects a formidable vitality, a vitality which French people were hardly aware of, having been overcome by a mixture of historical weariness and numbness.

A Tragic Sort of Stoicism

In a most striking manner, what *Copse 125* illustrates above all is the nobleness of its author's feelings. It is a book that focuses on war, written by a courageous combatant in the aftermath of a painful defeat, one that was aggravated by the unjust and humiliating conditions imposed by the victors. The ink of the Treaty of Versailles had barely dried, and yet, although the shadow of defeat is present throughout the book, in vain would we look for a single word of resentment, a single trace of hatred for Germany's enemies of yesteryear.

On the contrary, what we encounter is evident esteem and even sympathy for those whom Jünger had fought against with unbridled fury. The reason is not that he could ever doubt his own rights, even for a single moment– that is not the issue here. Indeed, going back

---

of its ideological content available to a new French public. What is quoted in this text of ours are extracts from this very same French edition.
14 TN: Charleroi's Comedy.
15 AN: A work published in 1934.

thirty centuries to reconnect with the ethos of the *Iliad*, he is willing to acknowledge the fact that his adversary is also within his rights. The actions of a Frenchman who kills a German in the name of his French fatherland are as justified as those of a German who kills a Frenchman in the name of the German fatherland. Each of the two armies is within its right. When one understands this, 'one honours heroism; one honours it everywhere and above all among the ranks of one's enemy.'

As for the only people who arouse the author's contempt, they are the pacifists. Jünger writes:

> We, too, have no lack of those who, like the Frenchman Barbusse, regard war as a material affair and, turning its negative side outwards, endeavour to run up on the other a temple of peace and happiness. They give as their reasons devastated towns and frightful sufferings — as though our highest duty was the avoidance of pain. They have no mind to accept the responsibilities that demand sacrifice of such corruptible treasures as life and property when a nation's greatness and its ideas are at stake.

Twenty years later, following yet another German defeat, these words would fall upon deaf ears among many. No, adds the writer, war is not a material event, for it is subject to higher realities:

> No — war is not a material matter. There are higher realities to which it is subject. When two civilised peoples confront one another, there is more in the scales than explosives and steel. All that either holds of any weight is in the balance. Values are tested in comparison with which the brutality of the means must — to anyone who has the power to judge — appear insignificant.

And in order to dispel any ambiguity regarding the very essence of his thinking, he insists further and states that war 'is a spiritual experience too; and a realisation of a strength of soul of which otherwise we should have had no knowledge. It is the point of focus in our lives. It decides our whole further development.'[16]

Jünger does not, however, attempt to conceal any of the horrible and unbearable sides of modern warfare. He thus describes all of its cruelty, as can be seen in the following passage of *Copse 125*, where he describes the explosion of grenades amid the scrimmage:

> The effect of the bursts, which at this range can fling a man in the air to come down like a sack, can be seen from the dead bodies lying all about beside and over one another just as death cast them down. Their faces and bodies are riddled by splinters [...]. The faces of those that lie on their backs are distorted, and their eyes wide open as though fixed upon a disaster from which there was no escape. Horror is fixed there like a mask — and one that no fantasy could devise.

The writer depicts this war in all of its frightening absurdity: young men chopped to pieces under the falling shells or burned to death by gas, crushed limbs, torn bodies, injured combatants screaming out in agonising suffering. Jünger experienced all of this himself in the flesh, since he was often injured. He describes death and the worst suffering with great precision, without artifice or complacency, while keeping a sort of cold distance. His aim is neither to shock nor to please and he remains completely honest. The conclusions that he draws from this ordeal are not, however, fraught with despair or resignation. They even reach far beyond the experience of his generation. What we can readily notice in them is a 'Heraclitean' type of contemplation of the challenges imposed upon men through the ages, challenges that occur in the framework of a cosmic struggle that will never come to an end:

> There is no eternal rest. There is only eternal movement that presses every smallest particle into its service.

---

16   AN: This is more or less what Thomas Mann wrote back in 1918, something that he would subsequently contest. See *Politische Schriften und Reden* [TN: Political Writings and Speeches] (*Considérations d'un apolitique*, Gallimard, 1971).

The Rejection of Nihilism

Bearing in mind the memory of the destroyed villages and the fields ravaged by shells, the young officer-writer adds:

> Hence, we must be as hard as stone. Fields will be tilled again and villages rebuilt and men multiplied beyond all need — but time and fate go by once and then no more.

His is a deeply tragic thought, according to which every generation must assume its role. In Jünger's case, the challenge was initially that of war; and what a war it was! Indeed, it would be the first major conflict involving the use of technological equipment. Faced with the resulting devastation, one might have been led to think that the ancient values of courage and heroism had forever been lost, drained of meaning by the flood of metal and fire. One might have been forgiven for thinking that culture was being crushed by the most absurd machines. Many men of this generation, including Céline and Drieu La Rochelle, thus sank into suicidal despondency. Jünger's reaction, by contrast, is the very opposite. Summoning all of his energy, he refuses to be crushed by such equipment and to submit to machines, choosing to perceive it as 'the expression of the human will that strives to dominate matter; intelligence cast in steel.' As for the war, the simple fact that it had lasted for so long sufficed to show that men had proven much more resistant than one had ever supposed:

> There is nothing so frightful that man cannot prove himself the master of in the end. And it is just when material resources seem to reach the point of annihilation that his courage and will power reach the zenith too.

Recalling the nightmarish landscapes that would become the daily setting of his very existence during those four years of war, never does Jünger lament — on the contrary!

Those frightful landscapes were our daily surroundings where destruction ruled over all and nothing stood except the might of the soul that no force can subdue.

Rare are the writings of soldiers imbued with such tonicity. And yet, this soldier was the very opposite of a braggart or a bully. In his account of the great German offensive of March 1918, he voices his scruples about the act of killing, although this occurred at a time when the fury of repeated battles had already seized him:

> The occupants, too, of a number of dugouts built in the sides of a sunken road rushed out and fled. […] My Englishman lay in front of it, a mere lad. I had shot him right through the head. There he lay, his face relaxed. I forced myself to look him in the eyes. Often have I gone back to this moment and remembered this dead man. There is indeed a responsibility of which the State cannot relieve us. It is a score that we have to settle with ourselves; for it seeps into the very depths of our dreams.[17]

The philosophical intuitions recorded in Jünger's text, the reflections that he initiated on the topics of total mobilisation and the essence of technology, all of it heralded the ideological debates that all of Europe would end up experiencing and which would never be as intense as those that raged in Weimar-era Germany. The advent of the Third Reich would eventually put a stop to such debates. The notion that mental energy is indeed superior to the titanic powers unleashed by the global domination of technology would, however, subsist in Jünger beyond this tragic period.[18]

The response experienced by the writer in his own country, but also in a certain part of Europe from the 1930s onwards, testifies to the fact

---

17 AN: *Storm of Steel*, French edition, pp. 395–396.

18 AN: France-Marie Frémeaux very rightly emphasised the nobleness of such a perspective in the note that she dedicated to Ernst Jünger in her *Dictionnaire de la Grande Guerre, 1914–1918* [TN: Dictionary of the Great War, 1914–1918], Robert Laffont, 'Bouquins' edition, 2008. One can also consult Isabelle Grazioli-Rozet's textbook simply titled *Jünger* and published by Pardès in 2007.

that, regardless of location, people aspired to counter the materialistic interpretation of war or peace. This impulse bore within it the human spirit's first victory over nihilism, that is to say, over the tendency to reduce everything to its most base element.

CHAPTER III

WEIMAR AND THE CONSERVATIVE REVOLUTION

In *Copse 125*, which was published in 1925, Ernst Jünger announces, with remarkable prescience, the emergence of actors of a new type that would dominate German and European history during the 1920s and 1930s. He thus writes:

> I see in old Europe a new and commanding breed rising up, fearless and fabulous, unsparing of blood and sparing of pity, inured to suffering the worst and to inflicting it and ready to stake all to attain their ends — a race that builds machines and trusts machines, to whom machines are not soulless iron, but engines of might which it controls with cold reason and hot blood. This puts a new face on the world.

In both Moscow and Rome, in Warsaw as well as in Berlin, the war had indeed given rise to a new type of man that supplanted the futile phrasemongers of the previous era: men who, in the words of Nikolai Berdyaev, are inclined 'to transpose military methods to the very structure of life, practicing methodical coercion — a type of human that is fond of power and mindful of force and that manifested himself in both communism and fascism.'[1]

---

1 AN: Nikolai Berdyaev, *Les Sources et le Sens du communisme russe* [TN: The Sources and Aim of Russian Communism], Gallimard, 1951.

In the Chaotic Germany of the 1920s

In Germany in particular, the fate of these new 'leaders' heralded by Jünger would be imposed upon them by their own era. Indeed, this destiny of theirs had begun to take shape in 1914. For the survivors, it would truly be forged four years later, in the nightmare of defeat and revolution.

Following the anxiety and suffering endured by Germany during those years of war, several events, namely the request for an armistice in the first days of November 1918, the abdication of the emperor, and the proclamation of the republic in a context of utter defeat, would unleash a tidal wave of revolts. In the space of less than a week, the powerful Wilhelminian state machine would all but vanish. The mutinies in the country's fleet and army, which began in the first days of November, would be followed by Spartacist or anarchist uprisings in all major German cities.

On the evening of 9 November 1918, at a time when Wilhelm II had made the decision to seek refuge in the Netherlands, Berlin and the other major cities fell prey to the outbreak of Spartacist riots, that is, to the German version of Bolshevism, which had triumphed in Russia a year earlier. In Moscow, Lenin was convinced that the red revolution would extend to Germany. And it would indeed prove to be a very close call. The ultimate failure of this revolutionary project was due to the agreement sealed by socialist minister Noske with the *Freikorps*, an unforeseen phenomenon that had arisen from the chaos and rubble of the former imperial army. Against all expectations, the latter would reap success in Germany, while their equivalent counterparts, the 'White Guards', failed in Russia.[2]

Within the mutinous regiments, a few volunteers gather spontaneously around certain young officers or mere non-commissioned

---

2   AN: Dominique Venner, *Les Blancs et les Rouges. Histoire de la guerre civile russe, 1917–1921* [TN: The Whites and the Reds — A History of the Russian Civil War, 1917–1921], Éditions du Rocher, 2007.

officers that had just extricated themselves from the war. They are not mature enough to allow themselves to be insulted and mistreated by rioters and furious crowds. As people spit in their face and tear off their shoulder straps (which symbolise authority), and they themselves are chased through the streets, they decide to counter. In the deserted barracks, they regroup, creating small volunteer units that adopt the name of an improvised leader. These *Freikorps* members have the advantage of being professional, armed and audacious. Soon, they would be joined by students and secondary school pupils who had previously been too young to be mobilised and whose hearts were ablaze with the dark patriotism of defeat. One of them, Ernst von Salomon, would later become famous for his account of their breathtaking adventure in an intense book that young activists would read all across Europe.[3]

The fragile socialist government of November 1918 was in dire need of them. Indeed, the police and army having vanished, they represented the Reich's last rampart in the face of insurrection. At the behest of minister Noske, the *Freikorps* would save a republic that its members were not even fond of. On two occasions, in December 1918 and January 1919, they would reclaim Berlin before intervening throughout the Reich to crush the red uprisings. This would be achieved by means of cannon fire and machine guns, with hundreds of deaths and quite a few atrocities perpetrated by each side. For a long time, Germany thus found itself in an endemic state of civil war. The final act of this era of armed unrest would be the Munich Putsch on 9 November 1923, which would throw a spotlight on Adolf Hitler's name.

After 1923, and until 1930, the Weimar Republic would experience a period of relative calm. It was then, during those few years, that a swarm of different movements emerged, as did the various nationalist newspapers in which Ernst Jünger would go on to play a major role. Through a principle of reciprocity, they would enable him to reach one of the peak moments of his life.

---

3   AN: Ernst von Salomon, *The Outlaws* (*Die Geächteten*, 1930). Published by Plon in 1931 and reprinted by Bartillat in 2007.

At the Heart of the Conservative Revolution

The history of this German revolutionary Right would be echoed throughout Europe. It extends all the way until the great crisis of 1929–1930, which would fuel the powerful rise of the National Socialist Party—a rise that would prove fatal to it.

These years represent a period of exceptional excitement, a period that was very different to the one that preceded it. Rifles were stored in secret warehouses and were replaced by small newspapers and magazines. The militarised habits and violent overtones of the previous period did not, however, disappear.

Indeed, one saw the formation of a number of 'combat leagues' (*Wehrverbände*), often rooted in the *Freikorps* and recruiting largely among youth movements. These groups, whose variable numbers were perhaps close to one hundred thousand members throughout Germany, constituted the very breeding ground for a prodigiously dynamic movement of ideas. This current of ideas was later given the generic name of *Konservative Revolution* (KR), or Conservative Revolution, by Armin Mohler, who worked as Ernst Jünger's secretary for a period of four years, from 1949 to 1953.[4] In his doctoral thesis, which he defended in Basel, in 1949, he actually coined this concept, which was not in use at the time. This famous thesis, which was initially published in 1950, is based on its author's very extensive bibliographic research and was subsequently constantly expanded.[5] In the sense attributed

---

4   AN: Armin Mohler was born in Basel (Switzerland) on 12 April 1920 and passed away on 4 July 2003. He published a yet untranslated book centring around the years he spent with Jünger and entitled *Ravensburger Tagebuch. Meine jahre mit Ernst Jünger* [TN: Ravensburg Diary—My Years with Ernst Jünger], Karolinger, 1999.

5   AN: Armin Mohler, *Die Konservative Revolution in Deutschland 1918–1932* [TN: The Conservative Revolution in Germany, 1918–1932], translated by Henri Plard and Hector Lipstick, Pardès, 1993. French bibliography developed by Alain de Benoist. One can also have a look at *La Révolution conservatrice dans l'Allemagne de Weimar* [TN: The Conservative Revolution in Weimar Germany], published by Kimé in 1992, under the supervision of Louis Dupeux. Armin Mohler points

to it by Mohler himself, the expression 'Conservative Revolution'[6] was allegedly coined by the poet Hugo von Hofmannsthal during a lecture he delivered in Munich in 1927, titled 'Literature as the Nation's Spiritual Space'. In Mohler's mind, however, it encompasses a vast political, literary and artistic movement that developed in Germany between 1918 and 1933. Reaching its peak around 1925, this completely unstructured protean movement actually surfaced long before 1918. According to Mohler, it was generated by the crisis of the modern world and the 'dislocation of the old Christian framework which, for an entire millennium, had given the West its very structure'. In contrast to the reactionary Right, the KR was not disheartened by this development. Some of the greatest German thinkers and authors are indeed associated with it, including Thomas Mann (prior to 1918), Oswald Spengler, Werner Sombart, Carl Schmitt, Ernst von Salomon, Arthur Moeller van den Bruck, Ernst Kantorowicz, Gottfried Benn and Ernst Jünger, though many other less renowned individuals also contributed to its flourishing. Historically speaking, it was greatly influenced by two factors: German romanticism and the ideas of Nietzsche.

---

out that the concept of the Conservative Revolution could be extended to all of Europe. He thus mentions the Russian Dostoyevsky (1821–1881), Frenchmen Georges Sorel (1847–1922) and Maurice Barrès (1862–1923), the Italians Vilfredo Pareto (1848–1923) and Gaetano Mosca (1858–1941), and the Spaniards Miguel de Unamuno (1864–1936) and José Ortega y Gasset (1883–1956).

6   AN: Armin Mohler notes that Maurras had incidentally used the expression in his work entitled *L'Enquête sur la monarchie* [TN: Inquiry into the Monarchy] (1909): 'We will never succeed in revolution, especially a conservative one, in a reinstatement and return to order, save by means of certain administrative and military elements.' The expression 'Conservative Revolution' is, however, used in a restrictive sense here, namely that of a counter-revolution. The German meaning is, by contrast, very different.

The Influence of German Romanticism

A powerful intellectual and poetic current born at the end of the 18th century, German romanticism rebelled against the artificiality and rationalism of the French Enlightenment. Following in Herder's footsteps, it contrasted abstract universalism with the living and multifaceted reality of different cultures, in the context of which all peoples are bearers of their own original genius, of a soul that endures through time by adopting ever-changing forms and of which language is the expression.

In the wake of Marcel Brion, one of the French writers who would speak of German romanticism with the greatest possible empathy is Julien Gracq (1910–2007). In his description of Novalis, he penned remarks with the actual potential to ruffle the conformism of his somewhat lettered compatriots:[7]

> French classicism and German romanticism undoubtedly represent the two opposing points of maximal possible deviation. French classicism has bequeathed to us a collection of completed works. Amidst the library shelves, however, the only occasional motion that one experiences is that of a rat's tiny gnawing movements [...] As for the books that belong to German romanticism, the situation is indeed different: whatever the formal disappointment engendered by works that are sometimes flawed, often botched, and many a time unfinished, what each of them still bears for us is the noticeable sign of a promise whose scope infinitely exceeds that of its artistic means. We are thus haunted by the notion that there are far more things in motion there than the books have conveyed to us.

This remark fully applies to the works of Jünger, which reach beyond their formal perfection.

What the thinkers of the Conservative Revolution retained from Nietzsche's writings is his challenging of nihilism ('the death of God'), to which they respond with a new search for meaning. To them, both

---

7   AN: Julien Gracq, *Préférences* [TN: Preferences], José Corti, 1989, p. 250 and the next.

national religiosity and that of action perpetuate all that is ephemeral in one's individual destiny. The myth of the eternal return reinforces a cyclical vision of history that is in radical opposition to the linear and finalistic viewpoint that results from Christianity and which the Enlightenment proceeded to secularise. When understood in accordance with such a mental pattern and as part of its astronomical significance of returning to the initial point, the word 'revolution' takes on an uncommon sort of depth. It does not merely imply severance and upheaval, but also reversal and the completion of a historical cycle. Indeed, it bears within itself the promise of a new point of departure. As for conservatism, and contrary to its French meaning, it suggests neither immobility nor attachment to deciduous forms. In the mindset of German romanticism, it represents, in fact, man's awareness of the permanent and the essential, of all that resists time and that a revolutionary impulse will be able to free from any and all outdated forms. This notion of a revolution that would ensure the resurgence of a fundamental kind of order is a bearer of great dynamism. It rests upon the metaphysical conviction that the epoch in question is that of an interregnum that lies between an already dead order and another yet to come, a sort of 'zero point', as Jünger would say, starting from which everything becomes possible.

The Advocate of Radical Nationalism

Having become the dominant intellectual figure of the national-revolutionary current of the 1925–1930 period, Ernst Jünger himself did not participate in the irregular *Freikorps* fights whose memory permeated the movement. What he wrote about it in *The Worker* (1932), however, is evidence of the esteem that he had for the very meaning of their activity, though he himself had belonged to the somewhat opposite side of the *Reichswehr*:

> Just as during the 'la Fronde' war, one fought for the king against the king, the same is true of the *Freikorps* at the borders, volunteer associations

and isolated saboteurs who sacrificed themselves in spite of the State in the name of the State [*Reich*]. And it was precisely there that it turned out Germany still had a type of man that could be counted on and that was equal to the task of overcoming anarchy. The remarkable resurrection of the former lansquenets within these troops, who, after four years of war, left as volunteers to wage war in the east; the defence of Silesia; the mediaeval massacre of Rhineland separatists with clubs and axes; the protests against sanctions by means of explosives; the spilt blood; and other actions through which the infallibility and correctness of a secret instinct are manifested, are all signs that shall endure as touchstones for future historians to use.[8]

In the meantime, Jünger had made the acquaintance of Ernst von Solomon, who was *the* herald of the *Baltikum Freikorps*. He was also in fairly close 'technical' contact with Lieutenant Commander Ehrhardt, one of the most famous *Freikorps* leaders and one of the actors of the disastrous Kapp putsch of 1920;[9] a not very gifted man, it must be said, in terms of politics and the debating of ideas. Many other former members of the *Freikorps* would act as his companions during those few years.

---

8   AN: Ernst Jünger, *The Worker* (*Der Arbeiter. Herrschaft und Gestalt*, 1932), translated by Julien Hervier and published by Christian Bourgois in 1989, p. 316. In his book entitled *A German Officer in Occupied Paris: The War Journals, 1941–1945* (Julliard, 1965, p. 474), Jünger tempers this point of view by recalling the disappointing memory he had of the few weeks during which, at the end of 1923, he had acted as the correspondent of the famous Captain Rossbach in Leipzig. At the time, however, the *Freikorps* had been disbanded and had transformed into clandestine networks or mutual-aid associations, thus no longer playing the historical role which had been theirs until 1921.

9   AN: Regarding the Kapp Putsch (13 March 1920), readers are advised to refer to the 11th chapter of our study entitled *Histoire d'un fascisme allemand. Les Corps francs du Baltikum et la révolution conservatrice* [TN: History of a German Sort of Fascism — The Baltikum Freikorps and the Conservative Revolution]. At the time, Jünger was an officer in the *Reichswehr* and thus intervened in Hanover to disperse a Spartacist riot that had taken advantage of the Kapp Putsch.

Having already achieved great fame thanks to his war books, Jünger was not unknown to others when, in 1925, he launched himself into the tumultuous waters of the Conservative Revolution.

In his study of the movement's complex cluster, Armin Mohler distinguishes several thought currents, each with its own nuances and variations. Some writers close to the KR would, in fact, continue to greatly evolve during the 1920s-1930s, including Ernst Jünger, as we shall see, and even Thomas Mann, whose *Reflections of a Non-political Man* can indeed be regarded as one of the writings of the Conservative Revolution, which would not be the case at all with the works he penned in the aftermath of the defeat.

Moeller van den Bruck and Jünger

One of the writers that best defined the distinctive 'vision' of the German Conservative Revolution in the 1920s is undoubtedly Arthur Moeller van den Bruck. His line of thought is therefore interesting to mention in comparison with that of Ernst Jünger.

Belonging to the previous generation, Moeller van den Bruck would intervene earlier than Jünger in the debates of the time. Multilingual and possessing vast historical, literary and artistic knowledge, he lived in Paris and Florence and was passionate about French and Italian art. A translator of Barbey d'Aurevilly, Maupassant and Dostoyevsky (*Complete Works* in twenty-two volumes) into German, he himself published several political essays, notably *Das Recht der jungen Völker* (1919)[10] and *Das dritte Reich* (1923),[11] whose title would lead to confusion ten years later. Indeed, Moeller van den Bruck was in no way Hitlerian. What his book referred to was the German mediaeval myth of the *Reich*, which bears no connection to what Hitler would do with the notion. It relates neither to the French nation-state nor to a multinational empire of the Habsburg type, nor even to the centralised

---

10 TN: The Right of Young Peoples.
11 TN: The Third Reich.

system that would be established by Hitler. The historical form to which it does relate is an entirely mediaeval one, namely that of the Holy Germanic Empire.

Intellectually, Jünger shares several characteristics with Moeller van den Bruck: vast literary knowledge, a friendly attitude towards France, and a European mindset that did not yet exist at the time. Despite being active in quite close circles, they differed from each other in terms of their generational gap. Indeed, Moeller was born in 1876, almost twenty years before Jünger. He was thus too old for the decisive adventure of the war. He was a brilliant intellectual, but no more than an intellectual, lacking the military experience of his younger counterpart. Owing to his temperament, furthermore, he was a doctrinarian, which Jünger was not in any way.

As a disciple of Herder and Dostoyevsky and a good connoisseur of European art and literature, Moeller had acquired the belief that every people had an inner life (an inner mould) of its own, a homogeneous national style that transcends time; a specific spirit, the *Volksgeist*, transmitted across generations, a spirit that survives all historical incidents and circumstantial patterns. His perception of universal history was at odds with Spengler's, as he rejected the analogy that the author of *The Decline of the West* establishes between cultures and living organisms. Nor was he convinced of the accuracy of the theory of cultural cycles and the fatalism that arises from it. Unlike Spengler, he did not believe in the inevitable death of cultures. And yet, although Spenglerian 'pessimism' was foreign to him, he did not partake in liberal or Marxist 'optimism'. In his view, no nation is to be considered 'young' or 'old' because of its organic chronology: peoples are 'old' or 'young' according to their behaviour at a given time. 'Young' peoples are the ones that retain their bursting and pro-active vitality. By contrast, 'old' peoples are those who consider themselves to be 'fully developed'. Moeller thus criticises Maurice Barrès for his philosophical notion of 'the earth and the dead', which he views as the admission of an 'old" nation whose only recourse is to focus on its own past. Unlike Spengler, he believes that destiny cannot be quantified through an equation: 'History is the history of what cannot be calculated.' Indeed, there is always a chance of regeneration. The memory of the Carolingian renaissance or the Gothic rebirth validates his rejection of the Spenglerian law of irreversibility.

A Stimulus for Hope

Moeller regards liberalism as the main factor responsible for contemporary decadence and as the reason behind the dissolution of the *Volksgemeinschaft* (i.e. the national community). 'Liberalism is the ruin of peoples,' he writes in *The Third Reich* — which should be understood as moral ruin. This topic would subsequently be adopted by all the ideologists of the Conservative Revolution, particularly by the jurist and political scientist Carl Schmitt, who, in his work entitled *Der Begriff des Politischen* [The Notion of the Political] (1927), would go on to show that the essence of liberalism is that of individualism.

Moeller contrasts the cult of reason that stems from the Enlightenment[12] and acts as the source of all materialism with the notion of understanding and vital forces. In this respect, he was in agreement with the Jünger of 1925.

In *The Right of Young Peoples*, Moeller proposes a strategy that reflects an 'optimism' which, in some way, will be shared by Jünger when he speaks of 'heroic realism'. The best way to fight against an idea, he

---

12 AN: The Enlightenment is to be understood here as an ideology and not in the context of the complex, multifaceted and often positive historical reality of the Enlightenment's evolution of ideas, which asserted the necessity for every (European) man to think outside the limits of dogma and, in Montesquieu's case, the capacity of every people to adopt its own definition of good, in harmony with its own laws and culture. As part of his universalistic and mathematical vision, Condorcet would rebel against this differentialism, as to him, 'a good law must be good for all men, just as a truthful statement is true for everyone.'

says, is to overcome it from within, to take it to its endpoint until it reverses itself and becomes its own opposite:

> We shall once again write the word 'liberalism' as *freedom*. We shall once again write the word 'democracy' as *popular identity*. Likewise, we shall write the word 'socialism' in a completely different way: as *Reich*.[13]

Shortly after the revolution of November 1918, at a time when Jünger was still an officer in the *Reichswehr*, Moeller van den Bruck would become the head of a circle of writers and journalists hostile to both communism and liberalism, without any nostalgia, however, for the Wilhelminian era. In response to the signing of the Treaty of Versailles (on 28 June 1919), the circle would take on the name *Juniklub* (meaning 'June Club'). Its emblem is a ring, *the* Ring, a symbol of faithfulness and power (*Nibelungen*), and also one of harmony with the cosmos and the eternal return. Under the influence of his *spiritus rector*, the *Juniklub* would become the first genuine 'revolutionary-conservative' circle, one that is usually defined as 'young conservative' (*Jungkonservative*).

Following the crisis of 1923, during the stabilisation period that had begun for Weimar Germany, the *Juniklub* went into a state of crisis. Several of its members would disperse in search of political alliances, under the pretext of being 'realistic', a discreet term that often acts as a cover-up for opportunism and personal ambition. Heinrich von Gleichen, who had, until then, supported the efforts of Moeller van den Bruck, would instead found the *Herrenklub* (Club of Lords), thus revealing his support for the establishment. Feeling desperate as a result of the dispersion that had afflicted the school of thought that he himself had founded, and no longer believing in the possible appearance of the new political forces that he had been hoping to see in the immediate future, Moeller took his own life on 30 May 1925. Eight years later, in his preface to the French edition of *The Third Reich*, a young Thierry Maulnier would state: 'Moeller van den Bruck did not

---

13   AN: Moeller van den Bruck, *Das dritte Reich*, Alexis Rédier, 1933, reprinted by. Fernand Sorlot, 1981.

devise his suicide to be an act of renunciation, but rather a seed, wanting it to serve as a stimulus for hope and rioting.'

To our knowledge, Ernst Jünger did not have the opportunity to comment on Moeller van den Bruck's act. And yet, young Thierry Maulnier's words would not have been out of place had they come from Jünger's own pen at that time.

The Currents of the Conservative Revolution

The first KR current noted by Mohler for being the oldest of all is the one he terms *völkisch*. We know, of course, that this word has no genuine equivalent in French.[14] The term 'racist' is the least adequate. The current's guiding image is that of a constancy of 'Germanity', whether ethnic, linguistic or cultural. Referring to the writer Hermann Löns in the first German edition of *Copse 125*, Jünger states that he is 'of a *völkisch* nature, meaning that he feels the very heartbeat of the tribe from which he stems', i.e. the people of Lower Saxony.

It is, in fact, the Brandenburg gymnastics teacher Friedrich Ludwig Jahn (1778–1852) that is regarded as the father of the *völkisch* movement; a man considered to have ignited the passions of the nationalist youth of the 'wars of liberation' (1813). To a certain extent, *Völkism* thus coincides with Pan-Germanism and its desire to bring together, within one single *Reich*, all of the German communities that had dispersed beyond the borders.

A second current is that of the so-called *Jungkonservative* ('young conservatives'), whose dominant personality was, as already mentioned, the essayist Arthur Moeller van den Bruck.[15] Although a rarity within the Conservative Revolution, both mediaeval and even Christian elements are quite common among 'young revolutionary

---

14 TN: Nor in English, for that matter.
15 AN: *The Third Reich*, op. cit. Also by the same author is *The Right of Young Peoples*, which includes a preface by Alain de Benoist and was published by Pardès in 1993.

conservatives', including Edgar J. Jung, one of the future victims of Hitler's Night of the Long Knives purge on 30 June 1934.

A third current, which Armin Mohler terms *bündisch* (a term that can be translated as 'communitarian'), represents the very nucleus of this truly very vast youth movement, whose origin dates back to the *Wandervogel* of the late 19th century. Around 1925, *bündisch* movements (Eagles, Falcons, Artaman, Freischar Schill, Gueux, etc.) were well-represented within the *Jugendbewegung* ('youth movement'), whose numbers would, all tendencies included, total four million members in the 1930s.

The *bündisch* movement is characterised by the presence of a *Bund*, a type of organisation inspired by the strength of community ties, as opposed to the anarchic individualism of the old *Wandervogel*. Emphasis is placed on the unrestricted appointment of leaders and the self-education of an elite destined to conduct a true cultural revolution.[16]

Just like the youth movement, the *bündisch* mindset is hostile to the adult world, for it is as imbued with nationalism as it is with communitarian socialism. It would thus exert its influence on *Die Kommenden*, a weekly in which Ernst Jünger acted as a co-editor in 1930. Some of the oldest members of the current, such as Karl Otto Paetel and Werner Lass, who were both close to Jünger, would end up in the ranks of the opposition to the Third Reich and in certain National Bolshevik groups. Werner Lass would even join the Communist Party.

---

16 AN: French literary sources remain few when it comes to the youth movement and the *Wandervogel*. One can, however, consult Karl Höffke's (1896–1933) *Wandervogel — Revolt against the Bourgeois Spirit* (Pardès, 1985) and Hans Blüher's *Wandervogel — History of a Youth Movement* (Les Dioscures, 1994). One of the inspirations of the *bündisch* movement was actually the poet Stefan George (1868–1933), one of whose disciples was none other than Colonel Claus von Stauffenberg (1907–1944), the organiser of the assassination attempt against Hitler on 20 July 1944.

Jünger and the National Revolutionaries

The fourth current distinguished by Armin Mohler within the Conservative Revolution is that of the 'national revolutionaries', a current sometimes labelled as 'soldier nationalism'. Ernst Jünger and Ernst von Salomon are its typical representatives, each in his own way. This current, in fact, arose from the world war and from the revolutionary clashes that followed it. At an age of great malleability, a large number of young men were forever defined by the decisive experience of those storms of steel. This experience forged a worldview that broke with the past in a most radical fashion. Within their own generation, the men that were thus moulded constitute an active minority that was not overwhelmed by the ordeal. In this generation, the fundamental bourgeois aspiration for comfort, hedonism and security simply crumbled.

Between 1914 and 1923, tens of thousands of young men acquired a taste for a type of existence wherein one's indulging in risk led them to despise individualism and well-being both as values and as ultimate ends. To borrow some of Jünger's words, these youths belonged to a race whose members 'can gladly be blown up and still perceive the event as a confirmation of order'.

In his *Deutsche allein* (1931),[17] a characteristic book of the 'national-revolutionary' train of thought, Franz Schauwecker, who was one of the prominent authors of the movement, summarises its mindset:

> History, the world, and the nation must not be viewed from the perspective of an individual regarded as a supreme authority, but in accordance with the law of superiority that we are preparing to establish in Germany once again.

The path that leads to such an accomplishment clearly sets the national revolutionaries apart from other groups. In harmony with the future expression coined by the Italian philosopher Julius Evola, they were determined to 'ride the tiger', that is to say, to vanquish the modern world using its own weapons. Published in 1932, Jünger's *The Worker*

---

17   TN: Germans alone.

would come across as one of the greatest expressions of this very mindset. We will come back to this at a later point.

The vision of the revolutionary Right is not rooted in ethnic soil, as is the case among the *Völkischen*. And yet, as written by Schauwecker, it stems from a purely Germanic vision:

> There exists today a German sort of mysticism which originates from the war […]. For we have fought against the whole world. It was, indeed, a German fight. By losing the war, we actually won it. By suffering defeat, we have been granted the necessary condition for future victory. The war, prior to all that followed, was but purification and a path through the world.

A fifth movement, very different from the previous ones, has been linked to the Conservative Revolution: the peasant movement (*Landvolkbewegung*), which developed from 1928 to 1930 in Schleswig-Holstein, Hanover and East Prussia and centred around the enigmatic personality of an old-lineage farmer, Claus Heim.[18] Born from the economic difficulties pervading the peasant world, the movement became political, calling into question the Weimar regime as well as the Treaty of Versailles. Several former *Freikorps* members and intellectuals of the revolutionary Right granted the *Landvolk* their support, notably Ernst von Salomon, who was imprisoned in 1928 for having participated in the attacks orchestrated by the movement. He actually mentions this rebellious and deep-rooted adventure in his book entitled *Die Stadt* (1932).[19]

Campfires before the Reveille

The academic distinction between the various currents of the Conservative Revolution as established after the fact by Mohler must

---

18 AN: The main character in Pierre Granier-Deferre's film *La Horse* (1970), starring Jean Gabin in the main role, is somewhat reminiscent of Claus Heim's proud, silent, harsh and feudal nature.

19 AN: Ernst von Salomon, *The City* (*Die Stadt*, 1932), Gallimard, 1933. [TN: Translated as *It Cannot Be Stormed*.]

necessarily comprise an arbitrary element. In actual fact, there were more connections between them than their portrayal might suggest. Ernst Jünger would express this with a touch of poetic nostalgia in his *War Dairies — A Cottage in the Vineyard*, dated 23 September 1945, with the world having changed dramatically a few months earlier:

> Today, nationalist circles seem to me like campfires before the reveille. That was where things were decided; Berlin attics and Brandenburg cellars defined the style of the times. In the morning, the circle would disperse in search of exploits, as the sagas say. Some were lucky enough to fall on the battlefield. Others had to cross borders, were hunted down, murdered, executed, tortured, or, once surrounded, opted for suicide. [Others still] became potentates, police chiefs, proconsuls, agitators, or convicts, and were finally stripped of all meaning like a deck of cards that one shuffles after the end of the game.

Despite their similarities, oppositions were clearly noticeable in matters of foreign policy, particularly in relation to Soviet Russia. These differences partly overlapped with what distinguishes two German historical traditions, namely the Catholic Habsburg Empire and Lutheran Prussia. In the eyes of many 'young conservatives', the main enemy had been located in the east ever since the Bolshevik Revolution of 1917. The situation was quite different in the case of Jünger and the 'national revolutionaries', who were wrongly mistaken for 'National Bolsheviks'.[20]

---

20 AN: Louis Dupeux, *Stratégie communiste et dynamique conservatrice. Essai sur les différents sens de l'expression «national-bolchevisme»* [TN: Communist Strategy and Conservative Dynamics — An Essay on the Different Meanings of the Expression 'National Bolshevism'], Honoré Champion, 1976. In it, the author offers the following definition:

> "True" National Bolshevism is an ideology espoused by the most radical extreme right, whose representatives appropriate the socio-economic revolution of Soviet communism and ally themselves with it, as they believe that, thanks to conservative dynamics, Germany and traditional values will ultimately triumph in a communistic and Eastern-European context.

CHAPTER IV

THE GERMAN-RUSSIAN ALLIANCE

In April 1922, the Treaty of Rapallo formalised German-Soviet relations. It also paved the way for secret military cooperation between the *Reichswehr* and the Red Army. The German ambassador to Moscow from 1922 to 1928 and the rather reluctant architect of the German-Russian agreements, Count von Brockdorff zu Rantzau, enjoyed great support in National Bolshevik circles as a result of a reputation that was partly marked by Russophilia.

After 1920, and thanks to its opposition to the state of affairs that had resulted from the Treaty of Versailles, Soviet Russia seemed like a potential ally to a small part of the German national opinion.

Prussia's Russophile Tradition

Whereas sympathy for the East, which is discernible in most 'national-revolutionary' writings, has ancient roots in the northeast of Germany and specifically Prussia, it is virtually non-existent in the South and

> An interesting definition, but one that fails to take into consideration the aspect of Russophilia that is not Bolshevik in any way and is inscribed in the historical tradition of Northern Germany and Prussia. On the other hand, one could also wonder what the term 'extreme right' actually meant in the Germany of that era, since it is a ragbag of controversy rather than an actual ideological and political category.

West of the country. In his *Reflections of a Non-Political Man*, Thomas Mann wrote the following in 1918:

> In my opinion, there is no doubt whatsoever that the German and Russian natures are closer to one another than the Russian and the French, and incomparably more so than the German and Latin.

An identical opinion is encountered with Dostoyevsky, who, at the end of the previous century, had described Germany as a 'protesting country' in his *Writer's Diary*:

> The most characteristic and essential trait of this great, proud and peculiar people — ever since their appearance on the historical horizon — consisted of the fact that they never consented to assimilate their destiny and their principles to those of the outermost Western world, i.e., the heirs of the ancient Roman tradition.

It is quite natural that Lutherans and Orthodox Christians should target Catholic Rome and its presumed daughter, France, with the same level of execration. To do so, however, is to trivialise an entire cultural, political and even religious tradition, one of Celtic and Frankish origin, whether feudal or Gallican, in contrast with the Latin or Catholic tradition that one usually associates France with. One must remember that this multifaceted nation celebrates opposites with a great deal of diligence, whether François Villon and Malherbe or Molière and Bossuet. As we have already stated, esteem and sympathy were historically more common on either side of the Rhine than lack of understanding and hostility. One only witnessed the rise of aversion after the catastrophe of 1870 and, of course, after the disaster of 1914, and even more so on the Germanic side in the aftermath of the Treaty of Versailles.[1]

---

1   AN: Those interested in comparing the reciprocal caricatures that were so common in France and Germany between 1914 and 1918 should refer to Jean-Jacques Becker and Gerd Krumeich's *La Grande Guerre. Une histoire franco-allemande* [TN: The Great War — A Franco-German Story], Tallandier, 2008, particularly

Northern Germany and Southern Germany

In Germany, the borders that delineate people's feelings towards Russia coincide with the very ancient, cultural and historical border of the *Limes* and the Main. It divides Germany in two: a predominantly Catholic Germany, that of the South-West, which was subjected to Roman and Catholic influence; and another, that of the North-East, which evaded it. The former is associated with the Austro-Hungarian monarchy and was often at odds with Russia, with the latter acting as heir to the Prussian and Lutheran tradition and frequently seeking an alliance with Russia.

Established in the Margraviate of Brandenburg and stemming from a mixture of Germanic populations and Slavs, Prussia had always, until the days of Bismarck, pursued a cautious policy towards Russia, limiting itself to what it considered realistic, spurning all adventurous behaviour and preserving harmony with its great easterly neighbour, to the detriment of Poland if necessary.

Prussia undoubtedly served as a rampart for the European West in the face of the East. Over time, however, it learnt to deal with the threat, whose extent it was very well-aware of.

Unlike Napoleon or Hitler, who were both from the south of Europe and had fed upon imperialist traditions originating from Rome or Habsburg, no Prussian statesman ever fell into the trap of attempting to conquer Russia's vast expanses.[2]

In the 1920s and 1930s, the anti-Soviet and crusader-like slogans shouted by Hitler in Munich fell upon deaf ears in Prussia. Pondering the Thirty Years' War, the Prussian Hermann Rauschning perceived the latter as a product of Habsburg catholicity: 'a South marked by Spanish fanaticism and not by the cold realism of the Prussian North.'

---

pp. 106–109. One will thus see that Francophobia was much less cultivated in Germany than Germanophobia was in France during that same period.

2 AN: Jean-Paul Bled, *Histoire de la Prusse* [TN: The History of Prussia], Fayard, 2007.

In his work entitled *Prussianism and Socialism* (1920), Oswald Spengler highlights the imperialist, Catholic, baroque and, quite frankly, Spanish character which, in his eyes, typifies both the Habsburg monarchy and the South of Germany:

> Within himself, the Spaniard feels the presence of a great mission... He is either a soldier or a priest... The Spanish spirit longs to conquer the planet, establishing an empire on which the sun would never set... Vienna is, likewise, a creation of the Spanish spirit... [Austrian people] are both Habsburgian and Spanish, and would remain so even if no single descendant of the House of Habsburg were to survive.[3]

Let Spengler assume responsibility for these rather questionable views, which we are only quoting to highlight the presence of contrasting traditions.

The Birth of National Bolshevism

'National Bolshevism', whose importance is often exaggerated but which Ernst Jünger sympathised with, was fuelled by Prussian Russophilia. Ernst Niekisch, an unusual character and prominent figure of the current, felt the deepest possible hostility towards Hitler, mainly because of the anti-Russian crusade conducted by Bavarian National Socialism.

A state of mind rather than an actual thought current, 'National Bolshevism' does not imply that one is attracted to Leninism as such. It is, in fact, a combination of hopes and illusions aimed at an alliance between the two 'proletarian nations' against the capitalistic West. And it is these very hopes and illusions that are crystallised by the three successive crises experienced by Germany in 1920, 1923 and 1930.

The first crisis arose from the Treaty of Versailles, which deprived Germany of some of its German territories (East Prussia and the Sudetenland), while also forcing it to pay money for compensation

---

3   AN: Oswald Spengler, *Prussianism and Socialism*. Preface by Gilbert Merlio, Actes Sud, 1986.

(for so-called 'reparations'). Shortly after, the Russo-Polish War of 1920 would bring Marshall Budyonny's Red Riders to the gates of Warsaw. Lenin and Trotsky thus hoped that the revolution would set Germany ablaze. Within the German Communist Party (KPD), the Hamburg group, led by Erich Laufenberg and Fritz Wolffheim, introduces the idea of a national war against the West. This meets the approval of some prominent members of the Conservative Revolution such as Count Ernst zu Reventlow. In August 1920, however, General Weygand defeats the Red Army in front of Warsaw. The initiative of the KPD's Hamburg faction is therefore no longer on the agenda, and Moscow condemns it.

The second crisis breaks out in 1923. The occupation of the Ruhr and the soaring inflation arouse both national and social anger. Among the communists, the initiative comes from the very top. Karl Radek, the delegate of the Comintern, delivers his famous speech on 'Schlageter, the pilgrim of nothingness',[4] which results in an offer of alliance from Moeller van den Bruck. As soon as the crisis is brought to an end, however, the pressure drops without anyone venturing beyond mere declarations of their intention.

The Strasser Group

The third critical phase begins in 1930, coinciding with the peak of the global economic crisis and the reparations policy imposed on Germany by the Young Plan. The leader of the National Socialist Party's (NSDAP) left wing, Gregor Strasser, who was also, as must be

---

4   AN: On 15 April 1923, when the Ruhr was invaded by the French army, Lieutenant Albert Schlageter, who had fought in World War I and was a former member of the *Baltikum Freikorps*, used dynamite to blow up a railway bridge near Kalkum. Denounced, arrested, and court-martialled by the French, he was shot on 26 May 1923. This execution aroused considerable emotion in Germany. Schlageter would thus become a national hero. On 26 May 1933, Martin Heidegger, the rector of the University of Freiburg, would once again praise him in front of the assembled students.

emphasised, the head of the party in northern Germany (Berlin), suggests establishing a league of oppressed peoples, meaning Germany and Russia. For his part, Heinz Neumann decides to seek out, from within the KPD, a possible alliance with the nationalists. On both sides, however, this moderate openness was but a series of tactical manoeuvres that would enjoy some publicity thanks to the 'Scheringer path' (*Scheringer-Kurs*) incident.

There is also an incident that one must not forget and that prompted Jünger's reaction. Convicted in October 1930 for his involvement in National Socialist activities within the *Reichswehr*, Lieutenant Scheringer is soon disavowed by Hitler, in application of the legalist line that the latter forced his party to adopt after the failure of the 1923 putsch. Imprisoned, Scheringer is outraged by Hitler's sophistry and thus joins the KPD (in March 1931). At the time, other nationalists would also choose to join the KPD: Ludwig Renn, Count Alexander Stenbock-Fermor, Bruno von Salomon (the brother of the author of *The Outlaws*) and former *Freikorps* leader Beppo Römer, the hero of the battles of Upper Silesia. Ernst Jünger would declare himself scandalised by Hitler's condemnation of Scheringer, an attitude which, in his eyes, betrayed the vilest possible political opportunism.

All attempts at collaboration between the revolutionary Right and the KPD would, however, go up in smoke. The rise of the National Socialist Party (which went from 12 to 107 *Reichstag* seats during the elections of September 1930) and the anti-Soviet line espoused by its Munich leadership would completely obliterate the pro-Russian orientations of the Strasser group (Northern Germany). On 30 June 1930, Gregor Strasser submits to Hitler and the Munich group, while his brother, Otto Strasser, resigns from the party.[5]

---

5   AN: Gregor Strasser (1892–1934) would be tempted, in December 1932, to give in to the requests of his party's adversaries, who offered him the position of vice-president in the cabinet formed by General Schleicher. This would escalate his feud with Hitler and lead to him (and Schleicher) being killed during the purge of 30 June 1934. As for his brother Otto Strasser (1897–1974), he would

Ernst Niekisch's Unusual Journey

Shortly after 1925, National Bolshevism would find its primary theoretician in the person of Ernst Niekisch.[6] A teacher born in Silesia (1889), this avid reader had, because of his deficient eyesight, been a member of his country's auxiliary service during the Great War. In 1917, he joined the Socialist Party (SPD), becoming the editor of one of its newspapers. He was in Augsburg in November 1918, at the time when, in Munich, Kurt Eisner proclaimed the establishment of the Bavarian Council Republic after overthrowing the dynasty of the reigning Wittelsbachs.[7] The soldiers of Augsburg would elect him president of their own council (soviet). Following Kurt Eisner's assassination, he is elected chairman of the Central Committee of the Bavarian Workers', Peasants' and Soldiers Councils. He thus finds himself at the very centre of the movement, but objecting to some people's intention to establish a communist republic in Bavaria, he resigns. After the crushing of the Bavarian Soviet Republic by General von Epp's *Freikorps* in May 1919, he was arrested and remained in prison until 1921.

His further evolution is characteristic of this era of upheavals, when young Germans sought to find their way amidst the blurred landmarks. Ernst von Salomon summarised these uncertainties in a

---

emigrate in 1933 and not return to Germany until 1955, trying in vain to resume his political activity.

6   AN: Opposed to Nazism, Ernst Niekisch (1889–1967) was imprisoned from 1937 to 1945. Following Germany's defeat in 1945, he worked as a teacher in East Germany (GDR), but his independence would ultimately cast him into the opposition. A collection of his texts was published in France under the title: *Hitler, a German Fate and Other National Bolshevik Writings*, with a preface by Alain de Benoist (Pardès, 1991). See also Sebastian Haffner's portrayal of Niekisch entitled *Preussische Profile* [TN: Prussian Profiles], Gallimard, 1983.

7   AN: The Bavarian 'Council Republic' took a most bloody turn at the beginning of 1919. It was overthrown thanks to the intervention of General von Epp's *Freikorps*, who re-conquered Munich on 1 May 1919. In this regard, one can refer to our *History of a German Sort of Fascism*, op. cit.

well-crafted sentence of *The Outlaws*: 'What we knew, we did not want; what we wanted, we didn't know!' Indeed, positions were rarely immutable. Socialists would rally around nationalism, and nationalists would sometimes join communism without betraying any of their profound convictions.

Regarding Weimar's Intellectual Scene

Weimar historians have mostly neglected this unconcealed reality. At the time, interactions were indeed constant between leftist and rightist writers. Thanks to Niekisch, who would become his friend, Jünger made the acquaintance of the pacifist Ernst Toller, the anarchist Erich Mühsam, and the Marxist Georg Lukacs. At the same time, Bertolt Brecht dined with Ernst von Salomon and Arnolt Bronnen in the publisher Rowohlt's home, without this ever causing a scandal. The communist Piscator agreed to participate in a radio debate with the young Dr Goebbels. In the press, Moeller van den Bruck entered into dialogue with Comintern representative Karl Radek. The expressionist poet Gottfried Benn evolved from the Left to the revolutionary Right, while Werner Lass, initially a disciple of Rossbach and then of Jünger, joined the KPD. The ceaseless dialogue between these men reflects the reciprocal influence of their ideas. Some analyses of Jünger's essay on *Total Mobilisation* and the philosophical issues they tackled became the starting point of the work developed by the Frankfurt School between 1930 and 1947, whose influence extends all the way to the work of Jürgen Habermas.[8]

On 8 May 1945, the day of the German capitulation, Ernst Jünger would recall in his *War Journals* the strong impression Goebbels had made on him in the heyday of the Conservative Revolution, especially

---

8   AN: Jean-Michel Palmier, *Ernst Jünger. Rêveries sur un chasseur de Cicindèles* [TN: Ernst Jünger -Meditations on the Life of a Tiger-Beetle Chaser], Hachette, 1995.

when they met in the home of their common acquaintance Arnolt Bronnen:

> The ascetic and concentrated appearance that characterised the physiognomy of Doctor Goebbels was no mere pretence; for the will has great powers when it is focused on a single point. The infirmity of his leg had certainly played its part in this. Such men do not usually waste their time; they work while others dance or converse amidst wine bottles. Then they come out of their seclusion, to the general astonishment of others, and can make up for the time they have lost indulging in pleasure. […] In the moments when the will did not impose its mask upon him, [Goebbels] exuded an undeniable charm, which must have particularly affected women.[9]

The intellectual milieu of the Weimar period was devoid of any and all impervious or impassable barriers. Imprisoned during the year of 1921, Niekisch reads Spengler and Machiavelli. Having pondered their ideas, he comes to the conclusion that a social revolution in Germany must inevitably be preceded by national liberation, that is to say, by a struggle against the Treaty of Versailles. Following his release, he moves to Berlin, where he becomes the secretary of the textile workers' union. He then enters into polemics with the country's main socialist leaders, including Eduard Bernstein, condemning the German government's submission to French demands. He claims that the socialist party must champion the resistance of the German people to Western, and therefore French, capitalism. In 1925, while in Dresden, he takes charge of a socialist faction close to his ideas.

On 1 July 1926, he founds the monthly magazine *Widerstand* ('Resistance'), which would bring him fame and notoriety. The following year, the magazine would receive powerful reinforcements

---

9 AN: Born in 1897, Dr Joseph Goebbels took his own life in Berlin, in the hours that followed Hitler's suicide on 30 April 1945, as did his wife Magda, who had previously killed their six children. This tragedy was recreated in Oliver Hirschbiegel's 2004 film *Downfall* (*Der Untergang*). Although the film's depiction of Magda Goebbels is flawless, her husband's portrayal as a mere puppet is very foreign to what we know of the real character.

through the addition of both Ernst Jünger's signature and that of August Winnig.

Marxism, a Byproduct of Bourgeois Materialism

Born in 1878, former social democrat and trade unionist August Winnig would become, in November 1918, the *Reich*'s High Commissioner for the Baltic countries and East Prussia. His solidarity with the *Baltikum Freikorps* leads him to support the Kapp Putsch in March 1920, resulting in his exclusion from the SPD. He thus soon begins to promote a type of National Socialism comprising Spenglerian elements. He explains that Marxism lacks the ability to combat capitalism efficiently, as it is but a by-product of bourgeois materialism. Insofar as it does not reach beyond the superficial field of exclusively material interests, class struggle, defined in accordance with Karl Marx's notion of things, only aims to instil bourgeois values into the minds of workers. What Karl Marx's criticism of the bourgeoisie reveals, he says, is his desire to become a bourgeois himself. Winnig thus no longer defines the proletariat in terms of class, as Marx did, but as the German community of all workers. He states that the proletariat 'is, above all, part of a people, that is to say, part of a historical and biological whole whose vital laws are valid for it'. He goes on to add that the worker must understand that his enemy is no longer the German employer but, instead, international financial capital, and that workers must establish themselves as the sole true representatives of the nation. These ideas, which Winnig began to develop in 1930, would exert a certain influence on Jünger and his figure of the *Worker* (1932).

Through Winnig, the views expressed by Niekisch in *Widerstand* would ultimately impact young conservative and *bündisch* circles, as well as some former *Freikorps* members, particularly those of the Oberland League headed by Friedrich Weber. Winnig, however, never considered himself to be a National Bolshevik. Unlike Jünger, he would break with Niekisch in 1930, when the latter began to argue in favour of a union with communism, something that he would describe as the 'romanticism of the abyss'.

Secret and Unexpected Solidarity

Niekisch and Jünger first met in the fall of 1927. Bonds of intellectual sympathy are immediately established, bonds that would take physical shape through Jünger's active collaboration with *Widerstand*. Their collaboration would yield eighteen articles between April 1927 and September 1933. Niekisch would also forge bonds with Ernst Jünger's younger brother, Friedrich Georg, and several other members of his entourage, particularly the young and fiery neo-pagan Friedrich Hielscher. Despite their closeness, however, Ernst Jünger never became a National Bolshevik, though he did contribute to radicalising Niekisch's ideas, and those of his friends, by advocating an active sort of stoicism in the face of the challenges presented by modernity, an attitude that would be expressed through the notion of 'heroic realism', a very present concept in Jünger's *Worker*.

It seems, however, that the concept of 'heroic realism' was actually invented by the young Werner Best, who remained quite close to Jünger until about 1930.[10] A brilliant jurist endowed with a highly po-

---

10 AN: The expression 'heroic realism' appeared in an article by Werner Best (1903–1989) entitled 'Der Krieg und das Recht' [TN: The War and the Law] which was part of the collective work *Krieg und Krieger* [TN: War and Warriors], edited by Ernst Jünger in Berlin in 1930. That same year, Werner Best would join the NSDAP, adding to the ranks of its legal experts. He would later become a senior official of the SS (attaining the rank of general) and one of the organisers of the SD (Secret Service). Extending his protection to Jünger, he would be stationed at the Parisian headquarters of the occupation forces (*Wehrmacht*) until July 1942, when he was appointed as the *Reich*'s High Commissioner in Denmark. In addition to Ernst Jünger and Werner Best, other noteworthy contributors to the work *Krieg und Krieger* include Friedrich Georg Jünger, Friedrich Hielscher, Ernst von Salomon, and Wilhelm von Schramm, who was in Paris during the war and would become one of the actors of the 20 July 1944 plot, as well as its future historian.

litical mind and a future high official of the SS (after 1933), Werner Best had been a member of the *Jungkonservative* group before becoming a diplomat. Until 1929, he had collaborated with others on *Vormarsch*, the 'Gazette of the Nationalist Youth' financed by Captain Ehrhardt and run by Ernst Jünger and Friedrich Hielscher [aka Bogumil]. After the war, Ernst von Salomon would ironically mention in his *Questionnaire* the contribution that the author of *Storm of Steel* had made to *Vormarsch*:

> It was Ernst Jünger who gave the publication its importance through articles that were so witty and written in such a crystalline style that our readers, filled with the deepest respect, were under the impression that it was already quite lovely if Ernst Jünger himself was able to understand them.[11]

A Vitalist Vision of History

Remembering this time in the aftermath of the great disasters of 1933–1945, Ernst Jünger resorted, as already noted, to a poetic and cryptic phrase in his *War Journals*: 'Nationalist circles seem to me [...] like campfires before the reveille.' In a veiled manner, he alludes to the contrasting destinies of 'nationalists' under the Third Reich: some, including Karl Paetel, were in exile; others, such as Friedrich Hielscher, were involved in internal resistance; and others still actively cooperated with the new power, as was the case with Werner Best, though they remained faithful to their old alliances. Thinking about the past, Jünger adds: 'How is it that so many of those evenings still lead so vivid an existence in one's memory?'[12]

To those close to the National Bolshevik movement, Russian communism was only superficially Marxist in nature. It seemed to be, above all, a Russian phenomenon, a view which would, at a later point, be shared in France by General de Gaulle. Perceiving Bolshevism to

---

11   AN: Ernst von Salomon, *The Questionnaire*, Gallimard, 1953, p. 238.
12   AN: Ernst Jünger, *War Journals*, 23 September 1945.

be, in its own way, a national revolution is but one step away, a step that Moeller van den Bruck seems to have taken prior to his suicide on 30 May 1925. His vitalist vision of history and certitude that the *Volkgeist*'s permanent features always prevail over the contingent forms of politics reinforce his conviction that the spirit of peoples will always end up vanquishing the most universalistic ideologies.

The appeal exerted by the 'romanticism of the abyss' is, as a rule, very foreign to Prussian coldness. It is fuelled by the haunting desire to break with a West deemed hostile and decadent, in order to draw on the supposedly youthful and intact strength of the East. It cleaves to the dream of German-Russian domination over 'greater Europe'.

All things considered, however, this dream was rather less unrealistic than that of a Germanic domination over Russia, which would drive Hitler to start the German-Soviet War in 1941 and lead to the complete crushing of Germany four years later. When the National Bolshevik dream of a German-Russian condominium took shape in the 1920s and 1930s, Germany and Russia were still equal in terms of power, which would no longer be the case after 1945.[13]

The Flagship Writer of the Revolutionary Right

During the tumultuous years of the Conservative Revolution, the movement's vitality left the men who had fought on the front and those that followed in their footsteps with the feeling that they were, to use the words of Ernst von Salomon, 'the accursed bearers of creative forces', i.e. those who bore the future.

Ernst Jünger had taken his leave from the *Reichswehr* on 31 August 1923. He thus felt free enough to write as he wished. His notoriety had begun to impose itself thanks to the publication of *Storm of Steel*. However, what would ultimately turn him into the most prominent

---

13 AN: Renata Fritsch-Bournazel, *De Rapallo à Zavidovo. Réflexions sur le devenir des relations germano-russes* [TN: 'From Rapallo to Zavidovo — Reflecting on the Future of German-Russian Relations'], Cahiers du CREST, issue number 11, Polytechnic School, September 1993.

author of the revolutionary Right was his rather fiery collaboration with *Die Standarte* (The Banner), a newspaper launched in June 1925. It was, in fact, an addition to the *Stahlhelm* (Steel Helmet) weekly, which featured the most important collaboration between former combatants. *Die Standarte*, 'a contribution to the deepening of frontline thinking', was, at the time, headed by former *Freikorps* leader Helmut Franke. This paper would play an essential role in the attack-minded development of neo-nationalism. It is put on hold for the first time on 28 March 1926. Indeed, those in charge of *Stahlhelm* were concerned about the rather hostile attitudes towards the Weimar regime that they were being made to adopt. Now considered the 'weekly of neo-nationalism', *Die Standarte* would be published for a period of 5 months under the collective care of Ernst Jünger, Helmut Franke, Franz Schauwecker and Wilhelm Kleinau. In August 1926, however, the newspaper is banned, this time for good, following an article that praised the assassinations of Erzberger and Rathenau.[14]

In the aftermath of the ban on *Die Standarte*, Jünger and his whole team would seek refuge in the *Arminius* monthly, a publication financed by Captain Ehrhardt, the famous *Freikorps* leader who was compromised by the Kapp Putsch in 1920. This new press adventure would only last a year. Still supported by Ehrhardt, Jünger would, in 1927, join forces with Werner Lass, Rossbach's former deputy at the head of the *Schilljugend* and a future communist, to publish *Der Vormarsch* ('The Advance'). He would thus contribute to raising the standard of the publication, which, once again, depended on the efforts of Captain Ehrhardt, a ubiquitous character at the time, though

---

14 AN: Matthias Erzberger (1875–1921) was a *Zentrum* (Christian-Democrat) PM who, in 1919, campaigned in favour of Germany's acceptance of the Treaty of Versailles. For this reason, he would be assassinated on 26 August 1921. Walther Rathenau (1867–1922) was an industrialist and a politician, and 'the only man capable of turning Germany into a copy of Anglo-Saxon mercantile democracies' (Ernst von Salomon). He is assassinated on 24 June 1922 by two young officers of the German navy, Erwin Kern and Hermann Fischer, who would pay for it with their lives.

one characterised by indigent political thinking. A few months later, Jünger would leave the running of the paper in the hands of his friend, the neo-pagan Friedrich Hielscher.

From 1927 to 1930, Jünger also contributed tirelessly to the publication of Niekisch's paper, *Widerstand*, and during the first 8 months of 1930, he would act, alongside Werner Lass, as a co-editor of the *Die Kommenden* weekly, which was quite influential in the ranks of the youth movement.

Provocative Nationalism

These efforts would constitute his final acts of cooperation with the political press. He would not publish anything in 1931 and no more than about 10 literary critiques in 1932–1933. In 1929, as part of the first version of his *Adventurous Heart*, he had already clearly distanced himself from all collective action.

Based on the presence of numerous signs, one could feel the era changing. Around 1930, the circles of the revolutionary Right were experiencing a loss of momentum, as Hitler's new power, that of the National Socialist Party, began to rise.

During the Conservative Revolution's years of turmoil, Jünger was admittedly neither a street activist nor an ideologist. He did, however, impose himself in the newspapers and publications of the day thanks to his prestigious soldier aura and his magical style. In the words of Ernst von Salomon, he was the only author of the revolutionary Right whose writings sometimes aroused commentaries in the general press outside this narrow environment.

Aware of this influence, Jünger would even briefly foster the ambition of gathering the entire nationalist current around him. This illusory ambition would not, however, last long. As part of his 'schließt euch zusammen'[15] call, which was published in *Die Standarte* on 3 June 1926, he urges rival groups to establish a 'National Front'. The call

---

15 TN: Band together.

would go unheeded, drowned by the sterile arguments of petty leaders. Unification would, of course, be ultimately achieved, but only behind a true political beast, once the National Socialist Party initiated its ascension to power from 1930 onwards.

During the previous years, Jünger had clearly proclaimed his adherence to nationalism, and not the most moderate kind at that. Traces of it are encountered in the preface he penned in 1926 for a radical pamphlet authored by his brother Friedrich Georg and titled 'Aufmarsch des Nationalismus'[16]:

> We call ourselves nationalists and do not fear incurring the hatred of the educated and uneducated plebs, all these opportunists of spirit and matter. […] We do not demand anything universal. We reject it — starting with universal truths and human rights and ending with universal education and compulsory military conscription, universal suffrage and universal ignobility which is a necessary result of the previous point. […] We do not mule over benefit and practical gain, we have no need of comfort, we only require that which is necessary — that which fate desires.[17]

Three years later, in 1929, with a now altered perspective, he would seize the opportunity to specify that, in his eyes, nationalism is not an absolute notion:

> Nationalism is a highly usable flag to clearly determine the original combat position espoused by a certain generation during the chaotic years of

---

16 TN: The March of Nationalism.

17 AN: As translated by Karine Moeglin for the 48th issue (1995) of *Nouvelle école* [TN: New School]. This magazine also published one of the articles included by Jünger in the *Arminius* issue of April 1927, an article that reveals the rather strident tone he adopted at the time. One can also refer to the quite politicised preface the author included in the 5th edition (1926) of his work *Der Kampf als inneres Erlebnis* [TN: War as an Inner Experience] (1922), a preface comprised in the translation published by Albin Michel in 1934 under the title 'Our Mother War' (La Guerre notre mère).

transition; in no way is it, as is believed by many of our friends and enemies, the expression of a superior value: it refers to a condition, not to our aim.[18]

A Therapy for Defeat

During the main years of the Conservative Revolution, Jünger's metapolitical thinking never ceased to evolve. It was impacted by the previously mentioned events, and particularly France's military invasion of the Ruhr, which resulted in national commotion. It was, likewise, perhaps influenced by the two years which the former officer spent studying philosophy and biology at the University of Leipzig. This began as early as the second semester of 1923, under the philosophical authority of Felix Krüger and Hans Driesch. In the spring of 1925, his studies were interrupted by a training course at the Oceanographic Institute of Naples, which led him to discover a paradise of both fauna and flora. This experience would undoubtedly influence his future career as an entomologist and be responsible for the appeal exerted upon him by the Mediterranean garrigue.

The reservist duty imposed upon him by his *Reichswehr* officer status until August 1923 had not prevented him from preparing the powerful pages of *Copse 125*, whose content was probably impacted by the author's philosophical studies. Completed at the end of 1924, this work was officially published in 1925, as previously stated. It was specifically during the 1925–1927 period that Jünger's political journalist career was the richest.[19] After the trauma of 1923, Germany's 1918

---

18 AN: '"Nationalismus"' und Nationalismus' [TN: 'Nationalism' and Nationalism], *Tagebuch* [TN: Diary/Journal], 21 September 1929.

19 AN: Ever since the *Bibliographie der Werke Ernst Jüngers* [TN: A Bibliography of Ernst Jünger's Works] (Klett-Cotta, 1985) by Hans Peter Des Coudres and Horst Mühleisen, the studies conducted on the political articles published by Ernst Jünger between 1923 and 1933 have come a long way. One can refer in particular to the compendium headed and commented on by Olaf Berggötz and titled *Politische Publizistik, 1919 bis 1933* [TN: Political Journalism, 1919 to 1933], Klett-Cotta, 2001, 899 pages. This work brings together, for the very first

defeat seemed to him like a most purulent wound. He thus began to seek therapy through the formulation of a nationalist ideology devoid of sentimental pathos. His political vision did not attach any importance to the Left/Right dichotomy, as he believed that socialism and nationalism are not contradictory but, on the contrary, 'expressions of the same power'. In accordance with a phrase used within certain officer circles, nationalism would be experienced as one's 'altruistic duty towards the *Reich*' and socialism as one's 'altruistic duty towards the people'. The only clearly designated adversary is the 'bourgeois', the focus of the author's condemnation in *The Worker* (1932).

Cold Artistic Distancing

After 1927, however, one would notice a significant evolution in some of Jünger's writings, a detachment that would have been unthinkable a year earlier. His artistic temperament would thus visibly take priority over political polemics, which was in contrast with his very nature. Ernst von Salomon would offer a rather sarcastic testimony of this evolution in his account of their first meeting in his *Questionnaire*, shortly after his release from prison in 1929. In a house located in a working-class district of Berlin, at the top of a staircase reeking of cabbage, he describes the writer's room, which overlooked a railway. The place abounded in books. On the desk, one could see a microscope, while the shelves were covered with Coleopteran collections and bizarre wooden masks. Wrapped in a dressing gown and wearing a multicoloured beret, Jünger is working on a *Vormarsch* issue. Von Salomon writes:

> I was incapable of grappling with his books. I lacked the necessary magical and metaphysical organ [...] I was therefore almost naturally excluded from the community that had formed about him, from that group of disciples who seemed to naturally possess what I myself so sorely lacked; they

---

time, all of Jünger's known political articles of the 1919–1933 period, totaling 144 articles, whose re-publication the author had rejected when still alive.

crouched at the feet of the master and stared, with fascinated eyes, at the philosopher's stone that he held in his hands, not to use it, but to weigh it, calibrate it, analyse it and exalt it.[20]

What rose from behind this irony was the disappointment felt by a young activist who expected his elder to show him a political line that could direct and justify his actions. 'I soon had to acknowledge the fact that this expectation remained foreign to Jünger's mission.'

Ernst von Salomon's testimony highlights all that sets Jünger apart from the other authors of the nationalist movement. Jünger's 1923 novella entitled *Sturm* had already heralded this distancing, which would be even more palpable in his political-literary work *The Adventurous Heart*, published in 1929. What one notices in it is a deliberate contrast between the passages dedicated to the martial fury of combat and others that display cold artistic distancing. He thus visibly cultivates a tendency towards egotism that one could never imagine in a political actor.[21]

One could never sufficiently emphasise the fact that, in spite of the 'revolutionary Right' label used to characterise Jünger's positions within the Conservative Revolution, the line of thinking that was his at the time could never be interpreted in accordance with the French categories of the Left and the Right. To ascertain this, one must bear in mind both Jünger's obvious sympathy for the 'National Bolshevism' espoused by his friend Niekisch and his hope for a future alliance between the two outcast nations of the 1920–1930 period, namely his vanquished Germany and Soviet Russia.

---

20   AN: Ernst von Salomon, *The Questionnaire* (French edition), pp. 255–260.

21   AN: His former secretary, Armin Mohler, would state that Maurice Barrès' youth book, *Du sang, de la volupté et de la mort* [TN: Blood, Voluptuousness and Death], which is a sort of dandyist manifesto, had left Jünger shaken when he was still at secondary school (Armin Mohler, *Die Konservative Revolution* [TN: The Conservative Revolution], op. cit., pp. 671–672). One can also consult Banine's work titled *La carrière d'Ernst Jünger, 1920–1929* [TN: Ernst Jünger's Career, 1920–1929], Études germaniques, July-September 1979.

CHAPTER V

FRANCO-GERMAN DIALOGUES

IN FRANCE, the part of the public for whom Jünger could have been of interest only began to read his works belatedly, after 1940. His future friend Julien Gracq would only discover him fortuitously around 1942. Gracq would, in fact, write that Jünger's name had, until then, been completely unknown to him.[1] Despite the fact that the translation of *Storm of Steel* had actually been published by Payot as early as 1930, this was done as part of a collection dedicated to memories and accounts of the Great War, thus limiting its significance and impact. Two years later, the translation of *Copse 125* would see the light at the same publisher. Lastly, in 1934, for obvious reasons of editorial opportuneness at a time when Hitler was effecting a spectacular improvement of his country's situation (a fact that attracted French people's concerned attention to the rise of a nationalistic Germany), the publishing company Albin Michel released a translation of *Der Kampf als inneres Erlebnis* (*War as an Inner Experience*, 1922), opting for the more eloquent title of *Our Mother War*. Owing to its martial and anti-bourgeois philosophy amidst the turbulent circumstances

---

1 AN: *Dossier H, Ernst Jünger* [TN: File H, Ernst Jünger], op. cit., p. 347.

and fascist magnetism of the year 1934, this work was the most adequate publication to attract people's attention.[2]

Jünger, Von Salomon and France

It does seem to be the case, however, that prior to 1940, the most famous adventurous and nationalistic German author in France, i.e. the most widely read and the most influential, was not actually Jünger but Ernst von Salomon. His fiery tale filled with both fury and nobleness and entitled *The Outlaws* was published in Germany in 1930 and translated into French by Librairie Plon as early as the following year. A former Prussian cadet and a young volunteer in the *Baltikum Freikorps*, he had served a long-term prison sentence for his complicity in the assassination of Walther Rathenau. Ernst von Salomon succeeded in imposing himself immediately as a pure-bred natural writer, the greatest of his generation according to Roger Stéphane[3] and one of the 5 greatest innovators of 20th century literary imagination according to Robert Poulet.[4]

Before Malraux and in a very different genre to that of T. E. Lawrence (*The Seven Pillars of Wisdom*, 1922), Ernst von Salomon was the writer who endowed the political adventure with its most fascinating sheen. And no other era than that of the 1930s was ever more

---

2   AN: In his bibliography of Ernst Jünger, op. cit., Alain de Benoist points out three extensive articles dedicated to this book: one by Jacques Carton in *La France militaire* [TN: Military France] (17 April 1934), another by Karl Korn in *Cahiers franco-allemands* [TN: Franco-German Notebooks] (February 1937), and a third one by Wladimir Weidlé entitled *Ernst Jünger, prophète d'un monde nouveau* [TN: Ernst Jünger, the Prophet of a New World] and published in *Le Mois* in August 1938.

3   AN: Roger Stéphane, *Portrait de l'aventurier* [TN: Portrait of the Adventurer], Grasset, 1965.

4   AN: Robert Poulet, *Le spectacle du* monde [TN: Beholding the World], September 1977. The remaining 4 writers mentioned by Poulet are James Joyce, Marcel Proust, Franz Kafka and Céline.

receptive to the culture of revolutionary action and the feverishness of political romanticism, whether red, black or brown.

Within the French 'young Right', admittedly quite impervious to Germanic alchemy, its highly precocious leader, Thierry Maulnier, revealed that he had been a most enthusiastic reader of *The Outlaws*:

> In post-war Germany, one witnessed the rise of generations that were sufficiently manly to believe that one's service to certain causes was worth not shying away from murder or death.[5]

This rather obvious allusion to Rathenau's assassination was written in 1933. In France, the influence of Ernst von Solomon's book had thus spread to the circles of our nationalist youth. And there is no shortage of testimonies regarding this impact of his. Remembering the time when he was 17 years old and he participated, alongside other secondary school students, in the first resistance demonstration in Paris, at the Champs-Élysées on 11 November 1940, Alain Griotteray would write:

> We stood alone against everyone else. [...] My friends and I would immerse ourselves in Ernst von Salomon's *The Outlaws*. Those boys seemed like role models to us, since they were fighting in the *Freikorps* [...] despite the directives issued by Germany [...], which had submitted to its victors.[6]

An analogous testimony is encountered with Raoul Girardet, a future academic and renowned historian who, at the time, was a secondary school student and would become a very young member of *Action française* before the war:

---

5   AN : Thierry Maulnier, preface to the French translation of Moeller van den Bruck's *The Third Reich*.
6   AN: Alain Griotteray, *La droite était au rendez-vous* [TN : The Right Rose to the Occasion], Robert Laffont, 1985, pp. 219–220. Shortly after 1940, Griotteray would join the Orion network, which he would head, before being parachuted above Béarn in 1944. He would subsequently pursue a very eventful political and journalistic career, until his death in 2008.

It was a time when Ernst von Salomon's *The Outlaws* went round our group, as we handed it to each other in a most feverish fashion. It was with disconcerting ease that we identified with those tragic heroes. [...] We all dreamt of insurrection, attacks and barricades.⁷

No equivalent attitudes towards Jünger ever surfaced back then. One would have to wait until France's defeat in 1940; the beginnings of the occupation and the resulting severe trauma that afflicted France; the uniformed writer's privileged position in Paris; and the French translations of his latest books titled *On the Marble Cliffs* and *Gardens and Streets*, before he would actually begin to garner the attention of our critics and cultured public. Under the signatures of Henri Thomas, Ramon Fernandez, Pierre Drieu La Rochelle and Frederico Federici, the prestigious *Nouvelle Revue française* devoted four articles to them, which were published in quick succession over a period of four months, from 1941 to 1942.⁸ Jünger's introduction to the French public was thus guaranteed, and the praise would thereafter never cease. That a great German writer, a hero of the previous war, a nationalist in his youth, and a self-declared Francophile, should, to top it all, become an officer in the very powerful Parisian headquarters of the occupation troops, now that was bound to favour many things.

The Soldier and the Revolutionary

It is hardly surprising that Ernst von Salomon's readers and Jünger's have rarely been the same. The author of *Storm of Steel* did not indulge in the romanticism of the barricades. Indeed, military heroism has little in common with that of revolutions. There is no doubt that the soldier faces death and suffering, but he does so with the complete support

---

7   AN: Raoul Girardet, discussions with Pierre Assouline, *Singulièment libre* [TN: Remarkably Free], Perrin, 1990, p. 36.
8   AN: Alain de Benoist, *Ernst Jünger. Une Bio-Bibliographie* [TN: Ernst Jünger. A Bio-Bibliography], op. cit., pp. 160–161. A translation of *Gardens and Streets* by Maurice Betz was published by Plon in the spring of 1942.

of society and the necessary authority to bestow legitimacy upon his actions and grant him moral support, honours and distinctions. This is an essential difference compared with the revolutionary and the rebel, who, in addition to all the personal risks, must draw from his own justifications from within himself in order to be able to face the daily disapproval, hostility and repressive action of the society he is fighting against. A heroic soldier rarely becomes an authentic revolutionary. Their motivations and natures have contradictory, not to say conflicting, essences. During an interview with Ernst von Salomon conducted in his home on 21 June 1972, shortly before his passing, the former outlaw did not, despite his gentrified paunch, hide from me the fact that he viewed his friend Jünger's ever more 'convenient' evolution with a touch of irony.[9]

These differences would impact the 'reception' of the two writers in France. When the historical movement that had initially favoured Ernst von Salomon found itself reversed, it was Jünger's readership that benefitted from it. The marmoreal wisdom of *On the Marble Cliffs* (1939) would henceforth resonate more and more, since the Europe of the post-1945 period had chosen to withdraw itself from history. By means of a reciprocal movement, Ernst von Salomon's masterpiece would end up losing a major part of the appeal it had exerted in the days of the 'immense and red' romanticism of political struggles and revolutionary hopes.

The Right on Either Side of the Rhine

In the aftermath of the plethora of upheavals brought about by World War I, all European countries would experience an intellectual exuberance that mirrored its challenging of a now-outdated world. And it was in Germany, as we have already seen, that this flow of ideas would be at its most intense. Its wealth is still a source of fascination today,

---

9 AN: I give a detailed account of my visit to Ernst von Salomon at the end of the first edition of *Baltikum*, Robert Laffont, 1974.

as is the fact that it has remained heirless. Indeed, after the Second World War, all native and autonomous European thinking was done away with for a long time to come. Through its consequences, this war had put an end to the spiritual independence and historical role of Europeans, who were hence forced to live in the projected shadow of the two foreign and victorious powers and their ideological systems, until the day when one vanquished the other to impose its temporary hegemony. For a long time, Europe thus entered a state of dormancy, a state of affairs that could never be perennial.[10]

In post-World War I France, a specific type of effervescence manifested itself among the young and somewhat cultured generation. This, however, took place on an infinitely more modest scale compared to Germany. This agitation was present in some rather small circles, magazines and newspapers that had previously been gathered by a historian of ideas, Jean-Louis Loubet Del Bayle, under the generic title of *The Non-Conformists of the 1930s*.[11] The rebellion against a system deemed rotten and a country afflicted by decadence was the recurrent theme of these 'non-conformists', an attitude that the young Thierry Maulnier would summarise one day by giving one of his articles the following title: 'Will We Ever Free Ourselves from French Abjection?'. And yet, despite the presence of some pivotal phrases and good intentions, this current would never succeed in tearing itself free from a mixture of conservative reminiscences and vague, albeit fascinating, urges, remaining more or less trapped in the sentimentality of a Christian sort of personalism that rambles on about Man *ad infinitum*, defining him

---

10 AN: This idea is developed in my work entitled *Le Siècle de 1914* [TN: The Century of 1914], Pygmalion, 2006.

11 AN: Jean-Louis Loubet Del Bayle, *Les Non-Conformistes des années Trente* [TN:The Non-Conformists of the 1930s], Éditions du Seuil, Paris, 1969. The author mainly highlights three tendencies: the 'young Right' associated with the magazine *Combat* [TN: Struggle] and its organiser, the young Thierry Maulnier; the magazine *L'Ordre nouveau* [TN: New Order], created in 1933 by Robert Aron, Armand Dandieu and Alexandre Mark; and last but not least, the magazine *Esprit* [TN: Spirit], started in 1932 by Emmanuel Mounier.

as that bland and vapid abstraction that Joseph de Maistre himself had never encountered.

Franco-German Conflicts

Following its crushing defeat in 1870, France was almost entirely, and particularly within the Right, dominated by a thirst for revenge bordering on hatred of Germany. It was a historic novelty. One thus forgot about what had been obvious for Victor Hugo, when he wrote in *Le Rhin*: 'There is an intimate connection between the two peoples, an undeniable consanguinity. They come from the same origins.'

In his essay 'Die Geburt zweier Völker: Deutsche und Franzosen',[12] the mediaevalist Carlrichard Brühl emphasised the fact that until the 16th century, there had never been any border disputes between the French and the Germans. The Lorraine region was never the object of quarrels, and neither were the waters of the Rhine. With all due respect to a subsequent interpretation proposed in 1870, the battle of Bouvines itself had actually been, above all, a dynastic conflict.

The rivalry between Valois and Habsburg dates back to the 1477 marriage of future Emperor Maximilian I of Austria to Marie de Bourgogne, daughter of Charles the Bold, who wished to protect his rights in the face of Louis XI's greed. This rivalry was not, however, perceived in any way as a national conflict between the French and the Germans. And although in the 18th century, the French had an aversion to the Habsburgs, who were considered their traditional enemies, they were full of admiration for the King of Prussia, a German prince.

The antagonism between the two peoples would only awaken after 1870, against a backdrop of French defeat and territorial conflict relating to the Alsace and Moselle regions. Up until then, the Germans had had more reason than the French to be wary of their neighbours.

Indeed, the undertakings of the French crown had often left bad memories in the Germanic psyche. Francis I's alliance with the Turks

---

12   TN: The Birth of Two Peoples: The Germans and the French.

against Austria had, for instance, scandalised all of Christianity. During the next century, it was difficult to overlook the interventions of both Richelieu and Mazarin in the Thirty Years' War, as well as the Treaties of Westphalia, whose aim was to drive Germany into a state of division and impotence, while simultaneously facilitating French annexations. When the time was right, Louis XIV spared no effort to fuel the resentment of our neighbours. First came the *coup de main*[13] of 1681, at a time of peace, to seize Strasbourg. This event was, however, quite negligible compared to what followed during the winter of 1688–1689, when the Palatinate was methodically ravaged by the troops of Louvois, who set Heidelberg, Mannheim, Speyer and Worms ablaze despite the pleas of the Princess Palatine, who was the sister-in-law of the Great King.

Viewed from a Tyrolean or Prussian perspective, the Revolutionary Wars and those of the First Empire were, despite their equivocal message of individualist and bourgeois freedom, seen quite early on for what they truly were, namely plunder and conquest ventures. The appeal to the people was heard, of course, but everted by the peoples themselves, who turned it into the instrument of their national resistance to French occupation and the Parisian pretension to speaking on behalf of the entire world.

Propagated through its bayonets and plundering generals, the Napoleonic revolution generated but one response: the birth of German nationalism. Following Prussia's humiliation in the battle of Jena, the resentment harboured against France would result in the 1813 outbreak of the wars of liberation, which would only come to an end on the plain of Waterloo.

Saved by the Restoration and spared by the Congress of Vienna, France would then tend to its wounds. The memory of past glories and recent exploits would prove strong enough to protect it against a potential inferiority complex. Through the voice of its great intellectuals, Victor Hugo, Edgar Quinet, Jules Michelet, Hippolyte Taine,

---

13   TN: Surprise attack.

and Ernest Renan, the France of literature and universities set out to germanise without restraint. It longed to see in Germany a good pupil of the Enlightenment, the homeland of Kant, idealism, morality, and progress. 'I studied Germany and thought I had entered a temple,' wrote Renan in a letter dated 24 August 1845. 'All that I have found in it is pure, high-minded, moral, beautiful and touching'. This idyll would, however, be shattered by the European catastrophe of 1870.

Civilisation against Barbarism

Today, one cannot imagine the trauma that resulted from this sudden and absolute defeat. As written by Renan back then, 'the war between France and Germany is the greatest misfortune that could have befallen civilisation. The intellectual harmony, morality and politics of humanity were thus left broken.' In those days, the assimilation of Europe to humanity was a common delusion.

The French suddenly discovered that they were no longer the 'Great Nation' of yesteryear. They thus became resentful and surrendered to an inexpiable hatred for the Germans, revealing their own decline. Thus was modern nationalism born, the offspring of Jacobin passions, Boulangism and 'revenge'. Through a reciprocal sort of movement, the demons of Pan-Germanism would awake in Germany.

The war of 1914–1918 would soon bear these passions to their peak, with the French claiming to be at the head of 'the struggle of civilisation against barbarism', as Bergson wrote on 8 August 1914. Bainville expanded on this: 'Having become a strong nation, the Germans have embraced barbarism... They have returned to their primitive state and to their role of invading hordes.' (*Cent Ans d'illusions sur l'Allemagne*,[14] 1917) Through the voice of Thomas Mann (in his *Reflections of a Non-Political Man*), the Germans saw themselves, by contrast, as the defenders of art against intellectualism and of authentic culture against

---

14 TN: One Hundred Years of Delusions about Germany.

the cosmopolitanism and artificiality that they deemed characteristic of France.

The 'struggle for civilisation and lawfulness' waged by the Republic against Germany fostered a xenophobic propaganda of unequalled brutality. All means were thus acceptable when it came to instilling in our public opinion an absolute hatred of the Germans, in an effort to 'kill the beast so as to neutralise the venom', to use the words of Gabriel Langlois in *L'Allemagne barbare*[15] (Walter et Cie, 1915). Scholars were required to demonstrate that the 'Krauts' had always been loathsome and ultimately alien to the human race. As coldly stated by Dr. Edgar Bérillon, a distinguished professor at the French School of Psychology and a friend of Charcot's, 'to admit that a German is a man like any other, you must never have had the opportunity to carefully study a specimen of his race'.

This blind ardour incited Charles Maurras, the famous doctrinaire of the monarchy, to call for 'dethroning the House of Hohenzollern' and prosecuting its people 'before the assizes of the universe', in a sort of *ante litteram* Nuremberg Trial or International Criminal Tribunal. He even recommended 'executing Wilhelm and his sons by firing squad, "Unter den Linden" [or on] Wilhelmstrasse', without the necessity to convene any court whatsoever. Indeed, this flaring-up of hatred drove even the most intellectually capable people completely insane.

After 1918, the anger against a now starving, defeated yet still potentially powerful Germany would define France's foreign policy, as our country remained determined to preserve even the least justifiable clauses of the Treaty of Versailles.

Incidentally, one can hardly speak of a 'treaty' when all the stipulations had actually been imposed upon the Germans, without possible negotiations. Stepping down to protest against Clemenceau's intransigence, the British economist J. M. Keynes, who had hitherto acted as

---

15 TN: Barbarian Germany.

financial representative for the Treasury to the 1919 Versailles peace conference, summed it all up when he wrote:

> The policy of reducing Germany to servitude for a generation, of degrading the lives of millions of human beings, and of depriving a whole nation of happiness should be abhorrent and detestable, — abhorrent and detestable, even if it were possible, even if it enriched ourselves, even if it did not sow the decay of the whole civilised life of Europe. […] [It was] one of the most outrageous acts of a cruel victor in civilised history.[16]

By demanding that Weimar politicians sign the treaty without discussion, Clemenceau designated them as traitors in the eyes of their country's public opinion. One cannot say that the French Republic did its little German sibling any favours! In 1923, under the pretext of a delay in 'reparation payment', Poincaré ordered the occupation of the Ruhr, which led to unanimous resistance and bloody reprisals. The resulting chain reaction plunged the country into a state of terrible chaos. As was the case during the last year of the war, people would die of hunger while traffickers grew fat.

The High Chivalry of War

It was at this time that Hitler's rise began. And yet, despite harbouring the justified sentiments of a German patriot, Ernst Jünger would never express, whether at the time or subsequently, the slightest bitterness or animosity towards France and the French. Indeed, one must acknowledge the fact that not all French people had given in to the delusions of the old 'revenge' during those many years. Jünger would thus later mention several French writers whose books he had read, including not only Drieu La Rochelle but also Montherlant. He thus states:

---

16 AN: J. M. Keynes, *The Economic Consequences of the Peace*, 1919.

Just like Saint-Exupéry and Quinton, I rank him among the small number of individuals that belong to that high chivalry produced by the first Great War.[17]

Henry de Montherlant (1896–1972) had basically participated in the war of 14–18, although from a certain distance. He was, however, injured. He then published several works that indirectly related to it all, notably *La Relève du matin*[18] (1920). He would even become the secretary general of the ossuary of Douaumont.

As for Antoine de Saint-Exupéry (1900–1944), although he was too young to have participated in the Great War, he did join the knightly ranks of Aéropostale pilots in 1926. This rough experience of his would be mentioned in his first book, *Courrier Sud*,[19] published in 1929. At his own request, he was assigned, despite his age, to a combat squadron in 1944, only to be killed in mid-flight on 8 September of that same year. His truly beautiful story entitled *Pilote de guerre*[20] (1942) focuses on the desperate aerial combats of 1940. Jünger was, of course, unable to read this book at the time of his comment.

The third character mentioned by Jünger is understandably René Quinton (1865–1925), who was both a genuine combatant and a deep thinker. A first-rate scientist and reserve officer, he would voluntarily return to his military duties in 1914, at the age of forty-eight, serving as artillery captain. The end of the war would see him ascend to the rank of lieutenant colonel, having suffered eight injuries, received seven commendations and been awarded the commander tie of the Legion of Honour. In his *Maximes sur la guerre*[21] (Grasset, 1930, reissued by Porte-Glaive in 1989), which is a true treatise on warrior stoicism, he

---

17   AN: Ernst Jünger, *Gardens and Streets (Gärten und Straßen)*, translated by Maurice Betz, Plon, 1942.
18   TN: Morning Rotation.
19   TN: Southern Mail.
20   TN: War Pilot.
21   TN: War Maxims.

praises what his compatriots considered to be horrific. In his *Journals*, Jünger would speak of this impressive book on several occasions, and would even offer it as a gift to his protector, Colonel Speidel, with a dedication in which he used one of Quinton's maxims.

CHAPTER VI

THE PRUSSIAN SOCIALISM OF *THE WORKER*

IN 1925, the year of Moeller van den Bruck's suicide, Jünger was only taking his first steps in politics. At the time, he believed that the still little-known character of Hitler, just like that of Mussolini, heralded 'a new type of leader'.[1] Much later, in his *War Journals*[2] text dated 28 March 1946, he would have the honesty to describe the shock he had felt at the discovery of the future Führer, whose rise was only just commencing:

> I barely knew his name when I saw him in a Munich amphitheatre, where he delivered one of his very first speeches [...]. I was captivated, as if I were undergoing some sort of purification. Our immeasurable efforts, during those four years of war, had not only led to our undoing, but also to humiliation. Our now disarmed country was surrounded by dangerous neighbours that were armed to their teeth; it was fragmented, traversed by corridors, pillaged, and bled dry. It was a sinister vision, a vision of sheer horror. And now we looked on, as a stranger rose up and told us what had to be said, and everyone felt that he was right. He was saying all that the government should have said, not literally, but in spirit [...]. And it wasn't a mere speech

---

1   AN: As stated in an article published in *Die Standarte* on 13 September 1925.
2   AN: *A German Officer in Occupied Paris: The War Journals, 1939–1948*, translated by Henri Plard, op. cit., p. 477, notes of 29 March 1946.

he was giving, for he embodied a manifestation of the elemental, and I had just been swept away by it.

We know, of course, that in Jünger's words, 'the elemental' has a positive connotation and is synonymous with 'the power of the depths'.

Jünger Discovers Hitler

From the very outset, a connection seemed to have been established between the still little-known young leader and the young combatant made famous by the publication of *Storm of Steel*. Hitler had also been a valiant WWI soldier, albeit a less prestigious one. He would thus send Jünger the first edition of *Mein Kampf*, dedication included. By return of post, Jünger would thank him by sending him his own war books. On the cover page of *Fire and Blood*, he inscribed the following tribute dated 9 January 1926: 'To Adolf Hitler, the Führer of the Nation! Ernst Jünger.'

That same year, Hitler announces his intention to visit Jünger in Leipzig. The visit would, however, ultimately be cancelled, Hitler's route having been modified.

'This visit would undoubtedly have yielded no results,' comments Jünger soberly in his *War Journals*, 'yet it would certainly have been a source of misfortune.'

The following year, in 1927, Hitler offers Jünger a mandate to become a member of the *Reichstag*. The offer is turned down, for as Jünger would later state, to him, 'the writing of a single verse was of more interest than the representation of 60,000 imbeciles in the Parliament'. Much later, on the eve of his hundredth birthday, he would respond to a journalist by adding with an ironic smile: 'Later on, however, I would have equally rejected a similar offer from our highly esteemed Federal Republic had I been made one.'

Despite Jünger's refusal, this was not yet to be the divide. Indeed, on 27 December 1929, during the final period of his political commitment, Ernst Jünger would once again write in *Die Kommenden*:

From the very bottom of our hearts, we wish for the victory of National Socialism; for we know the greatest of its strengths and the enthusiasm that drives it; we apprehend the sublime aspects of the sacrifices that are to be conceded to it without the slightest doubt. And yet, we also realise that it will only be able to carve its way through struggle […] if it renounces all remaining contributions that stem from a now-bygone past.

The Turning Point of *The Adventurous Heart*

The reason behind the reservation expressed by Jünger is quite enigmatic. On the other hand, we know that, despite the article published in *Die Kommenden*, the former officer had already distanced himself from political action by and large. There are multiple reasons for this. During the year of 1929, he published the first version of his work entitled *The Adventurous Heart*. This marks a certain break with his previous writings and a clear withdrawal into the inner sphere of reflection, that of more or less fantastical dreams and a writer's formal concerns. His vitalist and Nietzschean philosophy did not, however, disappear. There was indeed no shortage of him praising action for action's sake or glorifying those who honour voluntary death. As for the virulence of the nationalist polemicist, it had not vanished either. Some sentences were penned in a sarcastic and scathing manner that no humanitarian mind could read today without a start of horror. Speaking of the Germans of his time, for instance, the Jünger of *The Adventurous Heart* (in its first version) wrote:

> We have a global reputation for demolishing cathedrals. This is not negligible, at a time when awareness of sterility causes a string of museums to arise from the ground. […] We Germans have not granted Europe one single chance to lose.[3]

---

3   AN: *The Adventurous Heart* (1929), translated by Julien Hervier, Gallimard, 1995. The quotes included here come from a partial translation made by Armin Mohler. Its form is thus slightly different from Hervier's. Under the same title of *The Adventurous Heart*, Jünger would write a new, very different text in 1938. This second version, which was translated by Henri Thomas for Gallimard

Europe is to be understood here as the embodiment of universalism, which ultimately leads to a highly provocative tirade when Jünger castigates 'humanism's logical attempts to honour man in every bushman rather than in us. Hence our fear, insofar as we are Europeans. Perfect, isn't it — and above all, we are not to be shown any pity! It is a position from which one can operate. This reference to civilisation's secret measurement unit, which is kept in Paris, implies that we shall continue to lose this lost war, until the very end.'

And yet, one does not encounter a single complaint on his part, merely a stoic sort of firmness:

> Long have we been walking towards a magical zero point, one that shall only be transcended by those endowed with invisible sources of energy.

The book, which comes across as a series of disconnected reflections taken from an undated journal, baffled the admirers of war and political writings. Jünger acknowledges seeking literary aestheticism instead, giving way to intentional futility and a desired dreaminess that would bestow upon his mature writings their mysterious or irritating appeal. A careful reading reveals, however, that the writer did not sever his ties to the combative spirit of the previous years: he had only stopped believing in the resources of collective action:

> Nowadays, one cannot labour for Germany as a society; indeed, this must be done in solitude, just like a man who opens a breach in a virgin forest, sustained by the only hope that, somewhere, among the thickets, others are engaged in the same task.

Rift and Dissent

Joseph Goebbels, who had crossed paths with Jünger several times at the end of the 1920s within the Berlin intellectual circle hosted

---

(1942), erases all nationalist content, with the Nietzschean spirit of the first version greatly attenuated, albeit not completely absent.

by Arnolt Bronnen, declared himself disappointed. Having read *The Adventurous Heart*, he would note the following in his journal on 7 October 1929:

> It is but literature. Too bad for this Jünger, whose *Storm of Steel* I have just re-read. It was a truly powerful book, a heroic one. Behind it lurked an experience of blood, a complete experience. Today, Jünger simply locks himself away and rejects life, and his writings are nothing more than literature.

The views of the two men would hence continue to drift further apart, as the tempestuous pace of German political affairs accelerated.

It is, however, necessary to put the events of the times into perspective. During the *Reichstag* elections of May 1928, the NSDAP (National Socialist Party) had only managed to obtain 800,000 votes and 12 seats (out of 491). Two years later, on 14 September 1930, following the great and global economic crisis that had struck the Germans with full force, the party would make a giant leap, going from 800,000 to 6,400,000 votes, its number of parliament deputies skyrocketing from 12 to 107. And that was not to be the end of things, for the Communist Party had also made great headway, especially in Berlin. From that moment on, the Weimar Republic seemed doomed by the rise of movements that were intent on fighting it and by a crisis plunging the Germans into unspeakable distress. One of the little-known reasons behind the success of the National Socialist Party lay in the unexpected support it had received from the female electorate, whose members had apparently been seduced by its promises of security and family policies.

The great era of the small groups of the Conservative Revolution was now over. Indeed, we had entered a new historical phase where politics had reclaimed all its rights. From that moment on, Jünger would walk increasingly alone.

Meeting Ernst von Salomon in 1929, he says to him: 'I have chosen a high observation post from where I can watch the bedbugs devour each other'.[4]

This was certainly the case, but the fact that the new Jünger had distanced himself from all war writings and had adopted a literary attitude does not imply that his interest in thoughts and ideas had suddenly vanished. This fact would be demonstrated by the publication, in the fall of 1932, of his work titled *The Worker*, which is undoubtedly the most political and most sensational text penned by its author, having been heralded two years earlier by *Total Mobilisation*, a much briefer text that had already revealed Jünger's new themes.

The Worker's Indictment of the Bourgeoisie

The Worker was originally published in the previously mentioned context. Following the elections of 1930, the NSDAP's accession to power seemed inevitable. However, it was precisely during this period that Jünger and the most prominent representatives of the revolutionary Right would exacerbate the differences separating them, while also expressing their own views, which were anything but moderate.

The first pages of *The Worker* constitute one of the most violent indictments ever directed against the bourgeois world, from which Germany, according to Jünger, had been preserved, which was certainly true of the era:

> In Germany, the domination of the third estate has never been able to impact the most intimate core that determines the wealth, power and fullness of a life. Looking back on more than a century of German history, it is with pride that we can acknowledge the fact that we have actually been poor bourgeois. This garment, now worn down to its very weft, was not made-to-measure for us. Under its tatters now appears a much wilder and more innocent nature than the one whose sentimental accents had, very early on,

---

4 AN: Ernst von Salomon, *The Questionnaire*, p. 241.

caused the quivering of its curtain, behind which time concealed the great spectacle of democracy.[5]

It is tempting, upon reading this, to admire the art of the writer and his still intact polemical vigour: 'No,' he insists, 'the German was not a good bourgeois, and it was when he was at his strongest that he was least so. In all the places where one thought with the greatest depth and boldness, felt things with the greatest vivacity, fought with the greatest fierceness, it is impossible to ignore the revolt against the values that the great declaration of the independence of reason had hoisted on the bulwark.'

It is indeed hard to prove him wrong, for nowhere but in Germany had the criticism of French rationalism, ever associated with such names as Descartes, Sieyès or Condorcet, been so sharp. At the end of the 18th century, the philosopher Herder had been the first to place such an attitude at the very core of his protest, which was, at the time, that of the entire German romanticism, so different in its own nature from our French literary romanticism, which remained purely emotional and individualistic. The great German authors would only be equalled in England by Edmund Burke and his precocious criticism of both the French Revolution and the Declaration of Human Rights.

Having become a political philosopher endowed with his own kind of language, Jünger insists on what had been responsible for preserving his homeland:

> This country has no use of a concept of freedom which, akin to a measure defined once and for all and inherently deprived of content, can be applied to any variable that is subordinated to it. On the contrary, what always prevails here is the notion that the amount of freedom enjoyed by a certain force corresponds most precisely to the strength of the bond to which it is subject, and that what manifests itself in the extent of dispensed freedom is

---

5   AN: *The Worker* (1932), as translated by Julien Hervier for Christian Bourgois, 1989, p. 39. All quotes are taken from this edition.

the scope of the responsibility that bestows upon this will its very justification and validity (p. 41).

The Hardships Accumulated Since 1918

In other words, freedom is not a metaphysical idea. Jünger and the Germans do not believe in freedom per se, but in freedom as a function, such as the freedom of a given force. This idea is the very opposite of the notion of 'cunning vote collectors' and 'freedom merchants'. The latter are 'prisoners of the moral scheme of a corrupt Christianity that transposes the biblical curse to the worldly relationship between the exploiters and the exploited […]. They thus prove themselves incapable of envisioning freedom under any other terms than one's deliverance from a certain evil.' (pp. 99–100).

One is thus allowed to savour the philosophical-poetic language through which Jünger hints at the notion of freedom which, at the time, Germans still kept intact in their very hearts. One can also readily appreciate the formulation of concepts that evade the dry language of universities:

> Our freedom manifests itself with maximal power wherever it is borne by the awareness of having been awarded in fee (p. 41).

This idea of active freedom 'awarded in fee' was one that, in a now bygone past, the French had undoubtedly shared with their cousins from across the Rhine. Their national history, however, developed in such a way that ancient feudal freedoms, those ancient freedoms of nobility, found themselves uprooted, as demonstrated by Tocqueville, Taine and many subsequent historians.[6]

---

6   AN: Alexis de Tocqueville, *L'Ancien Régime et la Révolution* [TN: The Old Regime and the Revolution] (1856); Yves-Marie Bercé, *La Naissance dramatique de l'absolutisme, 1598- 1661* [TN : The Dramatic Rise of Absolutism, 1598- 1661] (Éditions du Seuil, 1992) ; Arlette Jouanna, *Le Devoir de révolte. La noblesse française et la gestation de l'État moderne, 1559–1661* [TN: The Duty of

When reading Jünger, one understands that in his eyes, at the time when he wrote such words, it was in Germany and in Germany alone that the ideal conditions were met to cut the 'old umbilical cord' of the bourgeois world. From there, embracing the belief that the Germans were, as a people, destined to be both the agent and beneficiary of the *Worker*'s 'planetary domination' is but a stone's throw away.

In *Gardens and Streets*, which constitutes the first part of his *War Journals*, Captain Jünger, now mobilised in the *Wehrmacht*, which had just triumphed during the battle of France, shares his conversation with French officers who had been taken prisoner:

> Questioning them about the causes of [their] sudden collapse, I learnt that they attributed it to dive bomber attacks. Their communication, the arrival of reserves and the transmission of orders had thus been made impossible from the very beginning, after which their army had been hacked to pieces using rapid weaponry, as if with a leather knife. In turn, they asked me if I could specify the reasons behind our success, to which I replied that I considered it to be the Worker's victory, though they seemed not to understand the true meaning of my response. This is because they knew nothing of the years we had experienced since 1918 and the latter's teachings, which we had collected as if in hot crucibles.

It is hardly surprising that our philosopher-captain's French interlocutors were unable to understand a single part of his message, for the language he had used was too obscure for them, a language that had little to do with ordinary thoughts.

The Worker's Enigmatic Figure

Let us, for a moment, return to the title of the work, *Der Arbeiter* (The Worker). It is quite an equivocal title and, it must be said, a rather poorly chosen one in our opinion. Indeed, the 'Worker' in question

---

Rebellion — The French Nobles and the Birth of the Modern State, 1559–1661] (Fayard, 1989); Jean-Marie Constant, *La Folle Liberté des baroques, 1600–1661* [TN: The Insane Freedom of the Baroque Era, 1600–1661] (Perrin, 2007); etc.

bears no relation whatsoever to the proletarian defined by Marxism, except in terms of brutality. Synonyms such as 'worker' or 'toiler' do not foster understanding. In no way is the book itself a treatise on political economy revolving around the social classes and workers ever so dear to the communist vulgate. This *Worker* is not a social 'type' in any shape or form, although he is, admittedly, the opposite of the bourgeois, which is undoubtedly one of its best definitions available. It is, in fact, a character that embodies the technical and martial domination of the times, a sort of Titan, as Jünger himself would subsequently state.[7]

Concerning the origin of Jünger's perception of a decisive paradigm change that led to the advent of the *Worker*, Julien Hervier proposes an explanation that is worth mentioning.

The author's experience of the Great War, the first genuine industrial war, was certainly instrumental:

> What ultimately changed were the mental structures, as the battlefield, with all its "armies of machines" and "worker battalions", became a factory [...]. All these war elements stem from modern technology, including not only guns, planes and tanks, but also the trenches themselves, now an immense labyrinth built by an army of trenchers [...]. The soldier was thus transformed into the *Arbeiter* [...]. He is at the service of the machine [and] trapped in the immense mechanism of universal technology. [...] This is not merely a psychological observation, but a record of a historical phenomenon. Indeed, as part of a highly Hegelian vision, Jünger believed that this entire process was governed either by the "spirit of the world" (*Weltgeist*) or "the spirit of an era" (*Zeitgeist*).[8]

---

7   AN: For an interpretation of the concept or 'figure' of the *Arbeiter*, one can consult Louis Dupeux's contribution to *Dossier H, Ernst Jünger* (op. cit.) [TN: File H, Ernst Jünger] entitled *Ernst Jünger, du nationalisme absolu à la gnose totalitaire de l'Arbeiter, 1925–1932* [TN: Ernst Jünger, from Absolute Nationalism to the Totalitarian Gnosis of the *Arbeiter, 1925–1932*].

8   AN: Julien Hervier, introduction aux *Journaux de guerre, I: 1914–1918* [TN: Introduction to the War Journals I, 1914–1918], p. XXXVIII–XXXIX.

The Notion of 'Figure' and 'Form'

Jünger contrasts the inorganic and inauthentic world of the bourgeoisie with that of the *Worker*, an updated version of the soldier, now free from all class connotations and dynamically united with technology in harmony with a heroic warrior approach. In order to highlight the powerful content of the very notion of the *Worker*, Jünger resorts to the term *Gestalt*, which, when translated literally, means either 'form' or 'figure', thus paving the way for every conceivable misinterpretation. We must indeed pause for a moment to ponder this highly present notion in *The Worker*. Using philosophical concepts only serves to muddle one's entire understanding. Although not a philosopher per se, Jünger had a deeply imaginative poetic mind, and that is how things are to be understood and interpreted. His 'figure' (*Gestalt*) of the Worker differs from Max Weber's Ideal Type and even more so from Plato's Idea, being their very opposite, in fact.

A quote from *The Worker* (p. 66) can thus set us on the right track:

> The vital, inalienable and sublime right that [the individual] shares with stones, plants, animals and stars, is his right to a "figure". […] All the great moments of life, the ardent dreams of youth, the intoxication of love, the fire of battle, coincide with an awareness of the "image," and memory is the magical return of the "image" that moves the heart and persuades it of the imperishable nature of these moments […].

This quote, in which the author has men share a 'figure' with stones, plants, animals and stars, suggests a highly immanentist sort of content. Men are thus inseparable from the sacred world of nature. And here is how they can realise themselves:

> The bitterest despair in life consists in not having fulfilled oneself, in not having lived up to oneself (p. 67).

If we are not fulfilled in our very being (that of a fish if one is a fish, that of a deer if one is a deer, that of a tree if one is a tree, that of a 'worker' or 'soldier' if one is a man [*vir*⁹], that of a beloved and/or mother if one is a woman), one simply cannot be a 'figure'. In other words, to possess a 'form' and be a 'figure' is to embody one's own 'genius' (the *daimon* of the Greeks), which animates a specific life. Without our *Gestalt* (figure), we are nothing. That is apparently the meaning of *Gestalt* as understood by Jünger: the fact of *being* (existing) or not being at all.

One can also perceive the 'form' as being a matrix. The Worker is only categorised as a 'figure' because of his relationship with the original 'form'. He only realises himself by expressing the 'form', by conforming to it. Jünger suggests that within the world of Workers, which is analogous to the pyramid of the former Prussian army (one of his favourite models, in fact), the category of each being is determined by his relationship to the 'form', that is, in harmony with the living principle of the new State. What is thereby suggested resembles a military structure whose hierarchy is merit-based (based on one's adequacy in relation to the 'form') and mirrors the Prussian system of free obedience. 'Total mobilisation' will thus be achieved, one whose purpose is 'not to ensure progress, but bestow power'.

Jünger had therefore every reason to believe that Hitler and his party had falsified this very idea by replacing the spiritualised notion of the Prussian State with that of race.

---

9   TN: Meaning 'man' in Latin.

CHAPTER VII

THE MYTH OF PRUSSIA AND THAT OF RACE

THE PRUSSIAN IDEA OF THE STATE, a highly spiritual one, has little in common with the purely administrative, individualistic and functional notion of the State that has prevailed in France since the days of Louis XIV.

So what *is* Prussia? 'Prussia is not a nation; it is the unadulterated and serious face of life.'[1] This poetic statement, which one would readily believe to have been penned by Ernst von Salomon himself, was actually made by a French writer who understood the mystery of Prussia, a creation of the mind and a political construct alike.

To Be Free and To Serve

Speaking of *Prussianism,* Spengler proposes a more historical definition:

> This word comprises all that we Germans possess not with regard to vague thoughts, desires, and ideas, but rather in terms of will, duty, and power, all of which are endowed with the strength of destiny. […] To be free — and to serve: there is nothing more difficult than these two things; only peoples whose mind and very being is rooted in such capacities and that can truly be free and serve have the right to aspire to a great destiny. Serving — therein

---

1 AN: Jean Grosjean, *Clausewitz,* an account published by Gallimard, 1972, p. 14.

lies the style of ancient Prussia [...]. There is no "I", but a "We", a collective feeling to which everyone commits their entire existence. The singular is of little importance and must sacrifice itself in the name of the Whole. Here, the notion of "every man for himself" counts for nothing, for what matters is "everyone for everyone else", including inner freedom in the noble sense of the term, namely that of *libertas oboedientiae*, freedom in obedience, which has always characterised the best elements of Prussian education.[2]

And Spengler goes on to specify that Prussia is the actual heir of the Teutonic Order. Indeed, its founders acted as 'servants to the notion according to which the State is designed to be a chivalric order.'[3]

A State conceived of as being a chivalric order; to be free and to serve: the Prussian notion of State cannot be summarised more accurately than this. According to Spengler, it was the Prussian army itself, that of Frederick the Great; of Scharnhorst and Gneisenau, of Moltke the Elder and the old Marshal von Hindenburg that had embodied this very notion.

This idea is in sharp contrast to the specifically Hitlerian conception of race. The historians who have worked on elucidating Hitler's mystery have not sufficiently noted that the founder of the Third Reich was not only a son of warfare, revenge and Pan-Germanism, a sincere and convinced proponent of National Socialism[4]. In terms of his fundamental ideas, he was, in fact, a product of 19th-century scientism and Darwinism. His racism owes nothing to the writings of someone like Gobineau.[5] His true master was the author of *On*

---

2 AN: Oswald Spengler, *Prussianité et socialisme* [TN: Prussianism and Socialism], *op. cit.*, pp. 51–54.

3 AN: Ibid., p. 55.

4 AN: For a fuller understanding of Hitler's racial Darwinism and the consequences of such a 'worldview', one can refer to the analysis included in the 6th chapter of *Le Siècle de 1914*, op. cit.

5 AN: Hitler's doctrine is, furthermore, very different from the historical philosophy of Houston Stewart Chamberlain as expressed in *The Foundations of the Nineteenth Century* (1899). In its Darwinist principles, it also differs from the

the Origin of Species by Means of Natural Selection, albeit in the latter's simplified formulation spread by popularisers at the time of Hitler's youth. Unlike other readers, his systematic mind, ever on a quest for absolute truth, was dazzled by it. What he ultimately drew from it was a simplifying and categorical imperative, one that was endowed with all the violence of religious extremism. That is what makes Hitler akin to Lenin and Marx's other disciples, for whom 'science' had replaced the certainties derived from the word of God. And since science and the future ordered him to do so, Hitler would, just like the Marxists, implement his plan without any regard for the suffering and damage that he would trigger. As for Jünger, he had anticipated this.

A Different Type of Historical Materialism

Due to its absolutism, Hitler's doctrine of race departs completely from the mundane acknowledgement of the existence of races and their role in history, both of which were accepted by each and every person before the disasters of the Third Reich led to the prohibition of such views, down to the very idea of race, which, up until then, had never bothered anyone. 'The more I have travelled, the more I have acquired the conviction that races are the greatest secret in all of history,' wrote Lamartine, without ever being accused of 'racism' as a result — in the current sense of the word that now prevails in Europe, namely that of inciting others to embrace hatred.[6] Just like his contemporaries, Jünger was well-aware of the importance of being 'well-bred' within the framework of a nation's necessary breeding ground. Unlike Hitler,

---

idealist views developed by Alfred Rosenberg in *Der Mythus des zwanzigsten Jahrhunderts* [TN: The Myth of the Twentieth Century] (1930).

6   AN: As quoted by Sarga Moussa (the publication director) in *L'Idée de «race» dans les sociétés humaines et la littérature (XVIIIe-XIXe siècle)* [TN: The Notion of 'Race' in Human Societies and Literature in the 18th and 19th Centuries], L'Harmattan, Paris, 2005. While, since 1945, Europe has been unable to even bear the word 'race', the concept has retained all its legitimacy in the United States, where it is even included in the legal definition of the identity of individuals.

however, he did not consider this to be the sole explanation behind everything. Through four fundamental pages of his *Mein Kampf*, Hitler draws the Darwinist framework of his doctrine[7] when granting it, on top of everything else, a religious dimension of absoluteness by calling upon the Creator. What is thus presented is the expression of a cosmic vision that would inspire his historical-political creed and action to the very end. Let us summarise it all with a brief quote: 'The strong must dominate and not blend with the weak, thus sacrificing their own greatness.' The author of *Mein Kampf* specifies that if the process was reversed, 'all further and higher development would cease and the opposite would occur.'[8] Racial advancement is the highest aim towards which Hitler directs the actions of his own movement. By doing so, he reveals himself to be a rather unexpected heir of the Enlightenment, which advocated mankind's sustained progress.[9] His adherence to the principles of the Enlightenment is actually twofold, since he considered human 'advancement' to be the result of material causes (the betterment of races and their competition). This vision is in stark contrast to that of traditionists (and traditionalists), who, without neglecting the factors of physical improvement or degeneration, do not believe in human advancement in line with a general evolution of the species, but through constantly repeated personal and civilisational improvements stemming from an effort to surpass oneself.[10]

---

7   AN: One must under no circumstances confuse the work of Charles Darwin and the notion of Darwinism, which is but an outrageous simplification of his thinking applied to the social and political domains.

8   AN: Adolf Hitler, *Mein Kampf*, French edition, Nouvelles Éditions Latines, 1934, pp. 283–286.

9   AN: 'Convinced', writes Condorcet (*Fragment of justification* [TN: Fragment of Justification]), 'that the human species was unlimitedly perfectible, I regarded the task of hastening this progress as one of the sweetest possible occupations.'

10 AN: Regarding the 'traditionalist' interpretation, one should refer to our work entitled *Histoire et tradition des Européens. 30 000 ans d'identité* [TN: European

Just as one can find some valid observations in Marxism, not everything is obviously absurd in the content of *Mein Kampf*. What one must bear in mind is the aspect of scientific certainty characterising this doctrine, whose implementation would be ensured fanatically. With the Darwinist notion of the struggle of species acting as its sole reference axis, its intention was to materially realize the myth of a 'superior race'. Under the Third Reich, this idea would inspire an entire racial policy where one assumed that it was enough to apply eugenic measures and to erect barriers against miscegenation so that the virtues of old could return and the Aryan, the creator of a higher form of civilisation, could automatically resurface. This mechanistic interpretation was experimentally contradicted by the anatomy of the movement's primary beacons, Hitler himself and Goebbels. Despite their racially debatable physique, one cannot dispute, from a Hitlerian point of view, all that would always remain exemplary in the behaviour of these two characters. By contrast, many were the 'beautiful' and 'pure' Aryans who, in both Europe and the United States, engaged in a fierce struggle against the Third Reich. It would seem that racial appearance does not account for everything after all…

Ernst Jünger had sensed that, just like Marxism, Hitlerism was a distortion of Enlightenment rationalism, a sort of madness-afflicted reasoning. Hitler believed himself to have discovered the secret of the ideal City based on science and reason. What had once been experienced as immemorial, accommodating and flexible wisdom would be imposed with geometric rigour by a dictatorial law that would enact thorough and tyrannical rules to be enforced by legions of obedient and narrow-minded officials. This distortion of reason, it must be said, is not specific to 'totalitarianism'. Indeed, most modern societies have fallen prey to it, under the pretext of hyper-rationality and submission to the judgements passed by 'experts' and 'specialists'. And that is where the ambiguous world of the *Worker* comes in.

History and Tradition — 30,000 Years of Identity], published by éditions du Rocher in 2002.

Heidegger and the Nihilism of *The Worker*

Jünger's work did not go unnoticed. In 1940, without even knowing its author, Martin Heidegger would go as far as to devote an entire seminar to it. The latter would quickly be banned by the authorities of the Third Reich, who considered it incompatible with their ideology. Heidegger's reading of this work, preceded by that of Jünger's text on *Total Mobilisation* (1930), in which Nietzschean nihilism and the essence of technology seem closely connected, piqued the interest of the Freiburg philosopher, who would maintain an excellent personal relationship with Jünger following their first meeting in 1948. However, according to historian Ernst Nolte, a former student and close friend of Heidegger's, 'one must exclude, from the very outset, any and all assumptions that [Heidegger] had actually found a lot of positive aspects to *The Worker*. […] Whereas, in Jünger's eyes, an expression such as "workshop landscape" plays an important role, it is precisely this bellicose and technological aspect that Heidegger rejects. *The Worker* only interests him to the extent that it bestows a shape—one that is developed with particular clarity—upon what he feels is the most extreme antipole to his own thought.'[11] What Heidegger himself would say about *The Worker* is that it provides the reader with an exemplary description of the European nihilism that had stemmed from the war.

If one equates nihilism to the triumph of materialism, it is definitely a good call on their part. And yet, *The Worker* can also be interpreted as a challenge to nihilism, which one should combat using its own

---

11   AN: Ernst Nolte, *Siegfried Gerlich im Gespräch mit Ernst Nolte. Einblick in ein Gesamtwerk* [TN: Translated into French as *Entre les lignes de front. Entretiens avec Siegfried Gerlich*, meaning 'Among the Front Lines: Interviews with Siegfried Gerlich'], Éditions du Rocher, 2008, pp. 127–128. Regarding Martin Heidegger's fundamental aversion to the technological evolution of the world and of life, one can refer to the famous interview that he gave to *Der Spiegel* in September 1966, published on 31 May 1976, shortly after his death. Translated by Jean Launay for Mercure de France (1988) under the title *Réponses et questions sur l'histoire et la politique* [TN: Answers and Questions on the Topic of History and Politics], pp. 45–47.

weapons, thus driving it to its very limits, as Moeller van den Bruck implicitly proposed.

Unlike most of his other works, which Jünger continued to re-work from reissue to reissue, *The Worker* was never subject to any modification. Fearful of incorrect interpretations and controversies resulting from the changing times, Jünger refused to have it reprinted after the third edition of 1942. Yielding to the entreaties of Martin Heidegger, however, he would eventually agree to re-release the book in 1963. And yet, for a long time to come, he would refuse to allow a translation to be published in French, fearing in particular that the rational nature of the French language would end up betraying his thoughts. With the author's agreement, however, such a translation would ultimately be made by Julien Hervier for Christian Bourgois editions (1989).

A Manifesto of 'Heroic Realism'

Upon reading this work long after its initial publication, with the times having completely changed, one understands Jünger's reluctance to authorise a French translation. The author's violent condemnation of liberal democracy and glorification of a new, young and brutal type of elite, in communion with his demand for 'heroic realism', could indeed lead to every manner of confusion. It is hard not to view it as an authentically 'pre-fascist' manifesto, in the historical sense of the term and not the controversial one; fascist, but in no way Hitlerian.[12]

Very present in *The Worker* as part of the author's response to the challenges of technological domination, the attitude of 'heroic realism' would subsequently disappear from Jünger's mental universe, once his mind had undergone the great 'humanist' reversal heralded by the publication of *On the Marble Cliffs* in 1939. The notion of 'heroic realism', apparently created by Werner Best, his former companion in the

---

12 AN: The essential differences between fascism and Hitlerism (beyond any formal similarities) are presented in great detail in *Le Siècle de 1914* [TN: The Century of 1914], op. cit.

networks of the revolutionary Right, is quite explicit.[13] It consists in facing the harshness and cruelty of the world with a stout heart rather than fleeing or seeking refuge in dreams of illusory hope. Those who embrace this attitude can be touched by 'neither idealism nor materialism'. They belong to 'the type of volunteers who greeted the Great War with enthusiasm and still greet everything that has followed and will follow it'.[14]

Displaying great suggestive power, *The Worker* is a book that reflects the fiery passions of its own era. It is a first-rate document centring on the forces which, at the time, impacted Europe and most particularly Germany. 'What must arouse esteem in every foreigner that visits Germany', writes Jünger with great arrogance, 'are not the facades preserved since the days of old, nor the solemn speeches to celebrate the centenary of the classics, nor even the concerns that constitute the very theme of novels and plays; for it is rather the virtues of poverty, work and courage that now offer the visible sign of a much deeper culture than what the bourgeois cultural ideal could ever dream of [...]. Moreover, the more one leads a cynical, Spartan, Prussian or Bolshevik life, the better [...]. Only a strong awareness of oneself, embodied by a young and brutal ruling caste, could cut deeply enough to deliver us from the old umbilical cord with the necessary vigour.'[15]

In an almost mantra-like manner, Jünger returns to this expectation of a new type of elite, one that is not averse to savagery:

> The less this class will be cultured in the usual sense, the better. The age of general culture has unfortunately deprived us of having a considerable

---

13 AN: The expression surfaced on 28 March 1930 as the title of an article published in *Die literarische Welt*. It was allegedly coined by Werner Best, who, at the time, was a friend of Jünger's and would go on to become a senior leader in the SS.

14 AN: *The Worker*, p. 66.

15 AN: Ibid., p. 257.

supply of illiterate people [...]. Our hope resides in the new relationship to the elemental that has been bestowed upon the Worker.[16]

The 'elemental' is to be understood as the instinctive forces of life, which are stifled by rationalism and the bourgeois rule. Jünger thus radicalises the dominant themes, namely those of his own philosophy of life, contrasting the stagnant peace of the bourgeois world with eternal struggle, defined as an 'inner experience'. Such was the view that prevailed in the year of 1932. Driven by seismographic sensitiveness to period changes, Jünger would, however, soon turn away from all this, especially with the ever-deepening chasm of mutual hostility separating him from Hitler and his party.

The Prussian Party vs Hitler's Party

One could easily have thought that the above-mentioned arguments presented by Jünger in *The Worker* would have met the approval of National Socialist ideologists. This, however, was far from being the case.

Upon publication, the book was scathingly criticised by the party's press, a party that had not yet seized power. At the time, the NSDAP was even the focus of various manoeuvres intended to prevent it from assuming such power. Following some major electoral successes and the crippling of the Weimar Republic, Hitler would, as we all know, be appointed Reich Chancellor on 30 January 1933.[17] Three months earlier, in its Bavarian edition of 22 October 1932, the *Völkischer Beobachter* (an NSDAP organ) had dedicated an extensive article to the condemnation of Jünger's book, under the quill of Thilo von Trotha. In it, von Trotha criticised Jünger for his 'fundamentally individualistic attitude' and concluded by stating that by authoring such a book, Jünger was getting dangerously close to 'being shot in the back of the neck'. One

---

16 AN: Ibid., p. 260.
17 AN: In the 7th chapter of *Le Siècle de 1914* (op. cit.), one can find a precise account of the circumstances surrounding Hitler's rise to power and its results.

wonders what could have justified such a threat. The explanation would soon be given. Jünger, continues Trotha, 'disregards the fundamental question of blood and soil'. Indeed, nowhere in Jünger's work does one find a single trace of the racial Darwinism that characterises Hitlerian National Socialism. Additionally, nowhere in this cryptic book of his are the party and its leader mentioned or even hinted at, although they were already marching towards power. Of course, it is a constant aspect of all hegemony-minded political parties to strive to exploit anything that manifests itself in the domain that is theirs. There is more to this, however.

Within the doctrine presented in *Mein Kampf*, the Party (second only to the Führer himself) is the sole bearer of supreme values, a role that Jünger was implicitly denying it. To the National Socialists, *The Worker* was not an insignificant book by any means: its author was the dominant intellectual of both the 'frontline generation' and the Conservative Revolution. In its own way, the book itself describes the revolution being conducted in Germany, but without ever alluding to the National Socialist Party and its leader, who considered themselves to be the only legitimate actors. In other words, such a manifestation of independence on Jünger's part was, at the time, synonymous with a declaration of opposition.

Let us not forget the political situation that prevailed in Germany back then. Indeed, except for the weakened democratic parties, and the Communist Party, which directed its attacks against the social democrats, two forces were competing for power in 1932: the first was Hitler's party, which became the strongest in Germany after securing 38% of all votes during the elections held on 31 July 1932. 230 'brown shirts' were thus elected to be part of the *Reichstag*. On the opposite side was the final rampart against the brown tidal wave, in the person of Marshal Hindenburg, the president of the German Republic, and the *Reichswehr*. This bulwark, however, was not a massive party. To counter the Hitlerian party that they loathed, Hindenburg and his advisors considered resorting to a dictatorship relying on the army. It is within such a mindset that General Schleicher is appointed chancellor on 1 December 1932. Acting in accordance with what was expected of him, he strives to shatter the Nazi party by poaching some of its leaders, notably Gregor Strasser. The manoeuvre having failed to produce the desired results, Schleicher is abandoned by Hindenburg and the *Reichswehr* on 28 January 1933. Two days later, Hitler is appointed chancellor.

Although basically retired from politics, Jünger chooses his side: that of Prussia and the *Reichswehr*, against National Socialism. It may seem rather simplistic to express things in this manner, but the future, especially the 1941–1944 period, would reveal the profound complicity uniting Jünger with the part of the officer corps where the most resolute adversaries of both Hitler and his regime would be recruited. From 1933 onwards, a number of high-ranking officers of the *Reichswehr* would, in the secrecy of their hearts, watch with concern as Germany falls into the hands of an uncontrollable man and a party whose brutality and plebeian vulgarity is repulsive to them.

Increasingly Greater Reservations

Jünger never gave a clear explanation to his opposition to the new regime. He never, in fact, explained himself clearly on anything, abiding by the mythical turn, and by no means historical expression, of his own thoughts, which were spontaneously geared towards the veiled circumlocutions of symbols and literature. And yet, those of us who study history in a desire to elucidate its mysteries can readily interpret the writer's motivations. Indeed, everything points to the fact that what he favoured was a revolution from above, in accordance with the Bismarckian model. A total revolution, as heralded by his writings, but a controlled and regulated one, a new and enlightened sort of despotism. 'My concept of the State is Prussian', Jünger emphasises once more in his *War Journals*, on 29 March 1944, the day of his forty-ninth birthday.

Indeed, what Jünger essentially writes in *The Worker* is that it is not Rousseau's social contract but the Prussian military order that is to found the German state of the future. In it, the State and the army would be inseparable. This view of things was bound to displease the National Socialists, for whom the Prussian system was not a model to follow, as they intended to submit the State and the army to their own party. Jünger, however, had no desire to please the Nazis.

Sharing the aesthetical, moral, social and political reservations of many *Reichswehr* officers, the writer feared that Germany's new leader would lead the country to disaster. Suspected of complicity with the 'National Bolsheviks' of his friend Niekisch, he is targeted with a first raid in April 1933, initiated by the subordinates of the local police amidst the climate of general suspicion and latent civil war that characterised the first months of the new regime. For fear of further raids, Jünger proceeds to destroy his diary detailing the years that preceded the advent of the Third Reich, a great loss that deprives us of the milestones that could have allowed us to gain a better understanding of his evolution at the time. In November, he publicly declares his refusal to join the Prussian Academy of Writers, in which he had been elected on the 9th of June, declining thereafter all other official proposals.[18]

Over the following years, Jünger would never relinquish his increasingly greater reservations, while still refusing to emigrate and sever his ties to his own homeland. Opting for inner exile, he devotes himself to his entomological work and to penning texts that are truly timeless, until the publication, in September 1939, of his novel *On the Marble Cliffs*. The work is immediately perceived as a coded condemnation of the regime. He is denounced accordingly to Hitler himself

---

18   AN: To gain additional understanding of Ernst Jünger's political evolution, one can consult Julien Hervier's *Deux individus dans l'histoire*. Pierre Drieu la Rochelle, Ernst Jünger, op. cit., Philippe Migaux's *Ernst Jünger. Écrits politiques de jeunesse, 1914–1932* [TN: Ernst Jünger: Political Writings of Youth, 1914–1932], thesis, Paris Institute of Political Studies, 1980, and Horst Mühleisen and Hans Peter Des Coudres' *Bibliographie der Werke Ernst Jüngers*, op. cit.

by *Reichsleiter* Philipp Bouhler (1899–1945), the head of the 'Party's Control Commission for the Protection of National Socialist Writings'. Harbouring respect for the heroic soldier of the Great War that authored *Storm of Steel*, Hitler would, however, prohibit all persecution: 'No one touches Jünger!'

CHAPTER VIII

INTERNAL EXILE

It was by chance that the writer Julien Gracq discovered *On the Marble Cliffs* at the newsagent's of Angers station,[1] at the darkest time of the Occupation. He opened it while waiting for a train and could not tear himself away from it. He would later state that the novel was 'Jünger's masterpiece'. In *La Littérature à l'estomac*,[2] a famous 1950 pamphlet that targeted the commercialisation of literature, he would add the following:

> I would readily give up on almost all the literature of the past ten years for Ernst Jünger's *On the Marble Cliffs*.[3]

At a later time, he would expand further and write:

---

1 AN: Louis Poirier (1910–2007) was a geography professor before becoming known as a writer under his nom de plume Julien Gracq. A member of the Communist Party from 1936 to 1939, he published his first novel, *Au château d'Argol* [TN: At the Château d'Argol], in 1938. Mobilised in 1939, he was taken prisoner in 1940 before being released for health reasons in 1941. He then became close with the surrealists. He would ultimately rise to fame in 1951 for his refusal of the Goncourt Prize that he had just been awarded for his novel *Le Rivage des Syrtes* [TN: The Opposing Shore].

2 TN: Although this can be translated as 'Stomach Literature' or, more literally, 'Literature in the Stomach', the intended meaning is probably 'Palatable Literature', that is, literature of the non-commercial kind.

3 AN: Julien Gracq, *Préférences*, op. cit., p. 23. This collection adopts, among other things, the content of *La Littérature à l'estomac*.

This book, which saw the light of day at one of the turning points of history [1939], tells us not only about Jünger himself, but, through him, also about ourselves and our era […]. I believe that one should read *On the Marble Cliffs* as a quintessential book. It is filled with great imagery, with images that have been, and still are, those of our lives as men of the mid-twentieth century, of our joys and disasters. […] Those are the different faces of our very situation: whether moving or terrible, they are the framework under which the cards of destiny were dealt to us.[4]

The Warrior Who Withdrew from the World

These thoughts, expressed by Julien Gracq, summarise to a certain extent the purpose of our current book. Ernst Jünger is indeed *the* witness of the successive faces of European destiny throughout the cruellest of centuries. However, *On the Marble Cliffs* only relates this fate in a fleeting manner. This coded novel cannot be separated from the era that witnessed its birth, independently of any artistic judgment.

In the text that we have just quoted, Julien Gracq briefly points out the highlights of Jünger's career as both an author and a soldier, a career whose successive stages we are well-aware of: the endless reading endeavours during his childhood and adolescence, punctuated by adventurous outings into an untouched sort of nature; the founding ordeal of the Great War; the insolent heroism of a young assault troop officer covered in scars and forever marked by the exhilaration of the military attacks and the unrelenting harshness of the trenches; and the birth of the writer from the very moment that he removed his helmet. And what a writer he was! He would first become an author of war books and then a writer of political works that would turn him into the intellectual beacon of new radical thoughts that would be collected in his sensational manifesto entitled *The Worker*. And it was then that the one that people sometimes considered a herald of the victorious movement of 1933 suddenly turned away from it all in the most abrupt

---

4 AN: Ibid.

and unbridled manner. In response to the pleas made to him, he would dryly reply, 'There is no room for me in an army where Göring is a general.'

Jünger thus becomes a sort of inner emigrant. He travels and meditates before penning his breakthrough novel, *On the Marble Cliffs*, in 1939, a novel whose meaning was immediately understood in Germany. As the first copies come out of the printing house, a new war breaks out. Although Jünger is mobilised, the enthusiasm of the past has given way to resignation. The opportunities to wage battle would be rare and he would not complain about it very much. Having ordered his men to always respect the vanquished in the aftermath of the French campaign, he is appointed to the headquarters of the occupying forces. Apart from being on leave a few times and a three-month mission in the Caucasus, he spent the rest of the war in Paris, establishing friendly relations with all that the French capital had to offer in terms of talent. Indirectly involved in the plot of 20 July 1944, he evades the fate of a great many other officers. During a long life in which he would also experience other, less dramatic developments, he had overcome many a mortal peril while enjoying a strange privilege of invulnerability.

Summarising Jünger's life in his own words, Julien Gracq compares him to 'those mediaeval warriors who had one day chosen to hang their sword on the walls of a cloister'. Although the image itself is beautiful, the fact remains that Jünger's long existence was punctuated by a greater number of transmutations than this single change. It is, of course, true that *On the Marble Cliffs* did mark a clear break in the middle of his life, heralding the immense rift that would soon befall the mind and destiny of Europeans. We shall return to this later.[5]

This break in Ernst Jünger's life and work is a source of more than one enigma. The warrior, tempted by the dreams of a violent revolution, suddenly withdraws from the world and transforms into

---

5   AN: The historical context that saw the birth of *On the Marble Cliffs* is presented in Chapter IX under the title *A Farewell to Arms*.

a humanitarian and pacifistic hermit, collecting plants on the heights of the *Marble Cliffs*. And it is the unexpected that drives even the least curious onlooker to ask questions.

The Night of the Long Knives

To try to understand this change, it is necessary to go back to the years that followed the publication of *The Worker*, to Hitler's rise to power on 30 January 1933, and the full powers that Hitler was granted by the *Reichstag* on 23 March (by 441 votes to 94) for a period of four years, on the occasion of what has been described as a legal coup d'état.[6]

The following year, a revolt of the SA[7] was crushed through the bloody purge of 30 June 1934. This 'Night of the Long Knives' proved that Germany had entered an era of political violence the likes of which one had not seen for a long time, if one disregards the latent civil war of 1919–1923. This event was caused by several complex factors.[8] To put it very simply, the purge, which also targeted right-wing opponents, was the result of a manipulative plan hatched by the leaders of the *Reichswehr*, who wanted to neutralise the now troublesome SA.[9] For

---

6 TN: The *Reichstag* voted for Hitler's 'Enabling Act', which allowed him to pass (i.e. 'enact') laws without having to worry about any sort of interference on the part of the president or the German parliament itself.

7 TN: The *Sturmabteilung* was a paramilitary organisation that used violent methods and played a decisive role in Hitler's ascent to power.

8 AN: Regarding this event, its real causes and its repercussions, one can refer to the 7th chapter of *Le Siècle de 1914*, op. cit., entitled '*The National Socialist Revolution*'. One can, likewise, consult *Histoire d'un fascisme allemand* , op. cit.

9 AN: In 1934, following the 'integration' of the various veterans' associations, Röhm, the leader of the SA, found himself at the head of a potential army of 3 million men. On the other hand, the *Reichswehr* itself was limited to an official count of no more than 100,000 men, the real number totalling 200,000. As for Röhm, he did not shy away from making it known that the time had come for genuine SA fighters (their officials having stemmed from the former *Freikorps*) to seek revenge against the 'gentlemen' of the *Reichswehr*. In the interview book titled *Entre les lignes de front*, op. cit., the historian Ernst Nolte suggests

once, they had enjoyed the complicity of some of the highest-standing party leaders, namely Göring, Goebbels and Himmler, who also wanted to bring the all too independent SA back in line by eliminating its leaders.

This whole affair would be complicated by the unexpected political agreement between the leaders of the SA, who had the reputation of being 'socialists', and a fraction of the conservative or nationalist Right, whose members were secretly hostile to Hitler. This tendency was embodied by Vice-Chancellor von Papen and Munich lawyer Edgar Julius Jung, a prominent personality of the Conservative Revolution. The massacre would be legalised by a law dated 3 July and enacted in implementation of the above-mentioned full powers. Controlled by Goebbels, the press only allowed minimal information on the actual scale of the killing to leak. The rest would be revealed by 'word of mouth'.[10] A number of SA leaders were thus shot, including Röhm, but also some right-wing opponents such as Herbert von Bose, Papen's deputy, Edgar Jung, the brain behind the entire conspiracy, and General Kurt von Schleicher, the last chancellor before Hitler, who had been appointed in the hope of stopping him.

Prussian National Socialist Gregor Strasser, who had given in to Schleicher's manoeuvres and who Jünger knew well, would also be shot dead, as would many others. Only von Papen would be spared and placed under house arrest while waiting to be sent on a diplomatic mission to Vienna and Ankara.

Public approval of the purge would come from the very top of the State in the shape of a message from old Marshal Hindenburg himself

---

a further explanation. According to him, Röhm and his plethoric militia, who were unfit for waging a war of aggression, were allegedly liquidated to enable the creation of the future *Wehrmacht*, a much more effective instrument for the implementation of a territorial expansion policy.

10 AN: The authorities would acknowledge 83 executions, which are therefore indisputable. Published in exile, the nominative list of the *Weißbuch* (White Book) actually lists a total of 116 names.

(the president of the German Republic until his imminent death[11]), who expressed his 'admiration' for Chancellor Hitler's determination.

This was not, however, the position espoused by Jünger, who was outraged by the massacre. One would later find a transposition of the 'Night of the Longs Knives' in certain bloody depictions comprised in his book *On the Marble Cliffs*. Others, notably Ernst von Salomon, Oswald Spengler and Martin Heidegger, would make no secret of their disapproval either, in contrast with the jurist Carl Schmitt. Although opposed to the Nazis before their coming to power, Schmitt justifies the executions in the name of the higher law of political sovereignty.[12]

The Prussian Opposition to Hitler

As soon as Hitler took power in 1933, Jünger, Spengler, von Salomon and many other major authors of the Conservative Revolution became his virtual opponents. The new regime seemed to them a mere travesty of the authentic 'national socialism' they wished for. In accordance with the excellent thought expressed by the historian Ernst Nolte, '"national socialism" was not, until 1934, a protected trademark'. The concept did not yet belong to any man or a party that would distort its meaning. In the eyes of their opponents, if the new leaders of Germany were indeed gifted in terms of political skill and will, they lacked any genuine culture, moral stature and moderation. In the absence of such virtues, all of which were characteristic of the great Prussian reformers Gneisenau and Bismarck, these callous characters would only ruin Germany's chances of recovery.

Even at the time of the first great successes, as Hitler and his party set out to break the shackles of the Treaty of Versailles, their opponents

---

11   AN: Hindenburg would pass away on 2 August 1934. The referendum held on 19 August 1934 would then grant Hitler the dual status of chancellor and head of state (with 89.9% voting in favour amidst a participation of 95.7% of registered voters).

12   AN: David Cumin, *Carl Schmitt. Biographie politique et intellectuelle* [TN: The Political and Intellectual Biography of Carl Schmitt], Éditions du Cerf, 2005.

did not allow themselves to be taken in by such developments. Indeed, they had sensed that the racial and territorial domination plans devised by Hitler would only lead Germany and Europe towards a terrible catastrophe. Such would be the position adopted by General Ludwig Beck (1880–1944). Having been named Chief of Staff of the German Army (OKH[13]) in 1935, he would play a key role in the development of the *Wehrmacht*. Starting at the end of 1937, however, he would proceed to explicitly criticise Hitler's risky foreign policy projects. Condemning the planned aggression against Czechoslovakia, he would resign in August 1938. Having failed in an initial conspiracy scheme in 1939, he would take charge of the 20 July 1944 conspiracy to assassinate Hitler, which would ultimately lead to him being shot as soon as the plot was thwarted.

The internal exile in which Jünger, Spengler and others chose to seek refuge is often said to be due to their aristocratism and contempt for a plebeian type of National Socialism. This explanation, however, is too basic and dissatisfactory. Indeed, a large number of genuine aristocrats of old stock were not unnerved by the rather crude manners of the new masters, whose behaviour was often that of the *nouveaux riches*.[14] They even rallied with enthusiasm around the regime and its leader, who seemed to be achieving great success in a titanic work of liberation, unification and recovery in which all others had previously failed.

Over the course of time, positions would continue to evolve in relation to the National Socialist revolution and its leader. One had better be wary, therefore, of placing their entire trust in all that has been written in the aftermath of 1945, as memories do tend to undergo the occasional obscuration. It is not that the actual honesty of the witnesses

---

13   TN: OKH (*Oberkommando des Heeres*) literally means 'High Command of the [German] Army'.

14   TN: In both English and French, the *nouveaux riches* are defined as people who, having recently become rich, still retain the vulgar tastes and manners of their own origin.

should necessarily be called into question, but what was clear before 1945 might no longer be so afterwards. This is because the unconscious part of one's memory will always engage in a selective sifting process, especially among intellectuals, who are naturally tempted to add coherence to their past conduct in light of newly acquired principles.

Günter Grass and the Obscuration of Memories

A good example of such obscuration of memories is offered by Günter Grass. Since the 1950s, and particularly since the publication of his autobiographical novel *Die Blechtrommel*[15] (1959), which was adapted for the big screen by Volker Schlöndorff in 1979, the writer, who was awarded the Nobel Prize in 1999, had embodied the repentant conscience of righteous democratic Germany. Suddenly, however, during the summer of 2006, he revealed in his memoir that he had enlisted in the Waffen-SS at the end of 1944, when he was seventeen years old. This revelation caused quite a resounding stir in Germany. The confession appeared on the pages of his *Beim Häuten der Zwiebel* ('Peeling the Onion'), released on 16 August 2006 by Steidl publishing. Layer by layer, as if peeling an onion, the author proceeded to expose the different folds of his own memory.[16] It must be emphasised that back in 1944, nothing was known of the reputation that the double rune of the SS would subsequently acquire, with the SS even seeing itself as the very symbol of the virtues of the new Germany. At the time, the Waffen-SS owed its elite army prestige to the terrible losses that it was willing to suffer in the most dangerous combat zones of the West and the East.

The young Günter Grass was, in fact, only six years old when Hitler initially rose to power. He belonged to a generation that had been moulded by the regime's precepts, including the exaltation of such

---

15 TN: The Tin Drum.
16 AN: The work was translated into French under the title *Pelures d'oignons* [TN: Onion skins], Éditions du Seuil, 2007.

virtues as self-sacrifice and heroism. The future writer had first wanted to join Germany's submarine fleet, which was considered elite. The U-boats were, however, no longer recruiting. This is why the teenager fell back on the 10th Waffen-SS Panzer Division. Sworn in during the month of January 1945, Günter Grass took part in his Panzer Division's battles against the Red Army in East Prussia, where the Germans were decimated on 20 and 21 April by Konev's forces. Günter Grass would then be taken prisoner by the Americans. In his book, he swears that, while detained in a camp in Bavaria, he played dice with another prisoner, a young devout Catholic who was destined to priesthood and would become pope under the name of Benedict XVI.

Although Günter Grass had, in the past, already admitted to having been a rather enthusiastic member of the *Hitlerjugend* (Hitler Youth), which had been compulsory since 1938, before becoming a soldier in the last months of the war, he had never spoken directly of the Waffen-SS. 'What I had accepted with the pride and stupidity of my young age I then remained silent about due to the shame that surfaced after the war. The burden, however, continued to weigh on me and there was no one that could ease it,' he writes in *Beim Häuten der Zwiebel*. What burden? The young SS member Günter Grass had not participated in any sort of abuse. When he had first joined the Waffen-SS, the latter was perceived in Germany as endowed with an aura of military merit. As he says in his book, it 'even had a European element: indeed, its Eastern Front divisions comprised some French, Walloon, Flemish and Dutch volunteers, as well as a large number of Norwegians, Danes, and even Swedes (whose country remained nonetheless neutral), waging a battle that would, as was said, save the West from the Bolshevik tidal wave'.[17] So, yes, one does wonder what burden could have weighed on the author's conscience.

In *Die Blechtrommel*, the novel that made him famous, Günter Grass uses all his literary skill to castigate the *Mitläufer*, the 'follow-my-leader

---

17   AN: The Waffen-SS comprised approximately 500,000 men in January 1945, including 100,000 European volunteers.

conformists' epitomised by the millions of Germans who marched under the Third Reich's banners without ever questioning anything. But have people ever asked themselves any questions, especially in times of war? Did the Americans ask themselves questions during their country's quite illegitimate involvement in the attacks against Iraq in 2003? Did the British ask themselves questions in 1943 with regard to their terror bombings of German cities, which even allowed their mastermind, Sir Arthur Harris, to be knighted by the queen? Did the French ask questions during the summer of 1962, when General de Gaulle chose to abandon the French of Algeria and the *harkis*[18] to their cruel fate, amidst people's general indifference?

Günter Grass had been one those countless *Mitläufers*, a follow-my-leader conformist, at a time when the Third Reich still seemed legitimate to the majority of Germans. Afterwards, once the regime had been toppled in an apocalyptic sort of atmosphere, he aligned himself with the new way of thinking imposed by the victors, doing so with a talent that would earn him enormous fame. One could legitimately ask if he was thus not, once again, a *Mitläufer*, a mere follower instead of a free, critical and rebellious spirit. When one takes this reasoning even further, is it not the case that by publishing his *Beim Häuten der Zwiebel* one year before his eightieth birthday,[19] rather than by a strange and quite dangerous initiative inaugurated by the publication of his novel *Im Krebsgang*,[20] the writer suddenly relinquished his very ordinary position of *Mitläufer*?[21]

---

18 TN: The *harkis* were the native Muslim Algerians who served as auxiliaries in the French Army during the Algerian War of 1954–1962.
19 AN: Günter Grass was born in Danzig on 16 October 1927.
20 TN: Crabwalk.
21 AN: Published in 2002, *Im Krebsgang* relates the intentional torpedoing of the *Wilhelm Gustloff* by the Soviet navy on 30 January 1945, off the coast of Danzig, an event that resulted in the deaths of 12,000 passengers, including 4,000 children, all of whom were fleeing the Red Army.

When the Germans Voted for Hitler

With the horrendous images of the end of the Third Reich before our eyes, and faced with its warfare and procession of horrors, it is impossible to imagine today what the previous years could actually have been like, those years that bore witness to Hitler's spectacular successes in a context of peace, at least until 1938.

Under the shadow of the year of 1945, it is difficult to discern that the evolution which led to war and atrocities was unthinkable to the vast majority of Germans in 1933 and the subsequent years. No one could thus have foreseen a future that had no precedent. Indeed, what happened from 1933 onwards was an absolute historical novelty and, for this reason, impossible to anticipate. Regarding this, one can refer to the impartial statement of a German Jew, Hans-Joachim Schoeps, who was young at the time:

> It was impossible for anyone, between 1933 and 1935,[22] to predict, however remotely, the crimes that the National Socialists would one day commit. Anyone who claims otherwise is a liar.[23]

In 1933, and over the next five years, Hitler appeared to a large majority of Germans as a providential statesman who channelled all his efforts towards the sole objective of curbing the crisis while simultaneously striving to avoid a communist takeover. Even anti-Jewish propaganda, associated with the fight against 'stateless capitalism', seemed to fit into this action plan. And many were the Germans who, in good faith,

---

22 AN: This alludes to the enactment of the Nuremberg laws of 15 September 1935, which stripped German Jews of all rights stemming from one's German nationality, all in accordance with certain racial criteria.

23 AN: Hans-Joachim Schoeps, *Bereit für Deutschland. Der Patriotismus deutscher Juden und der Nationalsozialismus* [TN: Ready for Germany — The Patriotism of German Jews and National Socialism], Haude & Spener, 1970, p. 11. Quoted by François Fédier in *Introduction à Heidegger* [TN: Introduction to Heidegger], Political Writings, Gallimard, 1995, p. 13.

thought that once economic stability was restored, the regime would abandon its anti-Semitic fixation.

Having become chancellor, Hitler stripped away his image of a demagogical and irresponsible leader. He urged people to make the necessary effort to fend off a crisis that was not just economic, but also political and diplomatic. He acted and spoke as a chancellor who had come to restore German pride, and what he said found resonance in a Germany that had not only been crushed by the crisis, but also felt burdened by opprobrium. Since its defeat in 1918, it had been ostracised by other nations and denounced as being guilty and barbaric. Socio-democratic governments themselves had, in fact, denounced the famous article 231 of the Treaty of Versailles, which intended to impose upon the now defeated Germany the duty to declare that it alone was responsible for triggering the war. This lie was the condition geared towards decreeing a payment of 'reparations' whose monstrous financial burden (223 billion gold marks, reduced to 132 billion by the Young Plan and spread over a period of forty-five years) was meant to punish Germany and weigh down its economy, considered exceedingly thriving and dangerous on the eve of 1914.

Oswald Spengler Distances Himself

Among the celebrities of the intellectual world, the historian and philosopher Oswald Spengler (1880–1936) was one of the rare minds to distance themselves early from the new regime. He thus joined Ernst Jünger in this respect, although his reasons were actually quite different. There was never any personal relationship between them, even if Jünger had read and pondered Spengler's thoughts around 1925, immersing himself in his cyclical conception of history and 'morphological' vision, which constituted one of the most superior German ways of understanding the world. Unlike the former army officer, Spengler clearly expressed his concerns at an early stage.

In July 1933, a mere six months after Hitler's ascension to the position of chancellor and four months after the 'legal coup' through which he was granted full powers, Spengler publishes *The Hour of Decision*,[24] a work that would reap immediate success, even more so than *The Decline of the West*. 100,000 copies are sold in two months. The implicit criticisms comprised in the preface, however, lead to the book being banned shortly afterwards. The head of the Foreign Policy Division at the German Political Institute, Johann von Leers, declares Spengler a dangerous adversary of National Socialism.

Stemming from a deep thinker and a talented (and unquestionably nationalistic) political writer, Spengler's criticisms are all the more remarkable since the new regime had not yet produced any negative effects. From the very first line, Spengler is careful to emphasise: 'No one can have looked forward to the national revolution of this year with greater longing than myself.' He then goes on to specify:

> The sordid Revolution of 1918 I detested from its first day, for it was the betrayal by the inferior part of our people of that strong, live part which had risen up in 1914 in the belief that it could and would have a future. Everything of a political nature that I have written since then has been directed against the forces which had entrenched themselves, with our enemies' help, on the mountain of our misery and misfortune in order to render this future impossible.

In principle, the power that had been in place for six months seemed suited to satisfy those who saw no other alternative for the Reich but that of 'achieving greatness or perishing'. The author thus admits:

> But the events of this year allow us to hope that the decision in our case has not yet been made — that we, as in Bismarck's day, shall sooner or later again be subjects and not mere objects of history.

Barely had these lines been penned that veiled reservations towards the new power and its leader begin to emerge:

---

24 AN: Oswald Spengler, *Les Années décisives*, [TN: The Decisive Years], Mercure de France, 1934, reissued by Copernic in 1980.

> The man of action is often limited in his vision. He is driven without knowing the real aim. […] But much more often he goes astray because he has conjured up a false picture of things around and within him.

Alternating praise and critical comments, Spengler adds the following a little further on:

> I shall neither scold nor flatter. I refrain from forming any estimate of those things which are only just coming into being.

To him, it was therefore too early, despite all the possible reservations, to pass judgment on what was still in progress during that summer of 1933.

The Fear of a New World War

Hitler's all too easy victory did, however, worry Spengler. He feared that it would encourage presumptuousness in matters of foreign policy, the only sphere that truly mattered in his eyes:

> It is no time or occasion for transports of triumph. Woe betide those who mistake mobilisation for victory!

What Spengler is explicitly alluding to here is the excessive enthusiasm of 1914, using prudent language fuelled by a solid knowledge of history and the trappings of major politics.

> The seizure of power took place in a confused whirl of strength and weakness. I see with misgiving that it continues to be noisily celebrated from day to day. It were better to save our enthusiasm for a day of real and definitive results — that is to say, of successes in *foreign politics*, which alone matter.

To Spengler, success cannot result from impatient action, and nothing could have been further from the designs harboured by Hitler, who wanted to achieve all his aims in the next ten years through a mixture of cunning and violence.

Faithful to his interpretation of history and the certainty that a great policy cannot be implemented without a ruling caste endowed with the qualities of discipline, responsibility and level-headedness, Spengler does little to conceal his distrust of the type of man that stood before him. Unveiling the very depths of his thoughts, what he essentially writes is that he had high hopes regarding the ongoing revolution, but also viewed the latter as a source of major threats.

> No one can know what forms, situations, and personalities will arise out of this upheaval, or the reactions which may result from outside. Every revolution makes the external situation of a country worse, and that fact alone requires statesmen of Bismarck's order to deal with it.

To Spengler, who had shortly before had the opportunity to speak to Hitler and had judged him to be mediocre,[25] this implicitly meant that the new chancellor was not the man for the job. His concerns were all the more acute, as he saw great dangers looming on the horizon:

> We stand, it may be, close before a second world war, unable to gauge the distribution of forces or to foresee its means or aims … military, economic, revolutionary. We have no time to limit ourselves to home politics; we have to be "in form" to deal with any conceivable occurrence. Germany is not an island. If we fail to see our relation to the world as — for us in particular — *the* important problem, fate — and what a fate! — will submerge us without mercy.

All of us who know what happened next can appreciate these prophetic lines at their true value. The bloody purge of 30 June 1934, during which Gregor Strasser and General von Schleicher (both of whom he knew) would be killed, ultimately convinced Spengler that the new leaders were mere brutes unworthy of ruling the Reich. This opinion, however, was not widely shared at the time.

---

25 AN: As confirmed by Spengler's correspondence and quoted by Alastair Hamilton in *A Study of Intellectuals and Fascism, 1919–1945*, Gallimard, 1973, p. 175.

Carl Schmitt, Jünger's Unlikely Friend

Unlike Jünger, Spengler and Ernst von Salomon, several renowned intellectuals belonging to the same hard-to-define movement of the Conservative Revolution had initially hoped that the new chancellor would be the providential actor that would bring about their country's national recovery. I am thinking of the jurist Carl Schmitt, the writer Gottfried Benn and the philosopher Martin Heidegger.

Carl Schmitt (1888–1985) was, for a long time, part of the circle of Jünger's close friends. They had met at the beginning of 1930 and the mutual appeal exerted by these two superior yet different minds had been so great that Jünger would often speak of his 'unfathomable friend' and his 'invigorating'[26] company. What had also brought them closer before 1933 was their shared distrust of Western democracies. On the other hand, the two men would have divergent standpoints as soon as Hitler had risen to power.

The great jurist had published his major works at the time of the Weimar Republic: his criticism of political romanticism (1919); his book on dictatorship (1921); and his studies on political theology (1922), on the political form of the Roman Catholic Church (1923), on the notion of the political (1928), and on the concepts of legality and legitimacy (1932). Remaining rather on the fringes of the Conservative Revolution, he was hostile to any and all organismic thought and even rejected an entire part of the German political tradition in order to draw inspiration from Italian (Machiavelli), French (Joseph de Maistre), Spanish (Donoso Cortès) and English (Thomas Hobbes) authors. His Christian faith, which Jünger did not share, and his counter-revolutionary Roman Catholicism served as a basis for his philosophy of the State. He criticised liberalism, as well as the economic and moral doctrine of individualism, which he deemed incompatible with

---

26 AN: Julien Hervier, compendium, as published in *Ernst Jünger, War Journals II: 1939–1948*, p. 1309. In his notes, Hervier provides readers with the necessary references to Jünger's comments.

genuine democracy owing to the fact that the latter presupposes a political homogeneity of citizens and a similarity of views between the governing and the governed. In July 1932, he called for a vote against the NSDAP headed by Hitler, whom he considered dangerous due to his ideological and political immaturity. Supporting Chancellor von Papen, he even spoke out in favour of the *Reichswehr*-based national dictatorship project, arguing for a ban on both the Nazi Party and the Communist Party for being in breach of the Weimar Constitution[27].

Following in von Papen's footsteps, however, he would align himself with the new power from the beginning of 1933. On 1 May 1933, he would even join the NSDAP, whose ban he had called for shortly before. With regard to this reversal, the question remains open as to the role of Schmitt's opportunism and career concerns, which may or may not account for this. Appointed to the Prussian State Council in 1933, he also became the head of the National Socialist Association of German Jurists. His ambition was, in fact, to become the official jurist of the new Reich. Philosophically, he hoped to promote the idea of the State (the 'total' State, as he himself wrote) at the expense of the notion of Party. His theory was that there is no totalitarian state as such, only a totalitarian party whose ambitions are to be limited by the State.[28] At the same time, he firmly upheld the distinction, a fundamental one in his eyes, between what is political and what is not; between the public sphere and the private sphere.

These conceptions would be rejected by the Nazis, who would regard them as a surrendering of the prerogatives enjoyed by the Party and its leader in favour of the State, all the more so since Schmitt was also opposed to any biological racism that contradicted his own philosophy of history. For this reason, he would be targeted by ever-increasing criticism from 1934 onwards. In 1936, he is forced to resign

---

27   AN: For a more complete understanding of the period, one can refer to *Le Siècle de 1914*, op. cit.

28   AN: Carl Schmitt, *Ex Captivitate Salus: Experiences, 1945–1947*. Texts collected by André Doremus, J. Vrin, 2003, p. 111.

from his official functions, before being subjected to a public trial by the SS newspaper *Das Schwarze Korps*,[29] in two front-page articles published in December 1936.[30] Realising that he had deceived himself, he confines himself to his academic work, adding to the number of those who had embraced 'internal emigration', to which Ernst Jünger had long preceded him. This would not stop him, however, from being arrested by the American police in 1945. He would thereafter be imprisoned in Nuremberg until May 1947. In the meantime, he had been expelled from university and was without pension, depending on a few friends to survive. Plummeting into the blackest bitterness, he would thus indulge, on the pages of his own *Journal* (*Glossarium*), in venomous attacks against his friend Jünger, reproaching him for his apparent detachment and his gradual return to grace.

Gottfried Benn and Martin Heidegger

Another example of disillusionment is offered by the doctor and expressionist poet Gottfried Benn (1886–1956), who, at the time, was one of Germany's three great intellectuals alongside Carl Schmitt and Martin Heidegger, and a man who compromised himself through his involvement with the Third Reich. However, unlike the other two, he never had any personal relationship with Jünger, having, for a long time, even ignored the latter's activity. At best, he ranked Jünger in the category of soldiers that wrote books. Appointed vice-president of the short-lived Union of National Writers by the Nazis, he would, at the end of 1934, be removed from this position due to ideological differences and find himself compelled to withdraw into his role of military doctor and his own solitary reflections.

---

29 TN: The Black Corps.
30 AN: On this subject, one can refer to Alain de Benoist's study entitled *L'affaire Carl Schmitt* [TN: The Carl Schmitt Affair], published in *Éléments*, issue number 110, October 2003.

A much more famous (and more meaningful) case than Benn's is that of Martin Heidegger. During the autumn of 1932, the one who would become the most influential philosopher of his era was teaching at the University of Freiburg, engrossed in his work and devoted to the thoughts of both Parmenides and Anaximander. Suffice to say that he stayed away from all politics. Nevertheless, according to his disciple, the historian Ernst Nolte, the philosopher was 'a "national socialist" in the literal sense of the term, that is to say, that he intended to bring about class reconciliation in Germany while simultaneously harbouring respect for other peoples.'[31] He belonged 'to the *völkisch* tendency, which had been the first to target Hitler with criticism, from within National Socialism itself.' After taking some time off, he would return to Freiburg in mid-March 1933, Hitler having become chancellor six weeks earlier. From that moment on, Germany would plunge into a revolutionary process involving not only acts of violence, but also hopes that were boosted by various decisions judged favourably by the Germans, especially the youngest ones. Simone Weil remarks:

> Only pre-war generations remain attached to the regime [of Weimar]; ever since the crisis, which deprived them of all hope, Germany's youths have been driven by a violent hatred of capitalism, by a fevered longing for a socialist regime.[32]

That is what Hitler seemed to embody, which did not displease Professor Heidegger.

National Socialism and the Mindset of 'May 68'

German universities did not remain on the sidelines of the country's general trend. In Freiburg itself, National Socialist students were many indeed and demanded the right to participate in the running of the

---

31 AN: Ernst Nolte, *Among the Front Lines*, op. cit., p. 125.
32 AN: Simone Weil, *Œuvres complètes* [TN: Complete Works], part II, vol. 1, Gallimard, 1988, p. 217.

university. The most conservative professors were opposed to the idea, regarding this claim as a form of 'Bolshevism'. Nowadays, one would speak of a 'May 68' mindset. Rector Wilhelm von Möllendorff, formally elected by his peers during the previous month of December, is rejected by the students who epitomise the country's new direction. Faced with a stalemate, teachers turn to Heidegger, who is appreciated by the students. The titular rector himself convenes an emergency session of the university senate, resigns and suggests the candidacy of Heidegger, who is elected on 21 April 1933 amidst almost unanimous support, save for two abstentions.

The philosopher himself was no conservative. He was, in fact, very sensitive to the notion of bringing harmony to all those that participate in the German effort, be it workers, students, civil servants, economic executives or university professors. It was a topic that he himself would first develop in front of the students on 25 November 1933 (in 'The German Student as a Worker'), then in front of the workers of Freiburg on 22 January 1934, as part of two speeches that testify to the very spirit of the era.[33] He himself would join the Party on 3 May 1933, a decision for which he would obviously be criticised after 1945. It would seem that he was actually granted membership in the hope of exerting a positive influence on the course of events within the university, without being overwhelmed by the most zealous elements who Heidegger had already categorically banned from displaying anti-Semitic billboards on university premises and burning vilified books.

All the texts and speeches written by Heidegger at the time are proof of the illusions he was under. The latter, in fact, were common among most Germans, including the best. This would become obvious during the plebiscite of 12 November 1933, when Pastor Niemöller, the physicist Max Planck, the poet Gerhart Hauptmann, most bishops and even the Union of German Citizens of Jewish Faith urged people to vote for the *Führer*. The same choice would also be made by the young

---

33 AN: Text fully published in Heidegger's *Political Writings*, op. cit.

Claus von Stauffenberg, the future initiator of the 20 July 1944 assassination attempt.

Having simultaneously clashed with some of his conservative colleagues and with a minister who intended to exercise political influence on his decisions, Heidegger submits his resignation as the university's rector in February 1934. To clearly highlight this break, he even refuses to take part in the official power transfer ceremonies two months later.[34]

Revisiting this period after the war, Heidegger would state that, beginning in the spring of 1934, his illusions with regard to the new regime had almost completely dissipated. He then added:

> After the 30th of June of that same year, I was no longer under any illusions at all. Anyone who took up a position at the university could no longer be unaware, after this date, who he was involving himself with.

Heidegger thus joined Jünger and Spengler in their disapproval.[35]

---

34 AN: Regarding Heidegger's intentions and his disillusionment, one should refer to the very exhaustive study included by François Fédier in his introduction to *Political Writings*, op. cit. From 1938 onwards, it would actually be forbidden to mention Heidegger's name in the newspapers, discuss his writings and republish his works.

35 AN: For better understanding of the general context, one can refer to François-Georges Dreyfus's book entitled *Le IIIe Reich* [TN: The Third Reich], published by Le Livre de Poche as part of its 'Reference' series, 1998.

CHAPTER IX

A FAREWELL TO ARMS

Having been sent to the Caucasus on a short mission to which we shall return, Jünger would, while writing his *Journal* on the evening of 16 December 1942, report a brief combat episode in which he was unexpectedly involved, as he and the officers accompanying him came under Soviet machine gun fire:

> We jumped into the foxholes for cover and let the storm pass over.

What follows is a remark that revealed a new state of mind:

> I have long since passed the age, or better said the condition, when I find such things amusing.

Did he feel old, then?

Secession from One's Self

Twenty years, or a little more, had passed since the belligerent exhilaration detailed in *Storm of Steel*. Jünger had changed. He was now past that age, as he himself says, but also past that state of mind. He had grown to be a different man, and his innermost perceptions had changed, as had the times. During the first war, he had embarked on his journey with untainted enthusiasm. This time around, however, he had been mobilised with gloomy resignation to join the army of a regime he hated, to wage an unjustified type of war. We know this, as we have already reflected on the rift he experienced as a result of his ever more vocal opposition to the new regime, its men, its morals, its practices and its ambitions. This falling-out changed him to the core, for it went hand in hand with a departure from all his 'perceptions', from his warrior mentality and political radicalism, all of which had now been shed like a serpent's skin.

His former reference points destroyed, his fate would thus be to lead a life of unrest. For a certain time, he would search for substitutes in the Bible, albeit without becoming a believer. He himself would cease to be a role model. So vibrant was his sensitivity to the world, however, that he still retained his seismographic ability.

We must not delude ourselves regarding his motivations by imagining him to have been something he was not. Indeed, unlike Moeller van den Bruck and his friend Niekisch, Jünger was not a doctrinaire. He was, instead, an extraordinary writer, a writer who actually had ideas; and these ideas were subject to variation, without any concern for ideological coherence. We all know to what extent he had been involved as a transmitter of ideas within the nationalist and revolutionary movement. One can thus bring to mind what he wrote in 1927:

> We nationalists do not believe in general ideas. We do not believe in general morality. We do not believe in mankind, in a collective being endowed with central consciousness and uniform rights. On the contrary, we believe that the truth, rights and morality are all conditioned to the extreme by time, space and blood. We believe in the value of the individual.[1]

Such a nominalistic speech was undoubtedly a little too subtle for the less than crystalline minds characterising the ideological functionaries of the NSDAP. Indeed, those people had failed to understand much of Jünger's famous *Worker*, assessing this rich text in light of their own mantras. Such is the flaw of all ideocracies such as Nazism, communism and even democratism, unlike Italian fascism, which was not

---

1   AN: As quoted by Armin Mohler in *Nouvelle École*, issue number 42, p. 69, number 40.

based on dogma but on myth.[2] This is also the downside of all political parties that long to subjugate the independence of intellectuals to the requirements of their propagandas. They judge writers according to the latter's conformity to the simplifications of the prevalent dogma. Concerning Jünger, it was his rejection of anti-Semitism, his individualism, and his literary frivolity that were regarded as suspicious. .In the eyes of the guardians of orthodoxy, the former officer was some kind of dangerous deviant, in addition to being a supporter of an unconditional agreement with Russia. [3]For this reason, he would be suspected of having ties to the 'Black Front' (i.e. the National Bolsheviks), which could, at the time, have earned anyone a one-way ticket to the camps.

Human Incompatibility

Style-related and ideological differences were exacerbated by a certain resentment that Jünger harboured against such people. Having observed the leaders of the NSDAP rather closely, he quickly fell into a state of disgust. Indeed, he saw them as nothing more than callous plebeians that had transformed into status seekers and social climbers as soon as they had seized power, as was the case with Göring.[4]

---

2 AN: These differences are analysed in my book entitled *The Century of 1914*, op. cit.

3 AN: 'Under the Third Reich, in 1934, I declared myself in favour of unconditional friendship with Russia, in an article that resulted in yet another Gestapo raid in 1940.' Ernst Jünger, '*Second Letter to my Friends*', dated 8 August 1946 and quoted in '*Dossier H' Ernst Jünger*, op. cit., p. 344.

4 AN: Hermann Göring (1893–1946) had been a fighter pilot in 14–18, claiming a total of thirty victories. He ended the war at the head of the *Richthofen* squadron, having attained the rank of captain and been awarded the Order of Merit (just like Jünger). Wholeheartedly devoted to Hitler as of 1922, he would be wounded during the Munich Putsch of 9 November 1923. An NS *Reichstag* deputy from 1928 onwards, his larger-than-life and worldly personality favoured the Nazis' legal conquest of power. Having been appointed president of the *Reichstag* in 1932, Prime Minister of Prussia in 1933, and ultimately Air Traffic Minister, he would become one of the three leading figures of the regime, often displaying

Jünger himself stuck to his Prussian austerity. A human and ideological incompatibility had therefore developed between him and the leaders of the NSDAP. His friends and connections, who, just like him, belonged to a variety of tendencies within the nationalist movement, had for the most part become his opponents. The times thus imposed tragic choices upon people and emotional reactions often carried more weight than ideas. It is indeed a well-known process where strong opposition to a political-religious power such as the Third Reich drives 'heretics' to move further and further away from what they once had in common, to the point of denying what they had previously professed.

Jünger never made any attempt to explain this secession from his own previous self, just as a seismograph records the earthquakes that it announces or describes them without ever explaining them. In the absence of such explanations, Jünger demonstrated his secession with a highly characteristic formulation used in his previously mentioned schismatic novel, *On the Marble Cliffs*, published in September 1939, shortly after Germany had entered the new war.

'I Have Underestimated This Man's Talents'

Seven years had now passed since the publication of *The Worker* in 1932; seven years during which Hitler and his party had undertaken to transform Germany, causing the earthquake that we are all familiar with. Without explaining his own evolution, Jünger, however, did describe it in part after the end of the nightmare, as Germany and himself took part in another story and faced misfortunes of a different nature.

On 31 March 1946, eleven months after the apocalyptic downfall of the Third Reich, Jünger writes the following words in his *Journals*:

---

ostentatious opulence. Captured by the Americans in 1945 and brought before the Nuremberg Tribunal, he would reveal himself to be the bravest and most aggressive of the defendants. Sentenced to death by hanging, he would evade execution by taking his own life in his cell on 15 October 1946.

When I think about my personal development curve, I see that it has been drawn in a manner that went against the general evolution of things, and often in spite of me. [Concerning Hitler], the assessment went, for example, from "this man is right" to "this man is ridiculous", and then again to "this man is becoming sinister". Overall, it corresponded to the very extent to which it all proceeded from response to provocation. At the time of the great electoral successes and the seizure of power, I was already quite aloof from the events.[5]

He then goes on to state:

I have sometimes wondered whether I was not, from the very outset, and due to my over-high expectations, inclined to suffer as a result of this realisation, and whether I would have come to this point at all had I been a contemporary of Napoleon or Bismarck.

Resuming his critical examination, he continues:

Without any doubt, I had underestimated the man's talents: his passion-arousing dynamism, his instinctive manner of using simplifying concepts, which summarised the trend of the era of masses and machines. All of it was extraordinary, especially when one considers his origins. In this regard, his adversaries had a lot to learn from him. Traditionalist, aesthetic and moral scruples rendered one easily blind to these gifts, as did pure intellectuality. His ruin was, incidentally, far less the result of his gifts than that of his temperament and insatiable greed. […] Scarcely has a single human being, in all of modern history, attracted such amounts of enthusiasm but also hatred.

Jünger expands on his memories:

Early on, catastrophic dreams had already begun to oppress me. These were sometimes set in landscapes of ice, and at other times in regions on fire.

Within a few months of 1939, these dreams would be crystallised in the form of a brief allegorical novel that enchanted Julien Gracq: *On the*

---

5   AN: Ernst Jünger, *Journal de guerre et d'Occupation, 1939-1948* [TN: Journal of War and Occupation, 1939-1948], pp. 480-481.

Marble Cliffs. Julian Hervier wrote that this book epitomised Jünger's contribution 'to a resistance that does not openly declare its presence and retreats into the moral values of one's inner self'.

For his part, Jünger long denied any attempt to equate the evil forces unleashed in his novel to Hitler.[6] He always said that his intention was to describe a general phenomenon relating as much to Stalinist Russia as to other modern systems of oppression.

On the Marble Cliffs

The cryptic beauty of *On the Marble Cliffs* does not lend itself to easy reading. This allegorical novel testifies to an essential turning point in the life and thoughts of its author. It also anticipates the reversal of all that would soon occur in Europe. Jünger was all too familiar with the fate of the intellectual who is horrified to discover the abyss that separates his ideas from their distortion through the political practices of the era of masses.

Having previously been seduced by the enchantments of revolution and the allurements of an ever-evolving history, other Europeans would also distance themselves by the turn of the 1930s or 1940s. One thinks of Malaparte in Italy, Eliade and Cioran in Romania, and Maulnier in France. Conversely, some writers would not be able to bring themselves to do so, as was the case of Brasillach and Drieu La Rochelle, who would die as a result, or Malraux, who would benefit from it all. Not to mention, of course, the large battalions of intellectuals who, after 1944 and 1945, would now hasten to rally behind the cause of the victors, celebrating Stalin or the 'American way of life', whether in France or elsewhere. With this fact in mind, one cannot emphasise enough the lucidity and courage that every nationalist had to demonstrate when joining the ranks of the opposition at the time of the National Socialist rise to power.

---

6   AN: Particularly in his *Journal*, on 8 May 1945.

CHAPTER IX. A FAREWELL TO ARMS

The story which *On the Marble Cliffs* recounts seems, on the surface of things, to be taking place in an imaginary country, the Marina, invaded by barbaric and bloodthirsty forces that readers can readily identify as symbolising Nazism. Two brothers, immediately recognisable as the 'doubles' of both Ernst Jünger and his younger brother Friedrich Georg, witness this invasion of barbarism, a barbarism embodied by the presence of the Head Forester. Supported by some of mankind's rejects, this ringleader would destroy the Marina, a land of ancient culture. At first, the brothers' belligerent past leads them to resort to the use of weapons: 'Then we too felt the power of the instinct run through our limbs like a flash.' Later on, however, while reflecting on things in the depths of their hermitage, the two brothers would come to the conclusion that 'there are weapons stronger than those which cut or stab'. Their fairly ambiguous evolution is precipitated by the company of a wise man, Father Lampros, a man that allows them to discover the power of an undefined sort of spirituality. Nevertheless, the temptation to take action simmers on inside them.

> But when we discussed the situation more thoroughly in the herbarium or library, our decision was strengthened to resist with spiritual forces alone. Yet from time to time, like children, we fell back on that earlier world in which terror rules supreme. We did not yet know the full measure of man's power.

Evasive, Jünger would say no more about this 'immense power', leaving readers to understand things as they pleased.

The two brothers are eventually torn from their wait-and-see attitude by their ally, the old shepherd Belovar, but in vain. They would indeed be defeated by the hounds of the Head Forester, before being miraculously saved by the enigmatic golden serpents that guard their hermitage.

With these trials now behind them, they now achieve a state of serenity:

We continued our study of language, for in the word we recognised the gleaming magic blade before which tyrants pale. There is a trinity of word, liberty and spirit.

A nice turn of phrase, readers will think. However, speech can undoubtedly become a 'magic blade' when authenticated through one's life and actions. Furthermore, can't it also convey lies, poison the mind and shackle freedom? Indeed, everyone knows that swords often have two edges.

The Condemnation of the 'Mauretanians'

The particularity of the Marina lies in it being dominated by a mysterious political sect which Jünger calls the 'Mauretanians'. This term already appears in other works of his, notably in the second version of *The Adventurous Heart* (1938), in which the writer allows a certain condemnation of his previous commitments to shine through:

> Instead of persevering in my studies, I joined the Mauretanians, those inferior engineers of power.[7]

Through the image of the Mauretanians, an idea dominates the book itself, suggesting that any endeavour that strives to achieve efficiency in the political sphere is inevitably immoral and degrading. Jünger uses the image of the Mauretanians to express his newly acquired conviction that action, even when fuelled by the most sincere intentions, always remains on the surface of things. It is a bearer of pipe dreams and catastrophes. It is obvious that what the former national-revolutionary intellectual thus reveals are his own disappointments. Aristotle would have said that Jünger had become confused with regard to the level at which actions are to be judged; for one can only judge an action on the basis of its ends. Those that relate to politics are thus limited to its

---

7 In *Deux individus contre l'histoire*, op. cit., Julien Hervier explains the origin of the word 'Mauretanian', which stems from a certain character in *The Arabian Nights*, one of Jünger's earliest reading experiences.

sphere. What is to blame here, therefore, is not politics as such, but the delusions brought about by utopias that were, particularly in the 20th century, responsible for burdening politics with eschatological and moral expectations pertaining to religiousness.

Departing from the views expressed in *The Worker*, Jünger asserts that nihilistic eras do not require political reformers, but theologians. He would later realise his mistake. A relative truth does, however, subsist. Although, in such times, an active individual will retain his autonomy and power to increase disorder and destruction, he is denied this power for creative reasons. In other words, certain eras are simply not conducive to action, as they require one to withdraw into the background.

What Jünger strived to express in veiled form when penning his rather non-fictional novel entitled *On the Marble Cliffs* were the thoughts that plagued him at the time. It is therefore less of a novel than a fable with a 'moral' behind it. That is perhaps why the protagonists of this bizarre story have so little depth. They are not individuals but, in fact, archetypes: the aristocrat (Sunmyra), the clergyman (Lampros), the Mauretanian (Braquemart), etc. Their features thus relate to their role and not to their temperament or spirit. This approach would remain unchanged in Jünger's future allegorical 'novels', namely *Heliopolis*, *The Glass Bees* and *Eumeswil*. It thus betrays the author's demonstrative intention (to write a fable), but also a certain difficulty he had in creating genuine fictional characters.

'Leave Jünger Alone'

Despite the façade that concealed Jünger's true intentions in writing the 'novel', German readers did indeed interpret the content as a veiled condemnation of the regime. And it was the author's notoriety that accounted for the book's best-selling success, with more than 30,000 copies sold during the first few months. As for the *Reich*'s authorities, we are all familiar with their reactions thanks to the subsequent testimony of Jünger's old neo-pagan friend, Friedrich Hielscher (1902–1990).

This active leader of a politico-religious sect had infiltrated the highest positions of the SS through his disciples, in particular in the person of Wolfram Sievers, who was at the head of the *Ahnenerbe*, the cultural research institute of the SS. He would thus be able to make some first-hand disclosures:

> Himmler told his circle of friends[8] that following a request made by Goebbels to immediately arrest Jünger for his writing of *On the Marble Cliffs*, the Führer himself had said: "Leave Jünger alone."[9]

In the cultured circles of occupied France, the French translation of *On the Marble Cliffs* (1941) received a most favourable response that extended to resistance fighters. The essayist Jean-Marie Domenach, a contributor to *Esprit* magazine who joined the Vercors *maquis*[10] in 1943, testified to this:

> Gilbert Gadoffre made me read Jünger's book, *On the Marble Cliffs*.[11]

Gilbert Gadoffre was a professor at Versailles who specialised in English. A reserve officer injured in the clashes of 1940, he joined a resistance network very early on. He would subsequently be sent to Uriage during the summer of 1942 to infiltrate the executive school,

---

8   AN: Which Sievers was part of.

9   AN: As stated in the letter sent by Hielscher to Ernst Jünger on 18 November 1985 and published in the Jünger-Hielscher correspondence (1927–1985), Klett-Cotta, 2005 — quoted by Julien Hervier in *War Journals II: 1939–1948*, p. XXV, number 2. After the war, Wolfram Sievers would be imprisoned, sentenced to death, and ultimately hanged in 1947 by decision of the Nuremberg Tribunal. See also the same volume by La Pléiade, in the biographical note dedicated to Friedrich Hielscher, p. 1301.

10 TN: Underground resistance.

11 AN: Pierre Bitoun, *Les Hommes d'Uriage* [TN : The Men of Uriage], La Découverte, 1988, p. 116.

which the Vichy government endorsed, before joining the Vercors *maquis* as well.[12]

Immersing himself in the reading of *On the Marble Cliffs*, Domenach would say that what he had found in it was a reflection of a feeling shared by his comrades, namely that of being 'aristocratic defenders of democracy'. Let us not get caught up in the pitfalls of words and simply recognize the positive intent behind them.

Unexpected Protections

With Jünger having distanced himself from the new regime from the very outset, one cannot disregard the resulting reaction of a system that was notorious for being very vindictive. To be honest, it turned out to be quite discreet. After 1945, one would find out what Jünger himself had been unaware of at the time: that Hitler's protection had shielded him. As already mentioned, the Führer had remained an admirer of the young officer who had penned *Storm of Steel*. However, Jünger did realise that several former members of the various circles of the Conservative Revolution who had started their career within the Party itself, the SS and even the Gestapo were watching over him. Recalling the old days, he would state this in his *Journal* with a hint of nostalgia on 23 September 1945:

> The memory created a sort of truce between those that then clashed in opposing camps. I often had the feeling, at times of crisis, that such minds continued to take part in this — that they discreetly suspended ongoing prosecutions, whether by making a file disappear or by having a plane ready to take off when the time comes.

Among such men, one can name the previously mentioned Werner Best and Wolfram Sievers, but also Rudolf Diels.[13] Speaking to Jünger,

---

12 AN: Dominique Venner, *Histoire critique de la Résistance* [TN: A Critical History of the Resistance], Pygmalion, 1995, reissued in 2002, p. 168.

13 AN: A young and brilliant official of the Prussian police at the end of the Weimar Republic, Rudolf Diels (1900–1957) put together a political unit at the request of

Diels would later relate the circumstances that had led to an unexpected search of the writer's home in the Berlin district of Steglitz at the end of 1933.

Jünger having been denounced by a neighbour, two municipal police officers would, as mentioned earlier, conduct a search to find weapons. This was routine work in such troubled times, when denouncements were on the increase.

This little warning would have a twofold consequence. Jünger first began by discarding a large number of documents, including letters and diaries dating back to 1919, which were thus lost forever. Next, he would later note the following in his *Journal* (24 August 1945):

> The Steglitz incident made me regard Berlin as an unfavourable location. This led to my leaving an already marked house and settling in Goslar.

Goslar is a small town in the Harz Mountains. Jünger would stay there with his family beginning in December 1933, before moving again three years later (9 December 1936), this time to Überlingen, on the edge of Lake Constance. This would, however, only be another long stop before yet another departure on 1 April 1939 for the former presbytery of Kirchhorst, near Hanover, where he would reside with his family until 1 December 1948.

Jünger's Greatest Work — the Journals

Mobilised on 26 August 1939 to join the *Wehrmacht* (while keeping his former rank of lieutenant, which brought a bitter smile to his face), Jünger would immediately be promoted to the rank of captain, a rank that he would henceforth retain. He thus joined the Celle garrison. For many months, the author would undertake to write a genuine

---

the socialist minister Carl Severing. When Göring became Prussian Minister of the Interior in 1933, he tasked Diels with organising the agency that would later become the Gestapo (*Geheime Staatspolizei* or 'secret state police'), which he would head until April 1934.

diary, one that was actually dated this time. He would note various facts, sometimes even trivial ones, which would then often give rise to long and cryptic comments. Still, future readers would at least be spared any details concerning his gastric ailments or the kind of erotic performances that burden the diaries and memories of his less prudish peers. Nothing of the sort is, in fact, encountered with Jünger, despite the intimate phrasing of his thoughts. Indeed, he would restrict his texts to the strict expression of feelings and contemplations.

If one disregards the occasional prolonged interruptions, notably during the periods devoted to new books,[14] Jünger would actually never stop keeping this diary, which he started to pen on 3 April 1939, at a time when he was only beginning to write *On the Marble Cliffs*.[15] Developed throughout the war, these journals would constitute his greatest work, perhaps even rivalling his works of youth, as this was where he would reveal the best of his writing talent. Already in *Storm of Steel*, which had been a sort of undated journal, he had demonstrated his exceptional qualities as a diarist, while also displaying the 'seismographic' predisposition that we have previously highlighted. One would witness the latter in action over the course of the exceptionally dramatic decade or so that spanned from 3 April 1939 to 2 December 1948, by which time the second set of Jünger's *Journals*, revolving around the Second World War and its immediate aftermath,[16] found itself completed.

---

14 AN: The date of 3 April 1939 is that of the final version, in the translation revised by Julien Hervier for *War Journals II: 1939–1948*, p. 17. In the edition published by Julliard in 1965 (with a translation by Henri Plard), the *Journal* began on 25 April 1939.

15 AN: Originally titled *The Queen of Serpents*.

16 AN: Jünger would later use the collective title of *Strahlungen* [TN: 'Emanations' or, more literally, 'Radiations'] for the middle books of his World War II journals, which, however, excluded *Gardens and Streets*, published in 1942, and *A Cottage in the Vineyard*, which would be released in 1958. At a later point, it would also comprise these two volumes under the same collective title, thus eventually bringing together all of his journals, including *Siebzig verweht* [TN:

In fear of police reactions, Jünger's wartime *Journals* would be subject to precautions. Some names would therefore be encrypted. Hitler thus becomes 'Kniebolo', which could hardly have deceived anyone.

From the very outset, Jünger had penned his *Journals* with the intention of publishing them. The text's highly elaborate wording was therefore carefully reviewed prior to publication — as imposed by the author's literary concerns. However, in contrast to his youthful writings, the author would only scarcely conduct revisions on the occasion of new editions.

Reading Jünger's *Journals* offers readers deep insight into his years of war, at least in terms of the reactions and thoughts aroused by the numerous events, encounters, reading experiences and certain minor aspects of his daily life[17].

Courage in the Civil War

The writer had only just donned his uniform when *On the Marble Cliffs* came out of the printing house in Germany, at the end of September 1939. In November, he would be transferred to the 287th infantry regiment in Belsen, where he would be tasked with commanding the 2nd company. He thus soon sets off at the head of his unit, which is assigned to the defence of the Siegfried Line against the French positions.

Thus begins what he himself termed the 'strange war', whose routine is only interrupted by a few skirmishes and machine gun fire.[18]

In a letter to a friend dated 24 March 1940, he shares the following noteworthy impressions:

Normally translated as 'After Seventy']. According to Julien Hervier, the French word 'rayonnements' [TN: which is the French title of the collective work] refers, in Jünger's mind, to the very notion of radiation.

17 AN: For a more detailed chronology of Jünger's life during those years of war, one can refer to the critical report produced by Julien Hervier for La Pléiade's second volume.

18 AN: Jünger would be awarded the Iron Cross Second Class for saving a comrade injured by enemy fire.

CHAPTER IX. A FAREWELL TO ARMS

I am here at the head of a company, just as I was twenty years ago, and it is this activity that I prefer, as it is the most contemplative that one can engage in within the army. [...] It is indeed where one fights that one can hope to meet the lowest possible number of those individuals whose very contact is loathsome. I have already removed the word "German" from all my works, so as not to have to share it with them.[19]

It is a remark fraught with meaning when coming from such a former nationalist.

In the *Journal* itself, every opportunity is taken to escape the war and indulge in dreamlike digressions on the topic of flowers, stones and insects, all of which were now inseparable from his unique imagination. This routine of his is interrupted in May by the earth-shattering start of the real war, marked by the onslaught of Panzers and Stukas.

From May to July 1940, Captain Jünger is involved in the French campaign on horseback and on foot, standing at the head of his infantry company and only participating in the offensive from quite a distance. Following closely behind the front line troops, he briefly captures Laon, whose mediaeval library he protects against all threats of pillaging and depredation. He also proceeds to empty many bottles of good wine, the only plunder that this victorious soldier would allow himself at the expense of local inhabitants, who had abandoned everything and fled their homes to take the roads of exodus.

The penning of this *Journal* (which would later become *Gardens and Streets*) is interrupted in July by a long leave in Kirchhorst and would only resume on 18 February 1941, the date on which Jünger's *First Paris Journal* would be initiated. In the meantime, Jünger had had to contend with the visit of two Gestapo officers to Kirchhorst, whose presence had been far more alarming than that of the municipal police in 1933. After the war, Jünger would relate the incident in his *Journal* dated 1 September 1945:

---

19   AN: As quoted by Julien Hervier, op. cit., p. XXXIX.

I was in an advantageous position—in uniform, following a successful *blitzkrieg*, and not subject to their jurisdiction.

He did agree, however, to answer their questions in order to find out more about their intentions. It was not a personal matter, in fact, but a general investigation targeting the Black Front, that is to say, the National Bolshevik circles centred around the person of Ernst Niekisch, who, at the time, had already been in prison for three years.

Remembering the incident, Jünger would state that it was during this period that he understood how much fiercer the courage of a radical political opponent was compared to that of a soldier:

> Ernst Niekisch is one of those exceptional men who demonstrate their courage in times of civil war. I would never have believed, prior to these events, that such civil courage was so extraordinarily rare. [...] In comparison, the courage to wage battle seems normal.

We already knew that, of course, but coming from such a combatant, this comment has quite a lot of weight. A personal memory highlights the remark:

> There is one night that I remember; it was during our advance through France, back in 1940: we heard the cannon of the Chemin des Dames and saw the lightning flashes. How was it that I was not concerned about the danger taking shape on the horizon, but rather about the article written by some petty scribbler who had "pilloried" me in his magazine? This imbalance seemed so absurd to me that I reprimanded myself on two or three occasions—and yet my thoughts always strayed back to this sensitive matter.

A war hero can still shake in his boots, it seems, when entering the field of political conflict, where his own legitimacy is no longer guaranteed. This confession is thus a credit to its author.

Parisian Stays

Having returned from leave in January 1941, Jünger changes garrison several times. In April, he is assigned to Vincennes, and then again to

CHAPTER IX. A FAREWELL TO ARMS

Paris. This marks the beginning of several years of strolling through the French capital, never neglecting fine restaurants such as the Ritz, Prunier, Drouant and La Tour d'Argent. On 30 May, he makes the acquaintance of Colonel Hans Speidel, who served as Germany's Chief of Staff of the military commander in France. It would prove to be a decisive meeting.[20] Indeed, Speidel was one of Jünger's admirers, as well as the very soul of a small circle of officers united by the same veiled hostility towards Hitler's policies — this was the 'George Circle', alluding to the George V Hotel, where the colonel had set up his quarters. On 22 June, Jünger is transferred to the Parisian headquarters at Speidel's request, who places him under his own protection. Jünger would keep this position throughout the Occupation, even in the absence of Speidel, who, for a time, had been assigned to the Eastern Front before returning to France as Rommel's chief of staff.

As for Captain Jünger, he resided in The Raphaël, and was thus very close to another hotel, The Majestic, located on Avenue Kleber,

---

20 AN: Enlisted in 1914, Hans Speidel (1897–1984) participated in all the battles. While remaining in the *Reichswehr*, he simultaneously resumed his studies of history and economics, defending his PhD thesis in 1925. Appointed to the general staff in 1930, he acts as deputy to the military attaché in France, taking charge of the intelligence services from 1933 to 1935. Following the 1940 campaign, he is appointed chief of staff of General Otto von Stülpnagel, the commander-in-chief of the German forces in France, during the month of August. Beginning in March 1942, he acts as the chief of staff of various large units on the Eastern Front. Having risen to the rank of general in March 1943, he is named chief of staff of Army Group B from April 1944 onwards, under the orders of Marshal Rommel. Taking temporarily over from the latter on the night of 6 June 1944, he does not consider it useful to alert the German forces of the situation, despite the information transmitted by Colonel Helmuth Meyer. Compromised during the 20 July 1944 Plot, in addition to having previously disobeyed Hitler's order to destroy Paris, he is arrested on 7 September. Despite having been freed by a military court of honour, he would suffer a P.O.W fate until 1949. After his release, he would become military advisor to Chancellor Adenauer, participating in the creation of the *Bundeswehr* and the rehabilitation of the German armies. From 1957 to 1963, he would take command of the land forces of NATO's Central Europe sector, before retiring in 1964.

where the headquarters of the German military command could be found. He would have an office there until the departure of the German troops in August 1944.

Outside the administrative or strictly military tasks entrusted to him, Jünger enjoys great freedom. With the support of his superiors, he spends a lot of time exploring the Parisian artistic and literary environment. On 8 October, he meets Sacha Guitry for the first time while visiting the Vichy government's representative in Paris, Ambassador Fernand de Brinon. Four days later, he encounters Pierre Drieu La Rochelle at Embassy Counsellor Schleier's place. On 23 November, he is presented to Gaston Gallimard and Jean Cocteau, on the occasion of a reception held at Paul and Hélène Morand's home. Such encounters would then go on for a long time.

And here is an important intimate detail regarding which Jünger always exercised absolute discretion: during the month of October, he made the acquaintance of Sophie Ravoux, who appears in his *Journal* under various pseudonyms, including that of 'the Doctress'. This lovely and bubbly young woman had been born in Germany to a Jewish mother and had emigrated to France after studying medicine, marrying a French journalist, Paul Ravoux, and thus obtaining the French nationality. Despite the very coy attitude adopted by Jünger, one can infer that he had maintained very strong personal ties to the young woman until his departure from Paris alongside the German occupying forces in August 1944.[21]

---

21   AN: Regarding Sophie Ravoux (1906–2001) and her husband, as well as the anti-Nazi German journalist Joseph Breitbach (1903–1980), who was both Jünger's and the couple's personal friend, one can consult the biographical directory created by Julien Hervier for La Pléiade, volume II. Joseph Breitbach, who was also a close friend of André Gide's and someone very familiar with the *Nouvelle Revue française* [TN: A French literary magazine], had played an important role before the war by acting as an intermediary between German literature and French literature.

In Florence Gould's Literary Salon

At the beginning of 1942, the first part of Jünger's *Journal* is published by a Berlin-based house under the bucolic title of *Gardens and Streets*. The work is then translated into French by Maurice Betz and published by Plon at the end of May. In this book, our writer-officer shares a variety of exalted, poetic and Francophile sentiments, a fact that would play a major role in terms of the author's acceptance within Parisian literary circles. Lieutenant Gerhard Heller, a former lecturer at the École Normale Supérieure of Rue d'Ulm and the man responsible for maintaining the necessary liaisons between *Propagandastaffel* and those in charge of the French edition, would act as his intercessor. As early as 28 March, he would ensure his introduction into the literary salon headed by Florence Gould (1891–1983).

Born to French parents who had emigrated to the United States, this gracious and extremely affluent woman had taken Frank Jay Gould—heir to one of the largest fortunes in America—to be her third husband. Having settled in Paris, the lovely, elegant and sporty Florence would become, in the interwar period, one of the most prominent figures of the local high life, contributing, alongside her husband, to the launching of Juan-les-Pins. At the start of the Occupation, she would open a literary salon in her apartment on Malakoff Avenue, one that would become the most distinguished literary salon in a scarred yet hardly dethroned capital.[22] Florence Gould would take no notice of any restrictions. Indeed, champagne was always served before she invited guests to enjoy lavish meals washed down by the best wines and accompanied by genuine coffee. The splenetic Paul Léautaud would fall under his hostess' spell:

---

22 AN: Concerning the unblemished influence enjoyed by Paris during the Occupation, one can refer to *Histoire de la Collaboration* [TN: A History of French Collaboration], Pygmalion, 2002.

Pretty and glued to you whenever conversing, she was tall, slim, graceful, and delicate, dressed in an old-fashioned skirt.[23]

He also described her eyes as 'feline, or rather pussycat-like, radiating a sort of amorous languidness'.

Eclecticism was the rule in her sumptuous salon. One encountered there every manner of people, including collaborators, Pétainists, members of the Resistance and those who chose to remain indifferent. When the day of liberation finally came, Florence Gould would escape the brutal cleansing by making generous donations to the members of the French Resistance. And Thursday lunches would thus continue with other guests, notably François Mauriac.[24]

Throughout the Occupation, and despite his low propensity for such socialising and small talk, Jünger's presence would be one of the adornments of the famous salon. It was there that he would develop close relationships with Jean Paulhan, Marcel Jouhandeau, Marcel Arland and Paul Léautaud. These would prove decisive for his position in the French artistic and literary environment. Jünger would also attend an ever-increasing number of events and gatherings, visit Braque and Picasso in their workshops, and make the acquaintance of Banine, a very influential woman of letters who would fall in love with him, without ever getting what she wanted. She would hold no ill will against him, however, leading people to believe that he was rather asexual. What a reassuring delusion... After the war, Banine would become the most faithful and active Parisian friend to defend the image and work of her beloved captain.[25]

23 AN: Paul Léautaud, *Journal littéraire* [TN : Literary Magazine], Mercure de France, volume XV, 22 November 1943.

24 AN: In 1978, Jünger published, through the Klett-Cotta publishing house, a translation of a book written by his friend Léautaud and entitled *In Memoriam*. The translation was followed by an afterword including a dedication to Florence Gould.

25 AN: Banine (1905–1992), short for Umm-el-Banine Assadoulaeff, was born in Baku, Azerbaijan, into a wealthy and highly cultured Shiite family. Emigrating

The Céline-Merline Affair

Céline is the only high-calibre writer who was not on the same wavelength. Indeed, Céline never had much luck with Germans, apart from Karl Epting, the director of the German Institute, who was a long-established French speaker and Francophile, a passionate connoisseur of the French language and an admirer of Célinian linguistics. Contrary to what has often been said, either through ignorance or malice, Céline was never well received in Nazi Germany.[26] Some of his novels were actually translated by a small publisher based in Czechoslovakia, and the German press simply ignored them. Better yet, in 1938, *Voyage au bout de la nuit*[27] and *Mort à crédit*[28] were among the books whose distribution was banned throughout the Reich's territory. In his report of 28 January 1942, Dr Bernhard Payr, a dye-in-the-wool Nazi and the head of the *Amt Schrifttumspflege* (publishing supervision service), reproaches Céline for having 'questioned and dragged through the mud just about everything that human existence has produced in terms of positive values.' How prudish were they, the people of the Great Reich! The report would be used against Dr Epting, who would ultimately be sanctioned. It was specifically Epting, in fact, who had arranged a meeting between Céline and Jünger at the German Institute, on 7 December 1941. What a disaster!

Our captain-writer, however, was not indifferent to all forms of unbridled literature. Indeed, he had a certain weakness for some quite disturbed minds such as Léon Bloy's (1846–1917), whose works

---

to France after the 1917 revolution and several other adventures, she would then live in Paris, finding her place in the local literary world. She then wrote several books on Jünger, the most complete being *Ernst Jünger aux faces multiples*, op. cit.

26 AN: Alain de Benoist, *Céline et l'Allemagne, 1933–1945* [TN: Céline and Germany, 1933–1945], *Le Bulletin Célinien* [TN: The Célinian Report], 1997, and *Histoire de la Collaboration*, op. cit., pp. 207–216.
27 TN: Journey to the Edge of Night.
28 TN: Dying on Credit.

he read and re-read, probably because he had never met him face to face. Unfortunately, he did meet Céline — for two whole hours, during which 'Bardamu'[29] had engaged in his great gesticulatory theatrics. The aversion was thus instantaneous. One thus finds extensive traces of this aversion in the description that Jünger gives of the man in his *Journal*:

> He speaks with a manic, inward-directed gaze, which seems to shine from deep within a cave. [...] He spoke of his consternation, his astonishment, at the fact that we soldiers were not shooting, hanging, and exterminating the Jews — astonishment that anyone who had a bayonet was not making unrestrained use of it. [...] It was informative to listen to him rant this way for two hours, because he radiated the amazing power of nihilism.

Jünger had taken care to disguise Céline's name as 'Merline'. One cannot plan everything, however. When the *Journal* is eventually translated and published in France, Banine, who hated Céline, would restore his real name. The author of *Voyage au bout de la nuit*, who was being prosecuted at the time, would threaten to file a defamation suit. To calm the waters, Jünger would deny the fact that Merline was actually Céline, hinting at a typographical error. And that would be that.

The Idyllic Dreams of *Der Friede*[30]

Following a fairly short mission under certain German military headquarters in the Caucasus, Jünger returns to Paris in February 1943. He would then finish writing a manifesto entitled *Der Friede*, intended to serve as a call 'to the youth of Europe [and] the world'. It is also meant to be a guide for the opposition[31] to follow. The idea had secretly begun

---

29   TN: Ferdinand Bardamu is the protagonist of Louis-Ferdinand Céline's 1932 novel *Journey to the Edge of Night*. The fact that they basically share the same first name is what prompted Venner to refer to Céline as 'Bardamu'.

30   TN: *Der Friede*, or 'The Peace', is a work published by Jünger in 1943.

31   AN: Although it has been claimed that the manifesto was read and approved by Field Marshal Rommel, there is no proof of this. The former head of the

to germinate in the autumn of 1941, in anticipation of a German victory. When the project was resumed in 1943, the military and political situation had already changed. And yet, just like the conspirators of the 20 July Plot, Jünger espied the completely illusory hope of peace through compromise. Following the German defeat of 8 May 1945, however, once the text had begun to circulate in the manner of a *samizdat*,[32] all such expectations would, of course, be dissolved.

Under the (now moribund) Third Reich, the pacifism of the manifesto would have been equated with treason and could have led its author to the gallows. After Germany's defeat, it would come across as a plea, one that the victors would prohibit. In Germany, apart from a limited and almost secret circulation in typewritten and copied form, *Der Friede* would never be subject to a separate edition. In France, by contrast, the manifesto would be published through La Table Ronde in 1948. The translation (a difficult one, it would seem) was made by Banine in collaboration with combatant-writer Armand Petitjean, who added a preface of his own.[33]

Afrikakorps and commander of Germany's Army Group B in the face of the Allies' summer 1944 landing bore no connection to the July 20 Plot and would undoubtedly have condemned the latter. Amidst all the confusion that characterised the era, such claims constituted a tragic misunderstanding that led Hitler to demand the secret suicide of the great soldier that Rommel certainly was (on 14 October 1944). With regard to this, one can consult Benoît Lemay's *Erwin Rommel*, Perrin, 2009.

32 TN: In the former USSR, the term *samizdat* was used in reference to a self-published work that was also banned.

33 AN: Armand Petitjean (1909–2003) was a student of the *École normale* and a contributor to the *Nouvelle Revue française (NRF)* before 1940. A friend of Jean Paulhan's, he was seriously injured in June 1940. He would then join the Vichy Youth Office (*secrétariat à la Jeunesse de Vichy*), attempting to grant it a more virile orientation. He would forge closer ties to the Resistance at the end of 1943 and, despite his mutilated hand, join the Moroccan battalions (1st army). He would thus participate in the fighting until Germany's capitulation and subsequently keep away from all political activity. In 1941, though, he had published a somewhat fascistic NRF essay entitled *Combats préliminaires* [TN: Preliminary

As part of a continuation of his diligent reading of the Bible during the years of war, Jünger now perceived the Church as an institutional and theological recourse capable of warding off nihilism. Everything in him had clearly begun to reel. During an interview with Julien Hervier conducted on the occasion of his ninetieth birthday, he would confide the following:

> I became particularly interested in the Bible during the Second World War. During the First, I was still a complete atheist.

He then goes on to specify: 'I am not a Christian.'[34] It was therefore not a matter of conversion, but a question of political rallying.

In France, *Der Friede* would be received differently; Maurrassian philosopher Pierre Boutang would view it as 'a ruse' on the part of a disguised pan-Germanist.[35] In *L'Homme revolté*[36] (1951), Albert Camus expresses the thought that Jünger is 'the only man of superior quality to give Nazism a philosophical veneer', which points, at least, to a superficial reading effort.

The first part of the manifesto, entitled 'The Seed', highlights the countless ordeals attributable to war and oppression systems. The second part, 'The Fruit', expresses the author's hope that these sacrifices would lead to universal peace, a peace whose mythical shape, as is often the case with Jünger, remains disconnected from real history.

Jünger's appeal to the President of the United States, urging the latter to display goodwill, and his openly declared hope for a 'transfiguration of the Russian Revolution [that must] be achieved on a metaphysical level' reflect an endearing sort of naivety. Before facing each

---

Clashes]. For more information on the topic, one can refer to our *Histoire de la Collaboration*, op. cit.

34 AN: Julien Hervier, *Entretiens avec Ernst Jünger* [TN: Interviews with Ernst Jünger], Gallimard, 'Arcades', 1986, p. 59 and 157.

35 AN: Pierre Boutang, *Les Abeilles de Delphes* [TN: The Bees of Delphi], La Table Ronde, 1952; reissued by Les Sirtes in 1999.

36 TN: The Rebel.

other off during the Cold War, the two victorious powers had only had one thing in mind (in 1944): to reduce Germany to ashes, thus forcing it to submit to their power and ideology. In February 1945, at Yalta, the two powers would agree to share Europe: in the West, an American protectorate that has yet to end; and in the East, ten European nations that would submit to the Red Army and the KGB. This Eastern yoke would only be broken in 1989 through the utter collapse of the Soviet system.

Completely taken in by his dreams of peace and of a mythical universal state, Jünger had failed to foresee this. He would, however, eventually come to his senses. Of all the content of his *Der Friede*, what would survive is his call for European reconciliation, namely that of the French and the Germans:

> Today, if ever, the hour for union has come and with it the hour when Europe, founding itself on the union of its peoples, attains sovereignty and constitutional form. The desire for unity is older than the crown of Charlemagne, but it was never so burning, so urgent as in our time.[37]

On this point, his prediction was correct. The Franco-German reconciliation programme outlined in *Der Friede* would be that of Robert Schuman, of General de Gaulle (after 1962), of Chancellor Adenauer, and even of the European Union, despite the great ambiguities.

Humanitarian Platitudes

Circulating clandestinely, the manuscript of *Der Friede* was never published separately in Germany. This small book, to which Jünger had always attached considerable significance, testifies, above all, to its author's great unrest and the intellectual reversal that heralded similar upheavals throughout Europe. In accordance with the dialectic of inverted mimicry, part of the opposition to Hitler sought its justifications

---

37 AN: Ernst Jünger, *Der Friede*, La Table Ronde, as found in the 1971 French edition, p. 77.

in various moral principles of Christian-Democratic inspiration — just as he himself had sought and found his own elsewhere.

In complete disarray, and deserting Nietzsche's precepts, Jünger would strive to anticipate the evolution of his contemporaries. In *Der Friede*, none would recognise any of the aspects that had once characterised the author of *Copse 125* or *The Worker*; neither in terms of ideas, nor even in terms of style. Its pitiful justifications and humanitarian platitudes summarise the intellectual chaos which Europe would have to contend with for a long time.

After the failure of the 20 July 1944 assassination plot, at a time when Colonel Claus von Stauffenberg and many officers were arrested before being executed,[38] Jünger would miraculously escape the repression. It would seem that he was still under Hitler's protection. The writer had been under no illusions regarding the endeavour's success, knowing all too well that such actions often backfire against those who attempt them. He had indulged in contemplations on Shakespeare's *Coriolanus* and remembered the fate of this Roman general, who, in a desire for revenge, ends up serving the enemy. During his mission in the Caucasus, in the fall of 1942, the young officers that he had spoken to had declared that on the front, the priority was to fight and that any attempt at conspiracy would be considered treason.

The severe repression that fell upon the conspirators thereafter, including individuals that he knew personally, attracted both his compassion and his admiration:

> Oh, how the victims are dying here, and especially in the smallest circles of the last chivalric men, of those freethinkers — the very people who are superior to the others, whose feelings and thoughts are but petty emotions. And yet these sacrifices are nonetheless important because they create an inner space and prevent the nation as a whole from falling into the horrifying depths of fate.[39]

---

38 AN: Concerning this plot, one can refer to the study published in issue 40 of *La Nouvelle Revue d'Histoire* [TN: New History Magazine], March-April 2009.

39 AN: Ernst Jünger, *Second Paris Journal*, 22 July 1944.

Burgundy and Strawberries

Shortly after leaving Paris on 15 August 1944, Jünger is demobilised. He joins his family in Kirchhorst, near Hanover, living in precarious conditions. Endowed with an energetic and practical mind, his wife, Gretha (Perpetua), had organised things around the immense house, which would soon be receiving swarms of refugees. She had cultivated the garden and transformed it into a vegetable patch. She had also taken the precaution of putting away and hiding some smoked hams. Amidst the terrible shortages that Germany would experience in the aftermath of its defeat, the household would not have to face complete starvation.

Despite having faced his own trials and tribulations, Jünger had, until then, enjoyed a state of grace resulting from his Parisian position, but also from a mental hygiene that had kept him sheltered from psychological destruction. He remained protected against horrors thanks to his apparent detachment, calculated coldness, and nurtured insensitivity. Anyone who reads his *Journal* is sometimes left amazed when, for instance, reading the following strange lines dated 14 March 1945:

> Piles of mail. Friedrich Georg calms me with one of his restorative letters, but nonetheless, he confirms that Überlingen has been bombed. At the very time of this peril, he was visiting Ziegler, the philosopher. I recognise in his report traits that are his alone: "People were killed and buildings destroyed. All around, the air was heavy with the scent of red cedars, cypresses, trees of life, firs, and other conifers, whose branches and foliage had been shorn off and crushed bythe shrapnel."

One wonders for a moment whether Jünger is not more preoccupied with the plant world than with the suffering of people. Still, one can readily gather that by uniting people and trees, Jünger manages to immunise his mind, preventing it from falling down the slope of his emotionality.

It is with such awareness that one must read his *Second Paris Journal* dated 27 May 1944, comprising words that leave so many critics gasping for air in virtuous indignation:

> Air-raid sirens, planes overhead. From the roof of the Raphaël, I watched two enormous detonation clouds billon upward in the region of Saint-Germain while the high-altitude formations cleared off. They were targeting the river bridges. The method and sequence of the tactics aimed at our supply lines imply a subtle mind. When the second raid came at sunset, I was holding a glass of burgundy with strawberries floating in it. The city, with its red towers and domes, was a place of stupendous beauty, like a calyx that they fly over to accomplish their deadly act of pollination. The whole thing was theater — pure power affirmed and magnified by suffering.

The image of strawberries floating in a glass of Burgundy as Jünger beholds the spectacle of a city caught in the throes of deadly bomb pollination, now *that* was a little bit too much! It was too much because the words came from a German officer contemplating a city that was still subject to his influence. The admirers of the Marquis de Sade were the first to choke, despite the scene being very juicy indeed; it did, after all, introduce strawberries into the domain of literature.

The Death of His Beloved Son

Let us return to a more serious context that will erase all accusations of insensitivity. What we are referring to is specifically Jünger's display of restrained pain upon being told of the death of his son Ernstel, a death that would henceforth weigh on him like a never-ending period of relentless grief.

At the beginning of 1944, the then seventeen-year-old teenager is at a naval cadet school in Wilhelmshaven. Soon, Jünger learns that his son had been thrown into prison for saying that he would gladly pull the rope that would be used to hang Hitler — a very serious situation considering the context of the time. In full uniform and accompanied by his wife, the writer would repeatedly approach both the military authorities and those of the navy (which were responsible for Ernstel), citing his son's youthful rashness as an excuse for his behaviour. He would ultimately manage to have his son shown leniency by the military judges in exchange for the boy's immediate recruitment into the army. This would prove to be a fatal mistake, as Ernstel would be killed in Italy on 29 November 1944, while on patrol in the vicinity of the Carrara marble quarries. Jünger would, however, not be notified of his son's passing until 12 January 1945.

Speaking temperately of his pain, Jünger writes the following in his *Journal*:

> Anguish is like rain that runs off in torrents and is only gradually absorbed by the earth. The mind cannot grasp it all at once. We have now truly become part of the one and only community of this war, its hidden brotherhood.

Jünger would thus experience the suffering that had stricken so many men and women all across Europe. Nothing of what characterised the lives of 20th-century Europeans would therefore be foreign to him. He would remain inconsolable. Every day, for the rest of his life, he would lose himself in contemplations at his child's grave.

Brilliant and sensitive, Ernstel had had the greatest possible admiration for his father and had dreamt of someday becoming his equal. And this is what Jünger wrote about it in his *Journal*:

> Such a good lad. Ever since childhood, he strove to emulate his father. Now he has done so on his first try, and truly surpassed him.[40]

Was he thinking of the audacity displayed by the boy when proclaiming his opposition to Hitler, as he himself had never openly done? Perhaps so, but he might also have been thinking of Ernstel's death in battle, one which he, the famous Ernst Jünger, had unintentionally escaped.[41]

---

40 AN: *Kirchhorst Diaries* (The Cottage in the Vineyard), 13 January 1945.
41 AN: Jünger had a second son, Alexander, whose courage in the face of the 1945 bombings he would also talk about. Having become a doctor, Alexander Jünger would remain close to his father and give him two grandchildren. Having been

CHAPTER X

FROM REBEL TO ANARCH

AMIDST THE apocalyptic red glow, Hitler killed himself alongside his last faithful acolytes, deep within the bunker of his Berlin Chancellery, on 30 April 1945. Across the world, and especially in Europe, his name would continue to reverberate in a most powerful manner. As for Ernst Jünger, he owes part of his notoriety to his having crossed paths with the former *Führer* of the German National Socialist Party and the Third Reich, before ultimately standing against him.

Machiavelli or Corneille

Several times already, we have attempted to understand the reasons that had led the former heroic soldier of 1914-1918 (who then became the most famous intellectual of the radical Right during the 1925-1930 period) to embrace dissidence. Additionally, we have listed the ideas that resulted in his being opposed to Hitler: his rejection of anti-Semitism and racial Darwinism, and his objection to Russophobia, as he himself wished for an alliance between Germany and Russia, even if the latter were Bolshevik. We have also spoken of Jünger's ever-growing aversion to the leaders of the brutal National Socialist Party, which he considered unworthy of embodying the new Germany.

---

left paralysed as a result of a surgical intervention, he would, sadly, commit suicide on 22 April 1993.

Stating all of this, however, is insufficient, as it does not account for the pacifistic and rather Christian reversal experienced by Jünger, whose former Nietzscheanism was asserted in *On the Marble Cliffs* (1939). We have admittedly elaborated on things, even dissecting at length what we termed 'secession from one's self', but there is more that needs to be said.

The expectations of a genuine historian, who feels compelled to understand even the most complex situations, require him to revisit this issue by taking a different path in analysing Jünger's dissent and the extreme changes that occurred within him. Indeed, one must not forget what he had been prior to the inversion of his 'perceptions'.

Around 1925, and until around 1930, Jünger had been a passionate yet utterly sincere intellectual. To use Ernst von Salomon's terminology, he lived *for* an idea and not *through* it. And although the idea in question gave him a reason to live, it ultimately caused him nothing but trouble, as he was both an idealistic and a profound thinker, and never a practical politician, although he did devote himself to political romanticism more than he would have been willing to concede.

Prior to 1930, while to some extent in a state of competition with Hitler, he had strived to rally the youth of the era around him so as to engage in rebellion. However, the only thing he would ever share with the future *Führer* was his nationalist hatred of Weimar. As for the rest, they would always be at odds. Among other things, he lacked what was necessary to achieve success in politics: the charismatic magnetism of a leader; ambition and opportunism; bad faith; an argumentative temperament; a penchant for demagogy; and both cunning and ruthlessness towards adversaries and competitors alike. Instead, what he had was a surplus of intellectual integrity, righteousness and poetic lyricism. In contrast, Hitler was a political beast bred for combat and success, a man willing to resort to every possible compromise, promise, alliance, brutality, and reversal. Hitler succeeded where Jünger himself failed, which bestowed upon the latter an element of nobility. Jünger thus set out to assess his real abilities, ultimately hating in Hitler what he himself was not. He was guilty of the typical mistake made by the idealists who wander into the realm of politics. He did not understand in time that politics is a domain that belongs to Machiavelli's world and not Corneille's.[1] He thus found himself hating Machiavelli.

When Jünger began to write *On the Marble Cliffs*, he was already perfectly aware of his mistake. Someone other than him, a much more gifted political beast, had taken over Germany, a 'head forester' that he would fight against alongside his 'Mauretanian' friends of the Black Front and certain *Reichswehr* officers, before laying down his arms as a result of his own weariness, confessing that every fight in the political sphere lacks purpose and is ultimately morally degrading.

It is within this new mindset that he spends the four years of the Occupation in rather pleasant conditions, protected by a few high-ranking officers and aware of the 20 July 1944 scheme, without, however, participating in it.

With this entire background in mind, we can now safely resume our analysis of Jünger's incessant evolution.

The Dissident Prevails over the Patriot

Returning from Paris, which capitulated on 25 August 1944,[2] Jünger arrived at his home in Kirchhorst on 4 September. Although he would evade the fate of the 20 July 1944 conspirators, he is demobilised and thus stripped of authority during the last days of October. On 5 January 1945, he is assigned to the local *Volkssturm*, a sort of territorial militia established towards the end of the war. On 3 April 1945, realising that any and all opposition had been rendered useless, he orders his men not to resist the American troops upon arrival. In the preceding weeks,

---

1 AN: Within the German and Prussian world, one could mention Heinrich von Kleist rather than Corneille.
2 AN: General Dietrich von Choltitz, the last German commander in charge of the *Place de Paris*, would surrender it without fighting on 25 August 1944, refusing to destroy the French capital as Hitler himself had ordered him to. As for Jünger, he had left a few days earlier.

German cities had been bombarded repeatedly,[3] and Jünger himself had witnessed this in the Hanover region. His childhood town had been targeted on several occasions. On 4 November 1944, he adds the following comment in his *Journal*:

> Massive detachment of aircraft overhead around noon, during which everyone in the [Kirchhorst] house gathered in our little air-raid shelter. First came a squadron of forty planes, which took heavy anti-aircraft fire. […] Huge numbers of bombs followed, glistening silvery white in the sunshine. The anti-aircraft fire surged to full force […]. I watched the events from our garden […]. The roar of the squadrons darkening the sky is so strong that it drowns out the defensive fire and even the detonation of the bombs themselves. […].The incredible energy of our age — otherwise diffused far and wide — emerges from its abstract potential and becomes perceptible to our senses. The impression of the squadrons lumbering on undeterred even when planes are exploding in their midst, is mightier than the detonation of the bombs themselves. We see the will to destroy, even at the cost of one's own destruction. This is a demonic trait.[4]

Under the diarist's pen, this bombing scene is limited to a mere clinical description accompanied by a cold general conclusion on the demonic character of the world of machines. There is neither indignation nor

---

3   AN: As regards the terror bombings that targeted German populations and that had been ordered by Churchill with the support of Roosevelt, one can refer for instance to the investigation conducted by the historian Jörg Friedrich and titled *Der Brand. Deutschland im Bombenkrieg 1940–1945* [TN: The Fire: The Bombing of Germany 1940–1945], published in France by Éditions de Fallois in 2004. To find out about another aspect of German suffering, one can consult the study carried out by the historian Heinz Nawratil under the title *Schwarzbuch der Vertreibung 1945–1948: Das letzte Kapitel unbewältigter Vergangenheit* [TN: The Black Book of Displacement: The Final Chapter of an Unresolved Past], Éditions Akribeia, 2001.

4   AN: Ernst Jünger, *A German Officer in Occupied Paris — The War Journals, 1941–1945*. The reference date is mentioned alongside each quoted segment. The quoted words can also be found, albeit with slight variations, in Ernst Jünger's *War Journals II: 1939–1948*, op. cit.

complaints about the suffering of civilian populations subjected to these undertakings of death and terror. Not a word of protest either regarding the destruction of the works of art and beauty that the German cities had been prior to being reduced to rubble. Here, the enemy of Hitler's Reich seems to prevail over the German that one would expect to display solidarity in the face of his compatriots' misfortune. And that is where a revealing letter, dated 24 March 1940 and addressed to one of Jünger's friends, springs to mind:

> I have already removed the word "German" from all my works, so as not to have to share it with them.

When he speaks of 'them', it is obviously the Nazis that he is referring to. One is sometimes left wondering if Jünger's hostility to the regime did not often extend to virtually everything German.

Until the mid-20th century, all sides and countries were thus in the grip of a massive mobilisation of peoples — by means of force, persuasion or fascination — behind a charismatic leader, an ideology, a myth or a collective passion. And everywhere, the dissidents and rebels chose to espouse moral secession from their native community, a community which, in their eyes, had given in to collaboration with the systems that they themselves were fighting. To the Europeans fulfilling different commitments, whether fascist or anti-fascist, communist or anti-communist, it is Jünger that somehow bears witness to this collective tragedy, one that has been imposed upon them by a merciless sort of destiny.

The Arrival of the Americans

On 23 January 1945, however, a slightly different remark would surface in the *Journal*, dictated in part by Jünger's professional perspective:

> The Russians have entered East Prussia and Silesia. New efforts to halt this breakthrough while the butchering continues in the West. The energy and the sheer athleticism of the will remain astonishing.

Soon, however, reservations start to emerge:

> Of course, this quality only shows itself as we are heading downhill—its only trait and accomplishment being mindlessness and decline.

New indications of the situation's development are dated 11 April 1945. That morning, the American vanguards pass through Kirchhorst. The former officer makes the following observation:

> At nine o'clock, a powerful, ever-increasing grinding sound announces the approach of the American tanks. [...]As always in such situations, unforeseen things happen [...]. Then a solitary hiker appears and remains standing on a forest path not far from the barrier. At the moment when the first gray tank with its five-pointed star appears, he releases the safety catch on his pistol and shoots himself in the head. [...] Seamlessly, slowly, yet irresistibly, the flood of men and steel surges past. [...] A good thing that Ernstel cannot see this; it would have hurt him too much.

The mentioning of his beloved son, who had been killed in combat on 29 November 1944, is indicative of a hitherto invisible pain: the pain of a defeat that is not merely that of a hated regime, but also that of the homeland. Other Europeans, no matter the place, have also experienced this:

> Recovery from such a defeat will not be the same as after Jena or Sedan. This portends a change in the lives of populations; not only must countless human beings die, but much of everything that used to motivate our deepest being perishes in this transition.

And let us also point out the following words again, penned on the same date and resulting from the same trauma:

> We are capable of recognising necessity, even of understanding and desiring and loving it as well—and yet at the same of being overcome with intense anguish.

The thought is not hard to decipher. The 'necessary' in question is obviously the end of Hitler's regime. As for 'intense anguish', it refers to the crushing of the German homeland.

Disasters and Tribulations

Throughout the *Journal*, the days of pain begin to stack up. Indeed, Kirchhorst was pillaged by the first American troops and Jünger himself was almost shot dead by a Colt-wielding looter. Practical and determined, Perpetua sends her husband to the attic once again, where he would be shut in among his books, so as to avoid a fatal manifestation of his fearlessness. With the accuracy of a seismograph, the *Journal* records various facts that reveal the immense catastrophe and the resulting tribulations, including the following notes on 9 May 1945, the day after the German capitulation:

> The roads are covered with millions and millions of wanderers, overwhelmed by the misery of inconceivable migrations. Our little cemetery has, likewise, reaped this harvest, receiving the bodies of the children and adults whose flight has come to an end here. Our guest is a young Berliner who lost everything in the looting. Her father had vanished on the Caucasus front and her mother escaped the terrors of the Russian invasion by ingesting poison.

Three days pass, punctuated by a series of sinister tragedies. On 12 May 1945, after noting the opening of a flower in his garden, Jünger remarks:

> We provided safe havens for the night to four men in vagabond rags, who, we could clearly see, had still fought in uniform a few days earlier. They were in a state of despair and convinced that the country owed its defeat to treason. "This time, the dagger thrust came from above"... It is likely that, some thirty years ago, I would have thought the same.

They had barely left when the car of two American journalists appeared. And we all know what happens with this kind of 'journalists', who come to investigate, pry and ask questions. They talk about the horrors of the concentration camps before wallowing in reflections on German cultural and scientific 'backwardness'. Even German medicine is thus alleged to be lagging behind, with the Americans having just discovered penicillin.[5] Jünger comments:

> A man who is more and more inclined to regard modern medicine as a calamitous power does not let himself be shaken by such arguments. Such discoveries occur every ten years and result, in the best case, in an acceleration of the pace of interactions, but probably also in a degeneration of the human race.

Was Jünger a eugenicist, or perhaps a pre-environmentalist? Whatever the case, at least he was not fooled.

Under the date of 16 May 1945, the *Journal* revisits the information which had begun to seep out, little by little, concerning the atrocities which the Germans of East Prussia and Silesia had fallen prey to. Jünger finds himself struggling with the new feelings that troubled him and thus insists:

> When, in my notes, I mention the Russians, the Americans, the Poles, the Germans and the French, they are all to be taken in the same sense, that of pawns in a game of chess. Each can be white or black.

His desire is not to cast blame on anyone:

> Murder, rape, pillaging, generosity, grandeur, all these behaviours have not been distributed one and for all among nations.

How can one fail to agree? Indeed, horrors and grandeurs are both bearers of mankind's potentialities. Jünger goes on to add something new, at least in terms of his feelings during recent years:

---

5   TN: A ridiculous claim to say the least, since penicillin was discovered in 1928 by Alexander Fleming, a Scottish physician and microbiologist.

"We cannot, however, strip ourselves of our belonging to our people. The nature of things dictates that the misfortune of our family, the suffering of our brother, affects us more deeply — and also that we are more closely bound to his guilt."

In the Face of Great Misfortunes

Reading the *Journal* allows one to follow the evolution taking place, day after day, in Jünger's mind, as the consequences of the defeat are exacerbated and news pours in regarding the atrocities that had been perpetrated, and were still being carried out, against the Germans. Long had Jünger been blind to this, his attention focused primarily on the suffering of the unfortunates who had to endure the Third Reich's cruelty. What testifies to his evolution are the words he recorded on 11 June 1945 after listening to Radio London:

> In the evening, the radio announced that the expulsion of the Sudeten German population was underway. [...] One spoke about terrible massacres. Some refugees report details which, in terms of infamy, exceed everything I have heard mentioned since 1917, and which I prefer not to commit to paper. [...] The news reached us via the London transmitter, whose indignation at the crimes perpetrated in our country I had often approved of over the past few years. But what are we to think of the satisfaction in which the story of these new atrocities was so evidently draped? While the voice of the well-fed man, accustomed to indulgent lunches, made my heart twist, I witnessed the indescribable misery stretched out along the roads near the border.

Talk about adopting a new tone… The writer thus discovers the truth about adversaries that had hitherto been credited with the noblest motivations.

Their propaganda had long reinforced his aversion to both the leaders of the Third Reich and their enforcers. And lo and behold, it is the great misfortunes which he now witnesses directly that reveal to him a different sort of reality. A rip now begins to spread through the fabric of his soul, as demonstrated by what he wrote on 20 August 1945, following a visit to Hanover. His childhood town is now no more than a pile of rubble:

> The misery, amidst these rows of ruin, has reached a degree that surpasses even that of the Russian cities that I have visited. One sensed that millions of beings did not yet have a roof under which they could spend the winter […]. They were all on the threshold of mass death.

From this sinister spectacle sprouts a new reflection:

> The theory of collective guilt has two parallel threads. For the vanquished, it signifies: I must declare myself to be in solidarity with my brother and his guilt. For the victor, it acts, in practice, as a driving force for indiscriminate pillaging.

This is a good summary of the predicament, and Jünger expands further:

> If the bow is drawn too tightly, a dangerous question may arise: was the brother truly so unjust?

Suicides in the Thousands

The *Journal* looks back on the recent past, as Jünger receives news concerning former comrades, contacts and friends, whether dead or alive, news which reach Kirchhorst through mysterious channels. It also abounds in factual information and comments on the consequences of the defeat, as seen on 20 December 1945, when Jünger went to Hamburg to visit friends:

> The stay in this razed city was depressing. […] I found out the details of Walter Franck's suicide, who had put a bullet in his own head, dying in the arms of his wife [following Hitler's death]. Stapel read me his farewell letters, which I found to be full of dignity. Among the huge number of suicides, there seemed to be many which Hitler's death had not only been

a signal for, but a secret justification; this was also Franck's case. Of all of Hitler's supporters, this historian had had one of the most astute minds.[6]

Jünger mentions many other suicides. Some of them are famous, including that of Air Force General Robert von Greim,[7] who had been appointed Göring's successor as head of the Supreme Command of the Luftwaffe during the last days of the *Reich*.

> So as to report for duty before Hitler, he asked the aviator Hanna Reitsch[8] to take him on a small plane to Berlin, which was already in agony. Tempelhof Airport had already fallen into Russian hands, so they landed at the Tiergarten airfield under violent enemy fire, which damaged the aircraft and injured Greim. The latter then went to the Reich Chancellery, put on his helmet, reported for duty and took the plane back to the South, once again amidst heavy anti-aircraft fire. Then, upon capitulation, he poisoned himself.

Gerhard Günther, one of the friends that Jünger met in Hamburg, would tell him about a night of terror spent in Pomerania on the arrival of the Soviets. He and other refugees 'had escaped from the castle of a Pomeranian property, into a pit dug in the middle of a clearing. A hail of bullets ripped through the surroundings, as if in a battue;[9] all the while, one could hear the screaming of women coming from the estate's farm, and one could also see the glow of the flames. The mistress of the estate, a young thirty-year-old woman, killed her entire

---

6   AN: A supporter of Hitler, Walter Franck (1905–1945) was a historian and the president of the *Reich*'s Institute for the History of the New Germany.

7   AN: Robert Ritter von Greim (1892–1945) was a former artillery officer who joined the German Air Force in 1916. He was the last field marshal to be promoted by Hitler, committing suicide in Salzburg on 24 May 1945.

8   AN: Hanna Reitsch (1912–1979) was an aviator who held around forty records, specialising in risky flights during the last part of the war. Imprisoned by the Americans in May 1945 for a period of 18 months, she would pursue her activities in India and Ghana.

9   TN: Beat hunting or battue is a type of hunting during which animals are driven through the woods in front of hunters.

large family, her old father as well as her children, by means of morphine injections, before shooting herself in the head. These places do not have names,' comments the diarist, 'for they can be counted in the thousands.'[10]

Jünger Is Banned from Publishing His Works

In the period following the German surrender of 1945, and despite his long-standing opposition to Nazism, Jünger suffered the fate of millions of his compatriots. The American occupation authorities had marked him as a nationalist writer, which, in other words, meant almost a Nazi. Just like Heidegger, he would, out of sheer dignity, refuse to fill out the de-nazification 'questionnaire' imposed upon his compatriots. Ernst von Salomon regards this as the most ironic, the most literary and the most 'European' (that is to say, the least American) expression of the protests of a German opponent of Nazism.[11]

Jünger's refusal to comply with the wishes of the occupying powers did not do him any favours. The Hanover region, where he had found his place of residence, was part of the English zone of occupation. The authorities of the area would thus make him pay the price of his mental independence by banning him from publishing any works, and the ban would not be lifted until 1949. This change would not, however, be the result of unexpected and sudden benevolence. Simply put, Jünger

---

10   AN: For a long time, the rape of more than two million German women at the hands of Soviet soldiers (between April and September 1945, with the encouragement of their superiors , as Ilya Ehrenburg shouted 'break their racial pride' on the radio) had been met with complete silence. In one way or another, every German family had borne such a tragedy, yet the shame and pain had been so great that no one dared to speak of it. Additionally, German suffering had to be silenced in the name of the Third Reich's victims. Next came the testimony of Marta Hillers in *A Woman in Berlin* (Gallimard, 2006 [TN: Originally released anonymously in 1954]) and, in October 2008, its adaptation by Max Färberböck for the film *Anonyma. Eine Frau in Berlin*, with Nina Hoss in the lead role. This time, the taboo had been lifted.

11   AN: Ernst von Salomon, *The Questionnaire*, Gallimard, 1953.

CHAPTER X. FROM REBEL TO ANARCH

and his family had chosen to emigrate to the French occupation zone, which was less fault-finding and censorious.

On 1 December 1948, the family would leave Kirchhorst, where they had lived since 1939, moving to Ravensburg, in the Rhineland, and thus escaping the British harassments. Jünger would therefore finally be able to publish his *War Journals (Radiations)*, as well as other works. His stay in Ravensburg would not last long, however. Indeed, in July 1950, Jünger and his family would depart for Wilflingen, in Swabia, where they would enjoy the hospitality of Baron von Stauffenberg, a close relative of the primary conspirator of the 20 July Plot.[12] This time around, the writer settles in once and for all, without, however, missing any opportunities to make numerous trips until his final days.

Echoing the uncertainties of the most aware and, therefore, the most troubled European minds of his time, Jünger watched as a number of certainties he had enjoyed under the Third Reich, prior to his country's defeat and the advent of the cruel trials imposed on the Germans, began to disintegrate. A new evolution of his perceptions was thus underway. His futuristic novel *Heliopolis*, which he would work on from January 1947 to March 1949, reflects his dismay. The compassionate perspective inaugurated by *On the Marble Cliffs* was still prevalent, but mixed with oneiric outpourings. Incidentally, this utopian novel, which is set in a new imaginary city, is not the easiest. Having read it, Jünger's wife, Gretha, would make a rather derisive comment fraught with a most biting intensity. 'She stated,' wrote the somewhat disappointed writer, 'that one had a sense of unease living under the same roof as a man capable of contriving such a text.'[13]

---

12   AN: Apart from subsequently moving into the house of the von Stauffenberg's head forester in 1951, Jünger would no longer change residence until the end of his days.

13   AN: As stated on 24 July 1949 and quoted by Julien Hervier in his introduction to *Ernst Jünger, War Journals II: 1939–1948*, op. cit., p. XLIX. Gretha Jünger would die of cancer on 20 November 1960. As for Ernst, he would get married

The mindset that characterised *Heliopolis* would be torn asunder shortly afterwards by the German publication of *Der Waldgang*[14] in October 1951. Once again, the times had changed.

The Forest Passage

The year was 1951, and six years had passed since Germany's crushing — six years characterised by mentality changes, especially in the West, and impacted by the Cold War, whose beginning historians trace back to 1948. Although the global conflict and opprobrium borne by Germany had not been forgotten, their memory would, for a time, be overshadowed by a nagging feeling of a threat that originated from the East. It is all a forgotten reality to which the events of the time bore witness. In France, the specific fear of invasion and massacres is very present indeed, as seen in the table talk of General de Gaulle who, although far from power at this stage, remained passionately attentive to current affairs.[15]

The work that Jünger published under the title *Der Waldgang* (The Forest Passage) reflects new undertones.[16] The work marks a complete break with the contemplative philosophy of *On the Marble Cliffs* and with the honeyed moral exhortations of *The Peace*. The behaviour adopted by the victorious powers of 1945 contributed to dispelling certain perceptions that the previous period had sown. As Jünger writes:

---

again on 3 March 1962 to Liselotte Lohrer, who he would often mention in his later diaries as 'the little bull', in reference to her zodiac sign.

14 TN: The Forest Passage.

15 AN: Dominique Venner, *De Gaulle. La grandeur et le néant* [TN: De Gaulle, Grandeur and Nothingness], Éditions du Rocher, 2004, pp. 211–212; Claude Guy, *En écoutant de Gaulle. Journal, 1946–1949* [TN: Listening to de Gaulle: Diary, 1946–1949] Grasset, 1996.

16 AN: Translated by Henri Plard as *Le Traité du rebelle, ou le recours aux forêts* [TN: Treatise on the Rebel, or the Forest Path] Éditions du Rocher, 1957; republished by Christian Bourgois in 1981.

After all, we are involved not simply in a national collapse but in a global catastrophe, in which the real winners and losers can hardly be known, let alone prophesied.

Looking back on the recent past in the light of the events of the early 1950s, which witnessed the confirmation of the enslavement endured by all the peoples of Eastern Europe as well as East Germans, Jünger distances himself from things so as to describe communist oppression, albeit without naming it as such:

> The hopeless encirclement of man has been long in the preparation, through theories that strive for a logical and seamless explanation of the world and go hand in hand with technical development. At first there is the rational encirclement of the opponent, then the societal one; finally, at the appointed hour, he is exterminated. No more desperate fate exists than getting mixed up in a process where the law has been turned into a weapon.

This description is, of course, valid for other systems as well, including those that strive to monopolise freedom:

> There exists no great word and no noble thought for which blood has not flowed.

In the absence of equivalents, the German title of the new work, *Der Waldgang*, was translated by Henri Plard for the French edition as 'The Rebel'. The word *Waldgänger* takes its name from an ancient mediaeval Scandinavian custom. According to the latter, any outlaws guilty of murder could be legally slain by anyone who met them. The outcast, however, also had the right to 'take the forest path' and take refuge in the woods, living freely there at his own risk. The French term 'maquisard' could have been chosen instead, but since it relates to a specific time and to a particular historical situation, it was not used by the translator.

Indeed, the 'rebel' that Jünger strives to define in his work is not a historicised character, even if the context that bore him was indeed historical. What influenced him was his memory of the French Resistance during the Second World War, as well as the topicality of Soviet threats during the dangerous period of the Cold War. A German, even one so far removed from everyday issues as Jünger was, could not turn a blind eye to the trauma resulting from the Berlin Blockade, which isolated the city's 'western' sector from June 1948 to May 1949, with the intention of ushering the entire former capital into the hands of Stalin.

The Poacher's Freedom

The mentioning of forests as sanctuaries of freedom can seem surprising when stemming from an author who, in *On the Marble Cliffs*, had on the contrary presented them as an accursed place. This new approach, however, is consistent with a centuries-old European tradition which has always viewed forests as archetypal places of regeneration. Such an interpretation is ubiquitous in the Arthurian cycle, as well as in many Celtic or Germanic legends that Jünger was familiar with. It was also present in the writer's childhood memories and imagination. It is, in fact, the meaning bestowed upon forests in *On the Marble Cliffs*, and not elsewhere, that constitutes an oddity.

On 19 February 1947, while the family was still living in Kirchhorst, Jünger's *War Journals* recount a particularly joyful memory that contrasts with the era's rather sombre concerns. And the framework of this memory is that of a forest described as a sanctuary. Jünger recollects:

> I go into the forest, tinkling with rime. On my way back, I meet young Haustein in front of his workshop, as he cheerfully beckons me in.

Young Haustein was half farmer and half forester. We would soon find out that he was also an unapologetic poacher. It was a world that Jünger knew well. In the short story entitled 'The Boar Hunt' ('Die Eberjagd'), published as an appendix to *Visit to Godenholm*, the writer would describe in connoisseur terms the atmosphere of a hunting expedition through the forest, emphasising the exhilaration that grips the young novice hunter before he is overwhelmed by a certain melancholy when faced with the death of the hunted animal.[17]

This time, hunting is only mentioned to highlight the pleasure of eating venison, a rare luxury in such periods of want. The young Haustein had 'shot a wild boar in the marsh'. During the Anglo-American military occupation that followed the defeat of 1945, Germans were prohibited from owning weapons and hunting. Indeed, Jünger himself had buried his rifles in his garden, while the number of wild boars increased. Properly gutted, skinned and dismembered, the one that Haustein had shot became a delicious roast prepared by the poacher's young wife.

> On the scrubbed table, the tenderloin was on display, alongside bread and butter; we pounce on it. The delicate flesh of a trespasser's back, one that had barely weighed sixty pounds, is a majestic feast indeed.

Judging by its weight, the wild boar had been about three years old, an age that guarantees tender and delicious cuts. 'The bread and the butter are just as wonderful,' Jünger adds. Those were 'home-made', of course — the products of freedom. Jünger thus comments:

> I cannot help but think of the Château d'Anet, the residence of Diane de Poitiers, where I had admired the statue of the breast-baring moon goddess. It was there, above the fireplace in the dining room, that I had read the proud motto: "No purchased dish is found on this table."

The 'eau-de-vie' that accompanies the roast 'is made by the family, under the moonlight.' We thus find ourselves in a world that evades all investigations and prohibitions. Homemade alcohol 'is a treacherous liquid full of earthy forces in a state of fermentation'.

Jünger expands further:

---

17 AN: Ernst Jünger, *Visit to Godenholm* (*Besuch auf Godenholm*), followed by 'The Boar Hunt', as translated into French by Henri Plard, Christian Bourgois, 1968.

The tenderloin gradually disappears, amidst conversations about hunting and the marshes; the bottle is, likewise, emptied, and a second makes its entrance. Haustein smokes tobacco that he himself had grown and begins to sing; his wife sits alongside us and joins him in singing:

"Little playful deer,
Why don't you fear
A hunter so direct
Tracking your every step"

Next, Jünger makes a cheerful remark: 'Five hours fly by, without my knowing where they had gone.' Still, it was time for him to think about taking his leave.

Outside, night had long since fallen; I can feel the liquor beginning to take effect. Some laundry is hanging in the meadow: it is frozen stiff and tinkles in the wind.

Upon reading further, one understands that Jünger had fallen into a state of sweet intoxication. He thus returns home with unsteady steps, but in a mood of sheer bliss. This seemingly bland story takes on more and more flavour when one is aware of the author's highly intellectualised personality, not to mention his love of intense experiences.[18] The return of such moments of freedom in the untouched world of the forest makes it all worthwhile. In their own way, the young Haustein and his wife are rebels living on the fringes of the surrounding society, a mechanised, regulated and monitored society from which they escape, leading a contrasting existence of peaceful happiness through the autonomy of a genuinely free life.

To interpret the figure of the *Waldgänger*, one should keep this seemingly purely anecdotal story in mind. It provides a familiar and illustrative complement to the political content of the treatise on the rebel.

---

18   AN: Ernst Jünger, *Annäherungen. Drogen und Rausch* [TN: Approaches: Drugs and Intoxication], as translated by Henri Plard, La Table Ronde, 1973.

Yoga Schools Are Not the Sole Remedy

Distancing himself from the praise of non-action that permeates *On the Marble Cliffs*, Jünger now writes:

> To defend oneself against injustice or tyranny, one cannot limit oneself to the sole conquest of interior realms.[19]

To act against all threats of enslavement is thus a moral duty:

> The issue cannot be reduced to the founding of yoga schools.

Rediscovering the overtones of his youthful writings, he even pens some lines that were now far removed from the bouts of sentimentality occasionally encountered in *The Peace*:

> The resistance of the forest rebel is absolute: he knows no neutrality [...]. He does not expect the enemy to listen to arguments, let alone act chivalrously. [...] He will not weaken the power of the adversary with concepts alone.

Jünger chooses to intentionally limit himself to generalities. His work thus acquires an element of timelessness, a guarantee of longevity that improvised writings are typically denied. Quickly gleaning a few examples to support his view, the author mentions, among others, General Malet, who almost managed to single-handedly overthrow Napoleon in 1813. On the other hand, he avoids any recollections regarding Colonel Claus von Stauffenberg and the other conspirators of the 20 July 1944 plot, whose beliefs he had shared without, however, approving of their actions. Indeed, none can readily adopt an absolute standpoint when it comes to the tragic choices posed by such an attack, unless one does as Jünger himself did by paying respect to the actors that sacrificed their lives in the name of an endeavour imposed

---

19   TN: The existing English translation does not mention injustice or tyranny, stating instead: '[...] and he means to defend himself. As we previously suggested, it cannot be limited to the conquest of purely interior realms.'

by the noblest, albeit unrealistic, intentions.[20] As already mentioned, Jünger himself did not behave like a rebel, although he did take some risks of his own. His reluctance to embrace direct action was not only due to moral factors, but also to the crisis of conscience experienced by an officer who was paralysed by the fear of harming his own country at a time when the latter was involved in a deadly conflict. Even when in loathsome hands, warring Germany remained his homeland.

Jünger's refusal to associate the figure of the *Waldgänger* with a specific historical setting is not a matter of intellectual or literary artifice. Throughout his work, Jünger always demonstrated that he did not think in historical terms, basing his thoughts instead on timeless myths. Therein lay his weakness and, more often than not, his very charm. Any mindset that remains disconnected from real history runs the risk of plummeting into abstractions and confused or unrealistic thoughts. Conversely, any attempt at strict historicisation can make one lose all sense of long-lastingness and permanence.

Jünger's rebel is therefore not a character that one could situate historically. He is, in accordance with the terminology favoured by the essayist, a 'figure', a timeless type who, for this very reason, can be revised to suit any time and age. Nothing is thus dated in this in-depth reflection on the timeless figure of the rebel, who displays 'determination to resist, and his intention to fight the battle, however hopeless' it may be. One thus understands that *The Forest Passage* is not a guerrilla

---

20 AN: Following Hitler's elimination, the conspirators hoped to obtain peace through compromise with the Americans and the English, thus preserving the borders of the *Reich* and acquiring the ability to focus on resisting the Red Army. It is all too clear that these unfortunates were completely unaware of the real intentions and motivations harboured by the new masters of the empire of the seas and oblivious to their decision to impose 'unconditional surrender' upon their enemy, an idea that had first been put forward by F. D. Roosevelt at the Casablanca conference on 24 January 1943 and approved by Churchill. As for Stalin, he would only express his full agreement with it at Yalta, in February 1945.

manual in any way, nor does it focus on the historical actions of various dissenters through the ages.

On the other hand, the work does comprise Jünger's new and profound reflection on contemporary nihilism. Distancing himself as much as possible, the author absorbs, with one single glance, the spiritual collapse of 'Western' man, who had now fallen prey to the economic and technological domination characterising the second half of the century:

> Typically, this person will be little developed ethically or spiritually, however eloquent he may be in convincing platitudes. He will be alert, intelligent, active, sceptical, inartistic, a natural-born debaser of higher types and ideas, an insurance fanatic, someone set on his own advantage, and easily manipulated by the catchphrases of propaganda whose often abrupt turnabouts he will hardly perceive; he will gush with humanitarian theory, yet be equally inclined to awful violence beyond all legal limits or international law whenever a neighbour or fellow human being does not fit into his system.

For a long time to come, this description would retain its veracity.

Through Jünger's use of an aphorism, one also perceives his return to Nietzschean ways:

> A spirited atheist always comes across more sympathetically than an indifferent man of the crowd, since he concerns himself with the world as a totality. Moreover, such a person is not infrequently open to higher possibilities […].

Theological Temptations

The reader cannot fail to notice Jünger's new evolution. Indeed, his reading of the Bible had gone hand in hand with his writing of the different segments of his Journal (*Strahlungen*), from 1939 to the end of the war. Just like the works of Herodotus, who was also very present in Jünger's life during the same period, the Bible encouraged him to indulge in timeless reflections, although there was nothing to indicate that the diarist was seeking some sort of divine consolation. Indeed, Jünger did not approach such texts with the mysticism of someone like Léon Bloy or Paul Claudel. Nor did he ponder it all from a theological perspective. Turning his back on Nietzschean thought, he believed, at the time, that certain Christian themes would enable him to find the political foundations of resistance to nihilism, which he equated with Nazism. In *The Peace*, he would thus write the following, for example:

> The true conquest of nihilism and the attainment of peace will be possible only with the help of the churches.

He insisted on this 'help', even speaking of the possible role of a 'State Church', without, however, taking sides in the quarrel between Catholics and Protestants:

> The only possible state church in Europe is Christian. [...] In the hell and whirlwinds of nihilism, it has proven, as always, capable of ensuring the salvation of millions of souls, not only before its pulpits and altars but also in the spiritual cathedrals of its doctrine and in the aura that surrounds the believer and assists him until the hour of his death.[21]

In 'Across the Line', a fairly brief text dedicated to Heidegger (1950), Jünger had already put his hopes into perspective:

> We must then establish that theology by no means finds itself in a condition capable of confronting nihilism. It fights much more against the rear guard of the Enlightenment, therefore finding itself entangled in the nihilistic discourse.[22]

The following year, in *The Forest Passage*, Jünger already seemed disillusioned with regard to any help from the Church:

---

21 AN: *The Peace*, translated by Banine and Petitjean, La Table Ronde, 1948' reissued in 1971, pp. 137 and 140–141.
22 AN: 'Across the Line', translated by Henri Plard, Christian Bourgois, 1997, p. 82.

In this regard there is the constant threat of rigidification and the consequent drying up of its beneficent forces. [...]; weakened by doubt, the edifice crumbles overnight—if it has not simply been transformed into a museum.[23]

What we could read in *The Peace*, a text that must be understood in its context of opposition to Nazism, was much more political than spiritual. Paying tribute to a publication by his brother Friedrich Georg on the topic of Greek myths at the end of 1946, Jünger would highlight what he viewed as the importance of ancient religious thought:

> These works are all the more important to me as my interest in Christianity has already given rise to errors in interpretation. Nowadays, one must always expect interpretations of the lowest quality.[24]

For his part, Heidegger had not been fooled by Jünger's philosophical contradictions. After reading 'Across the Line', he felt that Jünger had remained prisoner of ancient Western metaphysics, which he perceived as the root cause of nihilism.[25]

The Coherence of the Work

The son of a Catholic mother and a rationalistic father, Jünger was raised in accordance with conventional Lutheranism, though he would describe himself as an atheist during World War I. Without any interest in the philosophical implications of religion, he never ventured beyond a vague sort of religiousness. Julien Hervier thus states:

> In his moments of exaltation, he seemed to blend into an immense cosmic unity that had nothing to do with Christian perceptions.

---

23 AN: *The Forest Passage*, p. 77 (French edition).
24 AN: Letter to Gerhard Nebel, 31 October 1946. Quoted by Julien Hervier, *War Journals II* (op. cit.), p. XX.
25 AN: This opinion was expressed by the historian and philosopher Ernst Nolte during an interview conducted on 5 March 2008.

Revisiting Jünger's funeral, which took place in 1997 and involved a Catholic rite, Hervier would specify:

> Jünger had always had the desire to live in accordance with the rites of his own country. He therefore thought it necessary to adopt the religion of his own community. Swabia, however, where he had lived for a long time, was Catholic. Furthermore, German legislation requires one to declare the religion according to which burial ceremony is to be held. This was one of the primary motivations for his late conversion, so that his funeral could be conducted in harmony with the rites of his village and its people.[26]

Rejecting the compassionate imagery encountered on certain pages of Jünger's *War Journals* or *The Peace*, Julien Hervier believes, furthermore, that in Jünger's understanding of things, 'the universe rests on a dialectic of life and death wherein creation is born from destruction. [...] To a certain extent, he would never cease to identify with the agonistic essence of the world'.[27]

Jünger was not a doctrinaire, and his thoughts and work were not guided by a concern for logical coherence. In a letter to his friends, he would clarify his interpretation of his own evolutions:

> I must, above all, beseech my readers to consider my activity as a writer as one single whole, where one can distinguish different periods but no contradictions.[28]

To differentiate between the two major parts of his own work (namely that of his youth books, which was inaugurated by *Storm of Steel*, and that of his so-called mature books, initiated by *On the Marble Cliffs*), Jünger would resort to a biblical metaphor, speaking of his Old

---

26 AN: As stated by Julien Hervier in an interview given to Pauline Lecomte for *La Nouvelle Revue d'Histoire* [TN: New History Magazine], issue number 36, May-June 2008, p. 13.

27 AN: Ibid.

28 AN: First letter to his friends, dated 13 July 1946. These letters were published in 'File H', *Ernst Jünger*, op. cit.

Testament (works of youth) and his New Testament (mature works). He states:

> I would like to emphasise that far from distancing myself from some of its parts, I remain the guarantor of my work in its entirety.

And in the same letter, he goes on to specify:

> Only their combination can reveal the perspective from which I wish to be understood.[29]

This is indeed how we ourselves understood the work when likening Jünger to a seismograph. The latter's oscillations coincide as much with the writer's thoughts as with the eras that he heralded or shed light upon.

From Rebel to Anarch

If the Cold War did indeed give rise to *The Forest Passage*, the following period—that of Europe's historical dormancy–was the source of a new allegorical novel, *Eumeswil*, published in the German language in 1977, when Jünger was eighty-two years old. The work would be well received by most critics, who would regard it as being equally significant as his early works, despite the differences in style and mindset.

This novel describes a future in the aftermath of great nuclear catastrophes. In it, the imaginary town of Eumeswil is located on the Mediterranean shore, just like the one in *On the Marble Cliffs*. It is ruled by Condor, a tyrant in the ancient sense of the word. At night, the narrator (a man named Manuel) works as a bartender in a bar frequented by the tyrant's own entourage; but during the day, he is a history teacher surrounded by several characters of lesser importance.

---

29 AN: Third letter to his friends, dated 1 September 1946 and taken from the same source. It is in this third letter that Jünger writes: 'The relationship between texts such as *The Worker*, for instance, and others such as *Gardens and Streets* and *The Peace*, is similar to that of the Old and New Testament […].'

All of this rather convincing setting serves as a pretext allowing us to outline a new 'type', a new 'figure' which one would swear is that of the European forced to temporarily remain on the sidelines of history. And it was for him that Jünger coined the term of 'anarch', which he hastens to contrast with the anarchist. Indeed, the anarch is not the monarch's adversary. He observes the world around with both interest and detachment, standing ever aloof. He is an attentive observer that has renounced combat, but despite having relinquished all weapons, he has not been vanquished. What he is concerned about is, in fact, his integrity. Unable to be the king of the world, he is the king of his own self.

To clearly highlight the difference between the anarchist and the anarch, Jünger specifies that the former 'is dependent — both on his unclear desires and on the powers that be. He trails the powerful man as his shadow; the ruler is always on his guard against him. [The anarchist] is the antagonist of the monarch, whom he dreams of wiping out'.

His positive equivalent is the anarch:

> The positive counterpart of the anarchist is the anarch. The latter is not the adversary of the monarch but his antipode, untouched by him, though also dangerous. [...] After all, the monarch wants to rule many, nay, all people; the anarch, only himself. This gives him an attitude both objective and sceptical towards the powers that be.

To which Jünger then goes on to add that 'every born historian is more or less an anarch'.[30] We thus understand that the figure of the anarch is not only distinct from that of the anarchist and the political partisan, but also from that of the rebel.

And the thoughtful reader will immediately conclude that the temptation is strong enough for any lucid European to seek refuge in the attitude espoused by the anarch. Having been deprived of his

---

30   AN: Ernst Jünger, *Eumeswil*, published in French by Gallimard, 'Folio', 1978, pp. 56–57.

role as a historical actor, he withdraws into the position of a cold and distant spectator. The allegory is therefore crystal-clear. The great catastrophe of the two world wars drove Europeans out of history for several generations, as the excesses of manifested brutality left them long broken. Just like the Achaeans after the Trojan War, their will (both a source of grandeur and a curse to us Europeans) would fall prey to a type of nihilism that would plunge them into slumber. And similarly to Ulysses, they would thus have to sail across the open sea for a long time to come, suffering and learning a great many things before reconquering their lost homeland, that of their very soul and tradition.

EPILOGUE

A DIFFERENT EUROPEAN DESTINY

IS IT TRULY necessary to explain the subtitle of our book, *A Different European Destiny*? Beyond the darkness of the 20th century (for it was dark indeed from the European perspective), it is Ernst Jünger's figure that still stands out, pure and unsoiled, stemming from a century that witnessed the entombment of our immemorial civilisation and the interment of our own, separate destiny. Whether in times of war or periods of peace, it is his life that testifies to his having been an exemplary European. Ever wakeful within him was the immanent perception of a beautiful and dangerous world. A man of both action and contemplation, of high culture and great sensitivity, he managed, thanks to his unbroken fondness of France, to reconcile within himself the two brotherly and sometimes rival peoples born from the Carolingian world, a world that traced the visible outlines of the European body. With a presence sprawling through time like a solar arc, he allowed the perfection of his war and youth writings to act as a living echo not only to the *Iliad*, regarded as the founding poem of our presence in the world, but also to our ability to overcome obstacles and our aesthetical capabilities. In addition to this, Jünger embodies most of the traits with which all Europeans of good lineage identified at the time of their greatest glory.

Tragic Courage and Destiny

Has our destiny, then, truly been entombed? Despite such sinister impressions, my most profound conviction leads me to immediately rectify that thought. Considering all that my historical studies have taught me and what I know of the hidden treasures of our energy, I feel emboldened to think that Europe, defined as an age-old community of peoples, culture and civilisation, has yet to meet its fate, despite its appearing to have committed suicide. Struck in the heart by the devastation of a new Thirty Years' War between 1914 and 1945 and submitting to the utopias and systems imposed by the victors, it entered a state of dormancy.

In his writings, Jünger often alluded to destiny as if it were an obvious fact that did not require any explanation, just as others mention Allah, God, providence or history. The word 'destiny', which can be written in French either with or without a capital letter, depending on the context, has several meanings. When, in reference to one of his characters, a novelist states that 'his death gave him a destiny of his own', what he means is that the circumstances of the character's death have bestowed *meaning* upon his life, thus granting him a certain *quality*, a certain *status*. But when another novelist says that his character's destiny was to end up as a wreck or a hero, he defines destiny as being synonymous with the word *fate* or *fortune*, in the classic sense of the term. Analogously, one can speak of the destiny of a given people or a civilisation, that is, of its *existence* or its *historical future*. And one moves up a further level when, in the *Iliad*, Homer states that the gods themselves are subject to *Destiny*, this time with a capital letter. The episode is recounted in canto XXII when it comes to deciding Hector's fate in the face of Achilles' sword. Destiny is to be understood here as the *mysterious forces* that impose themselves upon men and even the gods and that human reason could never explain. What we are referring to here is not the divine providence of Christianity, which results from a divine plan that can allegedly be understood, at least in the eyes of the Church. This, however, is just another term for *fate*. In response to the latter, the Stoics and, in a different way, Nietzsche himself, speak of *amor fati*, meaning one's love of destiny, one's approval of what is, simply because one has no choice, for there is nothing else for us apart from what is real. This approval is contested by a major part of European tradition which, since the days of the *Iliad*, has glorified man's rejection of fate and doom. Let us now quote a fragment of canto XXII, which concerns the gods' decision. Pursued by Achilles, Hector suddenly feels abandoned:

> Out upon it, in good sooth have the gods called me to my death […]; but now again is my doom come upon me. Nay, but not without a struggle let me die, neither ingloriously […]. So saying, he drew his sharp sword that hung beside his flank, a great sword and a mighty, and gathering himself together swooped like an eagle of lofty flight that darteth to the plain […]; even so Hector swooped…

All that matters has thus been said. Hector is the embodiment of tragic courage, of one's uprising against the ruling of Destiny, despite one's awareness of its inevitability. Although all is indeed lost, one can at least fight and 'die a beautiful death'.

The Gordian Knot — Europe and Asia

If we consider the time that has elapsed and ponder the time that is yet to come, it is Ernst Jünger that offers us the perspectives of a different European destiny; a destiny that is completely at odds with what we still behold at the time when I am penning these words. As we fumble forward towards the dim dawn of an awakening future, it is Jünger who stands before us as the embodiment of a different way of being. The Europeans of the future will one day be able to build upon all that his life represented and rely on his spiritual journey to find their now lost face, a face that has been left disfigured. As if with a chisel on pure steel, Jünger engraved the traits of European permanence upon many of his writings, carving out a destiny that leaves little room for doubt and dismay. Never did he elucidate things with greater clarity as in *The Gordian Knot,* a work initially published in 1953.[1]

This work was visibly influenced by the times. On 16, 17 and 18 June of that same year, the working people of Berlin's Soviet zone rebelled and fought against the Red Army's tanks using nothing but their own bare hands, and were soon emulated by the entire population of the eastern part of Germany, which was subject to Soviet rule. The uprising was crushed by means of weapons, and the repression was bloody. In his book, Jünger himself did not allude to this, allowing the work to come across as a timeless reflection on the European spirit. Nevertheless, the implicit bitterness pervading the contemporary East-West conflict is noticeable, as are the sombre memories of the Hitler era, all of which are only hinted at on a small scale.

The contrast between the East and the West, and between Europe and Asia — such is the substance that fuels Jünger's reflections in his book. This is confirmed from the very first page thanks to the particular style adopted by the writer. Jünger writes that our memory and perception are made in such a way that they especially retain the splendour of wars and weapons through time. Marathon and Salamis, armies, phalanxes, elephant cohorts, the attacks of both crusaders and Saracens, naval battles, armoured divisions, debacles on ice expanses and in deserts, and the sacking of cities in the time of Demetrius Poliorcetes, Titus, Tamerlane and even our own: 'It is imprinted into the memory.'

This, however, is only the framework for reflections in both time and space. As for Jünger's statement, it is driven by a different ambition. As heralded by the very title of his book, he relies on the memory of the Gordian knot severed by Alexander the Great with a swing of his sword as he began his conquest of Asia. According to legend, dominion over all of Asia had been promised to the one who could unravel this elaborate knot, tied at the pole of a chariot belonging to Gordius,

---

[1] AN: Ernst Jünger, *The Gordian Knot,* translated into French by Henri Plard, Christian Bourgois, 1981.

king of Phrygia. How are we to interpret Alexander's sword stroke, then? Jünger's response to this myth delineates the very meaning of Europeanness, in contrast to all that defines the East or Asia.

Solar Principle vs Chthonic Principle

> The sword drawn for this purpose is spiritual: it is the means of free decision that separates, but also of power that dominates. The knot bears within itself a fatal constraint, the obscure implication of enigmas, the helplessness of man before the oracle. When looking at it a little more closely, one can see the coils of the serpent gleam, this embodiment of Gaia and her chthonic power. […] In the West, the slaying of the serpent is the first act of the true prince, that is to say, a mythical one. It is through such slaying that Heracles, still in his cradle, demonstrates his sovereignty.

One must ponder these complex words, for they shed light on the very meaning of the Gordian knot. The latter bears within itself 'the helplessness of man before the oracle' and symbolises the magical realm of Asia, which will subvert the crystalline freedom of the Western mind, a mind represented by the sword of the young conqueror[2] — which is why, Jünger explains, 'Alexander's idea would never have occurred to an Asian king; for none of them had thought of settling the matter with a sword'. When understood in this manner, Asia is actually a spiritual principle. It designates an existence that is subject to underground forces that evade the clarity of reason within a magical and despotic world. Jünger reminds us that Phrygia was ruled by Gordius, of whom nothing is known for certain, and that it 'was a kingdom of gold, among the kingdoms of gold. […] Alexander, too, was one of those princes adorned by the splendour of gold. Yet it was a different glitter to that of ancient kings: a sublime, separate light, a shimmering blaze borrowed from the sun and not from the chasms of Pactolus in the

---

2   AN: In both Jünger's book and our own comments, 'Western' is synonymous with 'European'. Likewise, the word West is taken in the old, traditional sense of the term, thus referring to Europe and not America.

very bosom of the Earth': a solar principle contrasting with a chthonic one — Athens versus Jerusalem, according to Nietzsche.

It is thus necessary to quote the following words, which clarify the twofold symbolism of gold:

> The sword used by Alexander to sever the fateful knot glitters with gold: it is a symbol of light. In the blink of an eye, and in a timeless manner, it asserts the reign of a new and more spiritual world. Its light topples magical cities such as Babylon, Tyre and Sidon with their treasures, the temples with their gods and their priesthoods [...]. In the flash of this sword stroke, a new awareness of time and space arises. It bears knowledge within itself, and even a hint of rationality, the sharpness of doubt, which disarms the ancient world and divides it. In stillness, the free spirit makes its decisions [...]. Henceforth, with this light now resplendent, one will perhaps experience circumlocution and error, but never turn back.[3]

In other words, the light of the European spirit and its freedom can no longer disappear, regardless of the misrepresentations or obscuration that may darken it temporarily, depending on the age and era.

Even Alexander himself fell victim to his own errors following his victory over Darius, with the Persians acknowledging him as the rightful successor. To the great discontentment of his Macedonians, he contemplated turning his Greek power into an oriental one. He thus surrounded himself with Asian pomp, and the Greeks themselves were required to prostrate themselves before his throne. Refusing to comply, Callisthenes would pay for it with his life.

> This Callisthenes was, in fact, related to Aristotle, of whom Alexander had said in his youth that he owed his life to Philip, his father, and that it was up to Aristotle to prove himself worthy of the name of man.[4]

Having been forgotten for the time being, Aristotle would not be eliminated.

---

3   AN: *The Gordian Knot*, French edition, pp. 12–15.
4   AN: Ibid., pp. 44–45.

Herodotus and the Greek Identity

The entire Western historical tradition rejects arbitrariness for being incompatible with the dignity of the sovereign. It perceives it as a shadow cast upon the fame of monarchs, upon whom it bestows the designation 'great'. This is not the case in the East, where, on the contrary, arbitrariness attests to the very greatness of the prince. If Harun al-Rashid, whose reign was full of atrocities, was called the Just, it is because we are faced here with a different notion of greatness.

Conversely, when referring to the *Iliad*, which is among the chief expressions of the European spirit, Jünger reminds us that Agamemnon, the head of the Greek coalition besieging Troy, was not vested with despotic power. Being a kind of feudal king, he was merely ranked first among his equals and peers. 'He summons the assembly of princes and leads the army into battle.' On the opposite side, the Trojans, who had been influenced by Asia, 'fail to produce a solar hero of Achilles' ilk, or such an astonishingly free spirit as that of Ulysses, whose cunning would lead to their city's downfall.'[5]

Apart from Homer perhaps, writes Jünger, 'no Western mind offers a more captivating spectacle of awakening than Herodotus. His work is suffused with the light of dawn, shimmering like the dew that refracts the sun.' Born in Halicarnassus in Asia Minor, Herodotus spent a major part of his life journeying through regions that were quite difficult to access. He thus saw Babylon, which still retained some of its splendour and the one hundred brass gates of its square enclosure.

> Long before Alexander, his eyes had gazed upon this paragon of magical power. To the north, Herodotus would reach the very confines of the Black Sea, and in Egypt, Elephantine. Driven by his unbridled enthusiasm to collect facts and traditions wherever he went, he stood at the head of our great travellers' procession, which stretched all the way to Vasco da Gama, Columbus, Cook, Humboldt and their emulators.

---

5   AN: Ibid., p. 33.

These intrepid travellers would never be rivalled by anyone in Asia. Although the latter did, admittedly, sometimes encroach into the West, it always took on the shape of conquering swarms charging behind Xerxes, Attila, Tamerlane or Genghis Khan. And all of the latter owed their greatness not to their discoveries, but to the terror of the massacres that they perpetrated.

Compared to such expeditions, whose sole purpose was to pillage or loot, what Herodotus inaugurated was truly novel. As pointed out by Jünger, the tireless discoverer states in his first book that the purpose of his work is 'to prevent human history from falling into oblivion, spread the glory of the great deeds and remarkable actions of both the Greeks and other peoples, and last but not least, to specify the reasons behind their wars.' Indeed, one of the distinctive features of all Europeans is that they are sincerely interested in other people, sometimes excessively so, even to the point of robbing themselves of their own standards. Cicero would thus rightly view Herodotus as the father of history as we understand it, defined as the art of observation rather than science and requiring a free mind that is open to criticising sources and perspectives alike.

Jünger rightly notes that Herodotus' innovation also lay in his clear perception of the immense shock resulting from the Persian wars, which were the first of many great conflicts between Asia and Europe and also the source of the unprecedented feeling that the Greeks would acquire of their own identity in the face of the discovery of a threatening sort of otherness. Jünger writes:

> In the clash between the Greek and oriental genius, freedom and despotism would, through their confrontation, shape a destiny that affects every man and every age of the world.

Herodotus' actions and words testify to a constant of the Greek spirit, one that was already present in Homer and would later be conceptualised by Aristotle:

> He believed that every display of unrestricted power aroused the wrath of the gods, and that the latter would punish it through crushing destruction. [...] One may wonder if this truth is not at the very heart of our conflicts and is not actually responsible for deciding their very outcome.

What he was thinking of here is, of course, Hitler and his excesses, to which he devoted many pages. On a more general level, he knew that, just like Alexander, Westerners are never immune to the hubris that results from wielding power and might. And yet they still bear, in their spiritual and historical tradition, the antidotes that will allow them to recover.

Freedom and Arbitrariness

> In every debate between East and West, the notion of freedom appears to be at the very core of their antinomy.

Jünger apprehends the word *freedom* in its two main meanings and touches upon each of them successively. Spiritual freedom is the first. It is the freedom of the 'free will', an innovation that Ulysses had already embodied: 'one of the types of Western man, an explorer and an inventor of the highest rank whose spiritual freedom never shrinks from anything and defies the gods themselves.'[6] Next comes political freedom, and the rejection of arbitrariness, whose limits and necessity Jünger clearly perceives:

> One of the disadvantages of liberal institutions is that they task many minds and viewpoints with the same charge. Movements that depend on negotiations, interests, and uncertain alliances are inevitably weaker than those gathered in one cluster by one single will.[7]

---

6 AN: Ibid., p. 18.
7 AN: Ibid., p. 32.

And that is why 'times of crisis always reaffirm the following empirical fact — that the will of a single person is swifter and more efficient than that of an assembly. In such a case, one will resort to the individual'. The Romans had previously formulated a precise theory regarding such crisis situations. They had invented dictatorship, which they kept as a contingency plan, 'as a drastic remedy, to be used in case of emergency'. For a brief period, one adorned dictators with ancient royal power. 'One sought him out at the plough, and then he returned to the plough'. The danger lay in the fact that every display of power could indeed abolish freedom for a long time to come. Precautionary measures, however subtle they may be, could never eliminate such a risk, as demonstrated by the history of Rome.

> As for whether despotism will be able to impose itself in the shape of a stable regime, one that none would dispute, it depends rather on basic freedom, that is to say, on the freedom of the *patres* of a people.

European history offers us numerous examples of this perilous balance. For the most part, it would be maintained during the ten centuries of the feudal Middle Ages and beyond, both within the Holy Roman Empire of the German Nation and in England, only to find itself disturbed in France with the establishment of an administrative and centralised monarchy supported by ecclesiastical powers, one that precluded the freedom of the *patres* and, in other words, ostracised the nobility. Never expanding on these examples, Jünger mentions, on the other hand, the power exercised by Churchill between 1940 and 1945. Better yet, he could have alluded to Mannerheim, Marshal of Finland. Indeed, both exercised Roman-style war dictatorship, a rule that the end of conflict would bring to a close. This type of power contrasts in a most meaningful way with Hitler and Stalin's, for instance, which could only come to an end with the death of the despot himself.

Immersed, since 1918, in an era of perpetual and dangerous upheavals, Jünger was no political theorist, but a superior mind that reflected on things based on his particularly rich historical experience. He never theorised about any specific forms of government. What he did instead was reflect on the demands of a European world made for freedom, while the Asian world flourished in despotism. Without venturing into the realm of potential political solutions, he only emphasised the fact that in the West, a 'good king' has always been a 'just king'. He then complements this reminder with a very telling image:

> In favourable cases, the will of a single person can harmonise with the spirit of the whole and transform it into actions. The governance remains, as in good households, almost imperceptible.

We all know that, ever since the disappearance of the *patres*, such harmony has long seemed out of reach. Still, one can, at the very least, bear it in mind as an action model.

In another part of his work, Jünger acknowledges how much 'we are troubled in our hearts whenever power, whether that of the despot or of the demos, money, ingenuity or elemental forces abide by their own law'.[8]

To describe oneself as troubled by such a development is an understatement. Indeed, the mere expression of such concerns is already a form of liberation as regards the deceitful claims that would have us believe that the unrestricted power afforded by money could actually be synonymous with freedom.

The *Iliad* and the Spirit of Chivalry

War is yet another field where the spirits of Asia and the West clash. Thanks to his relevant experience, the cruelties of the Second World War and the brutalities that followed the latter, it does seem legitimate for Jünger to devote many detailed pages to this very topic. Confined to the timeless even when historical, ancient or recent examples are called upon, Jünger's thoughts will never become obsolete, thanks to their comprehensiveness.

---

8   AN: Ibid., p. 135.

In spite of indulging in dreams of peace, Jünger was well aware that, regardless of its nature, armed conflict could never be eradicated. Europeans have, however, successfully managed to restrict violence through the ancient distinction made by the chivalrous spirit between one's armed enemy and one's disarmed foe.

Already in the *Iliad*, the violence unleashed by Achilles upon Hector's remains scandalised the gods themselves, whose indignation is not echoed in any shape or form by the great books of the Orient. Following the intervention of the Olympian gods, Achilles would relinquish all thoughts of revenge, sensitively welcoming the elderly King Priam and surrendering the body of his son to him so that funeral tributes could be paid.

So, what is a chivalrous attitude based on? Jünger himself rejects the notion that it is all rooted in reciprocity. He states instead that this attitude is, in all likelihood, associated with the image that one has of man and his dignity, meaning that it manifests itself all the more when we recognise ourselves in the person of our adversary. According to Jünger, the European combatant tends to comply with his own customs even when he encounters completely different behaviour to his own. Why? Because he does so, above all, 'out of respect for himself'.

Since the dawn of time, adds Jünger, we have witnessed two different laws of war: 'a superior form and a more barbaric one'. And this disparity reflects that of the West and the Orient. 'The Greeks fighting the barbarians and the Christians battling the infidels followed a harsher law' than the one they implemented among themselves.

> During the last war, the Germans waged two very different wars on the Eastern Front and the Western Front.

The consequences of this duality can already be perceived through the nature of the weapons used, some considered legal and others illegal.

One more remark: in the West, a soldier's right to surrender in a situation of hopelessness is included in the tacit conventions of military honour. Another prominent aspect of such 'laws of war' concerns the manner in which the dead are treated. The Western way, Jünger reminds us, is encapsulated in the following ancient adage: 'Those who fall in battle are to be honoured by both men and gods.' In virtually all European countries, one can nowadays find cemeteries where the enemies that perished in battle have been laid to rest.

> In doing so, not only do people do justice to yesterday's enemy, but also enhance the glory of their own weapons by endowing it with a gleam that ennobles it.

When cases of denied burial do occur, it is in a context of civil war, ethnic war or war of religion. Those defeated, perceived as 'traitors', 'barbarians' or 'heretics', must vanish once and for all and leave no trace. 'It is not a matter of chance,' adds Jünger, 'that we encounter the same principle of complete erasure in the fierce clash between the East and the West.'

As summarised by Jünger, one can determine the kind of conflict they are involved in by taking notice of three signs, namely the 'unrestricted use of weapons, denied burial, and enslavement'.

> The simultaneous presence of irreconcilables and the adjacency of noble and base traits present us with a major enigma.

But this is not unsolvable if we search for it in our hearts.

For we have seen the divine Achilles himself mistreat the fallen Hector in a manner that resurfaces in all eras of terror. [...] This grants plausibility to the hypothesis that these abysses are dug in man by his very own nature, which he discovers whenever order itself is at stake: when "everything is called into question". It is to the old telluric night that he returns, to the cyclopean, to the eyeless face, to a space without light.

It is a momentous thought that concerns all those who, by the workings of Destiny, have faced or will face extreme situations that invalidate the very order of things. Jünger develops his point further:

The myth, which always reaches into the very core of things, more fundamentally so than history itself, details the advent of a superior morality through the victory of the Olympians over the ancient world of the Titans.⁹

Such is the myth developed in all its depth by Hesiod in his *Theogony*. As for the legend of the Gordian knot, it is but its transposition.

The Artistry of Early Hunters

So where in the narrow European peninsula did it originate from, this mindset that we consider synonymous with 'freedom' and which constitutes the spiritual essence of Europe and its constant impulse towards beauty, excellence and respect for femininity? Where does the Western detachment from all magical powers and monstrous deities come from? Indeed, it is a detachment that 'draws a line of clarity across the history of our world'.

Jünger suggests that the origins of the 'European miracle' are more distant than commonly acknowledged. The most recent discoveries regarding prehistory have pushed back the boundaries of all that we thought possible. Our origins have thus been determined to go back tens of thousands of years. Admittedly, none can understand the reasons, but one does observe the effects summarised by Jünger in lines that imprint themselves on one's memory:

> If the artistry of early hunters moves us so much and speaks to us in a language greater than that of the ancient Orient, or even the more recent one, it is undoubtedly a sign that the very spirit of our spirit, the freedom of our freedom, resides in it.¹⁰

Jünger reaches even deeper into this reasoning and, quoting the Athenian reformer Solon, highlights the fact that sovereignty is rooted in an inner triumph. To free itself from dark forces and vile powers, 'the soul must be kept in check. […] There is a justice of forms and

---

9   AN: Ibid., pp. 57–69.
10 AN: Ibid., p. 16.

lines that gives us a feeling of beauty. It comes from afar, from the archaic dimensions and times when the walls of caves were being painted. Their appearance suggests that among primitive hunters, justice and freedom were already present in the meaning we assign to them today. By contrast, we perceive all barbaric taste as offensive. The world is full of works that remain captive of the fascination exerted by gods, demons and the forces of nature, wherever man fails to respond to them with his own freedom.'

At the time when these very lines are being penned, it has become all too clear that our world is now governed by barbaric forms presented as expressions of art. What we are obviously experiencing is a period of obscuration from which our ancient freedom has now vanished. The answer to such ordeals, however, has already been given. 'Such was the true meaning of Salamis,'[11] Jünger states.

Aiming Higher than One's Goal

Throughout history, as was the case in Salamis, there are always periods of extreme tension that arise, when the highest values of a civilisation depend on a handful of soldiers. As for Jünger's mind, it had every reason to be suffused with this fact. The lesson that the young officer of the German assault troops had been taught at the 'Storm of Steel' school had become one of the compelling ideas of his life, supported by the symbolism of the sacrificed position or 'lost position' (*verlorener Posten*). The origin of this expression dates back to the Lansquenets, to the crossroads of the 15th and 16th centuries. Faced with the impassable barrier of entire squares of Swiss spearmen, who were formidable adversaries, one had created a type of elite combatant, a sacrifice-ready warrior armed with a very long, powerful and two-handed sword

---

11 AN: Ibid., p. 136. In September 480 BCE, shortly after the Battle of Thermopylae (during which three hundred Spartans led by Leonidas himself had sacrificed their own lives), the Athenian fleet, under the command of Themistocles, would ultimately secure a decisive victory over the invading Persian forces, ensuring the survival of Greek civilisation.

whose height was greater than that of a man. Charging forward with slashing movements despite a great risk of being pierced right through, this warrior would hurl himself at the spear-bearing enemy squares in an attempt to shatter them. The entire outcome of the battle thus rested on his shoulders. In exchange for the great risks, the 'lost post' enjoyed great privileges and considerable respect.

In military language, the meaning of the expression 'lost post' would then evolve, referring to any mission of sacrifice. Its symbolism is encountered in German literature, among others in the works of Nietzsche.[12] Ernst Jünger would use it himself, giving it a broader meaning than that of the heroism of sacrifice. In *Heliopolis*, he writes for instance:

> One must always aim higher than one's goal. Only he who knows how to behave with regard to a lost post is equal to holding every post.

'To aim higher than one's goal' could be considered one of the mottos that apply to the life of the extraordinary soldier and author that Jünger was.

His exceptional physical and mental shape allowed him to reach the advanced age of almost one hundred and three years. However, it is not this feat which, in itself, commands respect, as it is better to die while in good shape at the age of twenty than to wallow in a pointless existence, decaying, bed-ridden and artificially kept alive against everyone's better judgement. Some medical advances have indeed increased the number of rather decrepit centenarians, in whose case even the slightest charitableness would lead one to wish they could put an end to such suffering. If respect and admiration accompanied Jünger into his old age, it is because he had reached this stage of his life without succumbing to decrepitude. Photos taken on the occasion of his one-hundredth birthday attest to the aristocratic firmness of his

---

12 AN: *Human, All Too Human*, 312 — 'There is an ambition for a forlorn hope which forces a party to place itself at the post of extreme danger.'

very face. And the television interview he granted in French on this occasion highlights the intact vigour of his sarcastic mind.

Showering in cold water every morning, he would go for a walk through the countryside on a daily basis and indulge in the daily practice of contemplative reading, transcribing his thoughts into his diary and never neglecting the beneficial effects of good wine and sleep. Such was the life of the very active hermit of Wilflingen, until the very end.

Conduct-Based Ethics

What is immediately striking about Jünger is his consistent moral and physical poise. Those who met him long after the war could never have imagined his slim silhouette without thinking of an officer, and specifically a 'Prussian officer'; a smiling one, of course, but upright and arched as if he were still under arms. Appropriate behaviour was a second nature to him and any deviation from it would have undoubtedly inflicted suffering upon him and proven impossible. The modesty and sentimental nobility displayed in his *Journals* provide ample proof of his moral demeanour. We are particularly struck by his refusal to engage in arguments with detractors and former friends such as Carl Schmitt, all of whom had surrendered to jealousy or bitterness. Another manifestation of his constant concern for proper conduct, one which now relates to the actual form of his works, had already asserted its presence during the rewriting of his first *War Journals*, before reemerging in the very special attention that he devoted, in all his writings, to developing a personal style that was highly enigmatic and devoid of any and all clichés.

In Jünger's case, conduct and demeanour were most certainly the result of his very temperament, but also of an extended education that reached well beyond his adolescence. We are all familiar with the influence exerted by his father through his intellectual rigour, and with the impact made by his more literary mother, both of whom were fine examples of superior effort-based discipline that went hand in hand with great mental freedom. One can also readily imagine the attendant effects of long-term and strict military training in an army that took military service very seriously indeed: four years of fighting in the trenches, his polished boots dug deep in the mud, the tiniest screw of his rifle kept clean and oiled regardless of circumstance. Next came a period of more than three years spent in the *Reichswehr* at a time of relative peace, and ultimately four years of officer duty in a *Wehrmacht* that could scarcely be accused of laxity, despite the pleasures offered by a Parisian city that fawned upon the victors. It is therefore hardly surprising that the former officer's stern demeanour remained detectable until the very end, despite his civilian clothing. It did, however, take more than acquired habits for Jünger to adhere to this; a desire to be like that and not different. This attitude of his is visible even in his pronounced appetite for all manner of transgression. He was indeed notorious for having a taste for wine and alcohol. And yet, everything about him contradicted his becoming a wine-guzzling drunkard. His fascination for extreme experiences had actually stemmed from the Great War, when he was part of his country's assault troops. 'Combat, wine, and love were a source of great exhilaration,' he would state in *War as an Inner Experience*. At the time, he was already experimenting with certain extreme and unusual states of consciousness, a curiosity that would never wane. He would then turn it into the very subject of his book *Approaches: Drugs and Intoxication* (*Annäherungen. Drogen und Rausch*, 1970). Just like the lover of Burgundy wines never sank into alcoholism, however, the experimenter of the effects of LSD would never become addicted to the drug. Ever his own master, he remained, and still remains in our memories, an example to follow in the most difficult of times, as we aim ever higher than our very goal.

Le Rembûcher, 21 December 2008

OTHER BOOKS PUBLISHED BY ARKTOS

Virginia Abernethy	Born Abroad
Sri Dharma Pravartaka Acharya	The Dharma Manifesto
Joakim Andersen	Rising from the Ruins
Winston C. Banks	Excessive Immigration
Stephen Baskerville	Who Lost America?
Alain de Benoist	Beyond Human Rights
	Carl Schmitt Today
	The Ideology of Sameness
	The Indo-Europeans
	Manifesto for a European Renaissance
	On the Brink of the Abyss
	The Problem of Democracy
	Runes and the Origins of Writing
	View from the Right (vol. 1–3)
Armand Berger	Tolkien, Europe, and Tradition
Arthur Moeller van den Bruck	Germany's Third Empire
Matt Battaglioli	The Consequences of Equality
Kerry Bolton	The Perversion of Normality
	Revolution from Above
	Yockey: A Fascist Odyssey
Isac Boman	Money Power
Charles William Dailey	The Serpent Symbol in Tradition
Ricardo Duchesne	Faustian Man in a Multicultural Age
Alexander Dugin	Ethnos and Society
	Ethnosociology
	Eurasian Mission
	The Fourth Political Theory
	The Great Awakening vs the Great Reset
	Last War of the World-Island
	Politica Aeterna
	Political Platonism
	Putin vs Putin
	The Rise of the Fourth Political Theory
	Templars of the Proletariat
	The Theory of a Multipolar World
Edward Dutton	Race Differences in Ethnocentrism
Mark Dyal	Hated and Proud
Clare Ellis	The Blackening of Europe
Koenraad Elst	Return of the Swastika
Julius Evola	The Bow and the Club
	Fascism Viewed from the Right
	A Handbook for Right-Wing Youth
	Metaphysics of Power
	Metaphysics of War
	The Myth of the Blood
	Notes on the Third Reich
	Pagan Imperialism

OTHER BOOKS PUBLISHED BY ARKTOS

	Recognitions
	A Traditionalist Confronts Fascism
Guillaume Faye	*Archeofuturism*
	Archeofuturism 2.0
	The Colonisation of Europe
	Convergence of Catastrophes
	Ethnic Apocalypse
	A Global Coup
	Prelude to War
	Sex and Deviance
	Understanding Islam
	Why We Fight
Daniel S. Forrest	*Suprahumanism*
Andrew Fraser	*Dissident Dispatches*
	Reinventing Aristocracy in the Age of Woke Capital
	The WASP Question
Génération Identitaire	*We are Generation Identity*
Peter Goodchild	*The Taxi Driver from Baghdad*
	The Western Path
Paul Gottfried	*War and Democracy*
Petr Hampl	*Breached Enclosure*
Porus Homi Havewala	*The Saga of the Aryan Race*
Lars Holger Holm	*Hiding in Broad Daylight*
	Homo Maximus
	Incidents of Travel in Latin America
	The Owls of Afrasiab
Richard Houck	*Liberalism Unmasked*
A. J. Illingworth	*Political Justice*
Institut Iliade	*For a European Awakening*
	Guardians of Heritage
Alexander Jacob	*De Naturae Natura*
Jason Reza Jorjani	*Artemis Unveiled*
	Closer Encounters
	Erosophia
	Faustian Futurist
	Iranian Leviathan
	Lovers of Sophia
	Novel Folklore
	Philosophy of the Future
	Prometheism
	Promethean Pirate
	Prometheus and Atlas
	Psychotron
	Uber Man
	World State of Emergency
Henrik Jonasson	*Sigmund*

OTHER BOOKS PUBLISHED BY ARKTOS

Edgar Julius Jung	The Significance of the German Revolution
Ruuben Kaalep & August Meister	Rebirth of Europe
Roderick Kaine	Smart and SeXy
Peter King	Here and Now
	Keeping Things Close
	On Modern Manners
James Kirkpatrick	Conservatism Inc.
Ludwig Klages	The Biocentric Worldview
	Cosmogonic Reflections
	The Science of Character
Andrew Korybko	Hybrid Wars
Pierre Krebs	Guillaume Faye: Truths & Tributes
	Fighting for the Essence
Julien Langella	Catholic and Identitarian
John Bruce Leonard	The New Prometheans
Stephen Pax Leonard	The Ideology of Failure
	Travels in Cultural Nihilism
William S. Lind	Reforging Excalibur
	Retroculture
Pentti Linkola	Can Life Prevail?
H. P. Lovecraft	The Conservative
Norman Lowell	Imperium Europa
Richard Lynn	Sex Differences in Intelligence
	A Tribute to Helmut Nyborg (ed.)
John MacLugash	The Return of the Solar King
Charles Maurras	The Future of the Intelligentsia &
	For a French Awakening
John Harmon McElroy	Agitprop in America
Michael O'Meara	Guillaume Faye and the Battle of Europe
	New Culture, New Right
Michael Millerman	Beginning with Heidegger
Dmitry Moiseev	The Philosophy of Italian Fascism
Maurice Muret	The Greatness of Elites
Brian Anse Patrick	The NRA and the Media
	Rise of the Anti-Media
	The Ten Commandments of Propaganda
	Zombology
Tito Perdue	The Bent Pyramid
	Journey to a Location
	Lee
	Morning Crafts
	Philip
	The Sweet-Scented Manuscript
	William's House (vol. 1–4)
John K. Press	The True West vs the Zombie Apocalypse
Raido	A Handbook of Traditional Living (vol. 1–2)

OTHER BOOKS PUBLISHED BY ARKTOS

P R Reddall	Towards Awakening
Claire Rae Randall	The War on Gender
Steven J. Rosen	The Agni and the Ecstasy
	The Jedi in the Lotus
Nicholas Rooney	Talking to the Wolf
Richard Rudgley	Barbarians
	Essential Substances
	Wildest Dreams
Ernst von Salomon	It Cannot Be Stormed
	The Outlaws
Werner Sombart	Traders and Heroes
Piero San Giorgio	Giuseppe
	Survive the Economic Collapse
	Surviving the Next Catastrophe
Sri Sri Ravi Shankar	Celebrating Silence
	Know Your Child
	Management Mantras
	Patanjali Yoga Sutras
	Secrets of Relationships
George T. Shaw (ed.)	A Fair Hearing
Fenek Solère	Kraal
	Reconquista
Oswald Spengler	The Decline of the West
	Man and Technics
Richard Storey	The Uniqueness of Western Law
Tomislav Sunic	Against Democracy and Equality
	Homo Americanus
	Postmortem Report
	Titans are in Town
Askr Svarte	Gods in the Abyss
Hans-Jürgen Syberberg	On the Fortunes and Misfortunes of Art in Post-War Germany
Abir Taha	Defining Terrorism
	The Epic of Arya (2nd ed.)
	Nietzsche is Coming God, or the Redemption of the Divine
	Verses of Light
Jean Thiriart	Europe: An Empire of 400 Million
Bal Gangadhar Tilak	The Arctic Home in the Vedas
Dominique Venner	For a Positive Critique
	The Shock of History
Hans Vogel	How Europe Became American
Markus Willinger	A Europe of Nations
	Generation Identity
Alexander Wolfheze	Alba Rosa
	Globus Horribilis
	Rupes Nigra

Printed in Great Britain
by Amazon